Federalism and Political Performance

This book fills a gap in current scholarship by considering not just the distinction between federal and unitary governments, but also whether this distinction makes a difference for public policy and policy outcomes. There is no comparable book available, and it should certainly be used widely in comparative politics courses.

AREND LIJPHART
Research Professor of Political Science,
University of California

In a world marked by continuing economic and political integration, over a third of the world's population is already governed under a federal system. *Federalism and Political Performance* examines the political potential of federalism. It considers the resistance generated amongst those who fear losing their livelihood or their identity, and explores the potential effects of the territorial division of power on peace, freedom, democracy, economic wealth and social security.

Federalism and Political Performance features a panel of international experts, who compare the political performance of federal and non-federal states, and evaluate the impact of different types of federation. It draws together focused case studies from a wide range of countries, including Russia, India, Spain, Germany, Switzerland, Australia and Canada. This thorough and authoritative volume is a valuable resource for students and scholars of Comparative Politics.

Ute Wachendorfer-Schmidt teaches at the Institute of Political Science, the University of Heidelberg, Germany.

Routledge/ECPR Studies in European Political Science

Formerly edited by Hans Keman, *Vrije University, The Netherlands*; now edited by Jan W. van Deth, *University of Mannheim, Germany on behalf of the European Consortium for Political Research*

The Routledge/ECPR Studies in European Political Science series is published in association with the European Consortium for Political Research – the leading organisation concerned with the growth and development of political science in Europe. The series presents high-quality edited volumes on topics at the leading edge of current interest in political science and related fields, with contributions from European scholars and others who have presented work at ECPR workshops or research groups.

Federalism and Political Performance

Edited by
Ute Wachendorfer-Schmidt

London and New York

First published 2000
by Routledge
11 New Fetter Lane, London EC4P 4EE

Simultaneously published in the USA and Canada
by Routledge
29 West 35th Street, New York, NY 10001

Routledge is an imprint of the Taylor & Francis Group

Typeset in Baskerville by Exe Valley Dataset Ltd, Exeter
Printed and bound in Great Britain by
MPG Books Ltd, Bodmin, Cornwall

British Library Cataloguing in Publication Data
A catalogue record for this book is available
from the British Library

Library of Congress Cataloguing in Publication Data
Federalism and political performance/edited by Ute Wachendorfer-Schmidt.
    p.   cm.
  Includes bibliographical references and index.
  1. Federal government.   2. Economic development–Political aspects.
  3. Federal government–Case studies.   I. Wachendorfer, Ute, 1950–

JC355.F3715 2000
321.02'3—dc21   00–036597

ISBN 0–415–21810–1

Contents

Figures and tables

Contributors

Klaus Armingeon is Professor of Political Science at the University of Berne, Switzerland. He has contributed to debates on corporatism, trade unions, consociational democracy, and social and economic policy from a comparative perspective. His publications include *Staat und Arbeitsbeziehungen* (1994), and *Deutschland, Österreich und die Schweiz im Vergleich* (co-edited with Pascal Sciarini; a special issue of *Schweizerische Zeitschrift für Politikwissenschaft*, 1996).

Klaus von Beyme is Professor Emeritus of Political Science at the University of Heidelberg. From 1959 to 1960 he studied at the Lomonossov University in Moscow; from 1961 to 1962 von Beyme was a research fellow at the Russian Center of Harvard University. From 1974 to 1999 he was Professor of Political Science at the University of Heidelberg. His scientific work comprises contributions to the comparative research of political systems (Eastern and Western Europe), political theory, and policy analysis (culture policy, housing and urban policy). His publications include *Der Gesetzgeber. Der Bundestag als Entscheidungszentrum* (1997); *Die Kunst der Macht und die Gegenmacht der Kunst* (1998); *Die parlamentarische Demokratie. Entstehung und Funktionsweise 1789– 1999* (1999).

Francis G. Castles is Professor of Political Science in the Research School of Social Sciences at the Australian University. His research interests are in comparative public and social policy and comparative politics. His most recent books are *Comparative Public Policy: Patterns of Post-war Transformation* (1998) and *The Welfare State: A Reader* (co-edited with Chris Pierson 2000).

Mireia Grau i Creus is a junior lecturer on Public Policy at the University of Murcia. She is working on a doctoral thesis on federalism in Spain. Her research focuses on public policy in Spain, Spanish politics, intergovernmental relations and policy analysis.

Alexander M. Hicks, who received his PhD in sociology from the University of Wisconsin-Madison in 1979, is Professor of Sociology and Political Science (adjunct) at Emory University. He is author of *Social Democracy and Welfare Capitalism: A Century of Income Security Policy* (1999), winner of the American Political Science Association's 2000 Luebbert Award for the best book in comparative politics published in 1998 or 1999. He is also co-editor (with Thomas Janoski) of *The Comparative Political Economy of the Welfare State: New Methodologies and Approaches* (1994).

Hans Keman holds the Chair of Political Science at the 'Vrije Universiteit' of Amsterdam. He is presently editor of the *European Journal of Political Science*. He has been Fellow at the European University Institute (Florence, Italy), the Australian National University (Canberra, Australia) and the Netherlands Institute of Advanced Study (NIAS). Among his recent publications are: *The Politics of Problem-Solving in Postwar Democracies* (1997); *Institutions and Political Choice* (with Roland Czada and Adrienne Héritier; 1998); *Doing Research in Political Science* (with Paul Pennings and Jan Kleinnijenhuis; 1999), and *Party-Government in 48 Democracies* (with Jaap Woldendorp and Ian Budge; 2000).

Thomas D. Lancaster is Associate Professor of Political Science at Emory University in Atlanta, Georgia, USA. His theoretical interests focus on the interaction of institutional arrangements, political attitudes, voting behaviour, and economic performance. As an analyst of comparative politics, his research tends to concentrate on western and southern Europe, especially the cases of Spain and Germany. Some of his recent work on federalism includes co-editing and contributing both to *Compounded Representation in West European Federations* (1999) and to a special issue of *Publius, the Journal of Federalism,* entitled *Federalism and Compounded Representation* (1999). Other major works include being a multiple co-author (with Michael Curtis, et al.) of *Western European Government and Politics* (1997).

Subrata K. Mitra is currently Professor of Political Science at the School of Politics, Nottingham University, UK. Governance, sub-nationalism, rational choice theory, quantitative applications in Political Science and South Asian politics and security are among his main areas of interest. His recent publications are *Culture and Rationality* (1999), *Democracy and Social Change* (1999), and 'Effects of Institutional Arrangements on Political Stability in South Asia', in the *Annual Review of Political Science* (1999). Professor Mitra is currently engaged in a comparative study of governance in six Indian States.

Martin Painter has been Professor at the University of Sydney since 1974, and in 2000 completed a five-year term as Head of Department.

His recent research has been on multi-level governance, particularly with reference to intergovernmental relations in the Australian federal system. He has participated in a joint project comparing public sector reform in Australia and Scandinavia, and is part of a team undertaking a comparative study of public officials' pay and rewards in Pacific Rim countries. In 2000–2001 he is director of a research project comparing bureaucratic elites in Thailand, Malaysia, Vietnam and Indonesia. Professor Painter is a National Fellow of the Institute of Public Administration, Australia, and was co-editor of the *Australian Journal of Public Administration* for six years. He was President of the Australasian Political Studies Association in 1995. His most recent books are *Collaborative Federalism* (1998) and an edited collection, *Managerialism: The Great Debate* (1997).

Stephen G. Tomblin is an Associate Professor in the Department of Political Science at Memorial University, where he has taught since 1985. His major research interests are in comparative federalism, regionalism, comparative public policy, and political institutions. In 1995 he authored *Ottawa and the Outer Provinces: The Challenge of Regional Integration in Canada* and is currently working on a book on New England and Atlantic regionalism. Professor Tomblin is currently engaged in a study on social and political restructuring and the implications for individual and community health in coastal communities in British Columbia and Newfoundland.

Ute Wachendorfer-Schmidt teaches at the Institute of Political Science, the University of Heidelberg, Germany. She is writing a habilitation thesis on 'Joint decision-making in unified Germany'. Her recent publications involve the comparative study of federalism, federalism in Germany, and policy-making in the European Union. She has also contributed to the study of third world politics and policies.

Series editor's preface

Since federalism is about the division of power between central and regional governments, debates about federalism affect the very core of politics in many states. Federalism seems to be an attractive attempt to combine the needs for effective government at the central level on the one hand, and requests for independence and identity at non-central levels on the other. Instead of trying to harmonize and standardize apparent differences, federalism aims at protecting distinctiveness without abandoning the idea of a national community. It has been practised successfully in either relatively large countries (such as the USA, Canada, India, Argentina, Germany) and in clearly divided countries (such as Belgium, Austria, Malaysia, Switzerland). In a world where independence is defined increasingly as national separatism, federalism could be a cure for many problems. The potential gains of federalism have been clearly recognized by the 'Founding Fathers' of the oldest functioning democracy in the world, who called their discussion platform not without reason *The Federalist*.

In the collection of essays presented in this volume the authors deal with the question: 'does federalism matter?' The answer is – not surprisingly – positive: yes, federalism does matter. The unique character of the contributions to this volume, however, is the broad approach to the advantages and disadvantages of federal versus unitary political systems for the performance of those systems in terms of policy-making. While there is certainly no lack of research from institutionalist perspectives or research focusing on the policy-making capacity of federal systems, only few publications aim explicitly at the relationships between these two areas in a systematic way. This systematic connection is realized here by arranging the various contributions in three broad clusters, each dealing with a specific perspective and research strategy.

After the editor presents an overview of the various approaches and conceptualizations of federalism in her introductory chapter, the first part of the volume is addressed to the role of federalism in several countries. Klaus von Beyme comes to the conclusion that federalism is stronger in the Russian Federation than it was in the Soviet Union, but that Russia is 'not yet a federal system' although there is definitely 'centrifugal regionalism'. In a similar way, extensive analyses of the developments in India by Subrata Mitra and in Spain by Mireia Grau i Creus reveal the complex and complicated nature of federalism in the process of establishing democracy. These three chapters contain a wealth of information on the relationships between central and regional government without following the conventional approach of taking US experiences as the point of departure and as the ultimate yardstick to evaluate federalism.

The question of the effects of federalism on policy-making is answered in several ways in the second and third parts of this volume on the basis of case studies and comparative statistical analyses respectively. The second part contains four case studies of well-established Western democracies and starts with a discussion of the complex system of German federalism by Ute Wachendorfer-Schmidt. In his examination of Switzerland Klaus Armingeon rejects the depiction of Swiss federalism as 'the worst of all possible worlds' and he stresses the high level of satisfaction among the Swiss with their political system as compared to American citizens. Long and complicated decision-making procedures are described by Martin Painter and Stephen Tomblin in their overviews of attempts to reform federalist aspects of the political systems of Australia and Canada. As Painter points out, money made available by the central government often provides the 'glue' to make parties stick to federal agreements. The provision of resources and regulations by central agencies is at the core of the comparative analyses presented in the third part of the volume. By using macro-indicators for divergent aspects of the political and economic systems in a number of countries, the performances of federal and non-federal states are contrasted. Frances Castles focuses on the consequences of fiscal decentralization for economic performance, Hans Keman discusses policy performances in relation to main characteristics of political systems, and Thomas Lancaster and Alexander Hicks are especially interested in the impact of neo-corporatist and federal features on economic performance. The analyses in the second and the third parts lead to the above mentioned conclusion that 'federalism does matter' – what becomes clear is that this evident relevance depends on a number of specific characterizations and developments and that there is no room for trivial generalizations in this area.

Yet federal systems do not only have benign characteristics. Sophisticated discussions of 'national' versus 'federal' aspects of constitutions by James Madison back in June 1788 cannot hide the fact that the distribution of power between centre and periphery usually implies a 'structural asymmetry', which can easily develop into a rather dangerous 'contradiction' with very high decision-making costs. Even if bloodshed is avoided, a lot remains to be desired. Federal processes are blamed for being slow and ineffective or even depicted as 'the worst of all possible worlds' in the case of Switzerland. A simple division of power between central and non-central government is a necessary but certainly not a sufficient condition for the successful pacification of divergent interests. What is needed is a legitimate compromise about the boundaries and range of national and federal competence, based on the idea of decentralization as well as on the recognition of the fact that sovereignty cannot be cleaved by definition. As the discussions of the developments of very different political systems in this volume show, this delicate balance is difficult to obtain and can only survive if the rules and regulations are explicitly attuned to the specific circumstances in a country or region. The rewards of federalism, then, are evident and possible disadvantages look rather unimportant when the alternatives of separation, oppression, and internal war are considered.

JAN W. VAN DETH
Series Editor
Mannheim, March 2000

Introduction

Ute Wachendorfer-Schmidt

The purpose of this book is to study problem-solving in federal systems, and to compare the political performance of federal and non-federal states, and of different types of federations. Political scientists may find this topic of interest, given the comparative aspect, and a general readership may also care to learn more about the political potential of federalism, a form of state organization that still represents a minority – 19 of the 193 sovereign states of the world – but that already rules over more than a third of the world population.[1] Finally, the theme of the book may attract the attention of those who are concerned with the potential gains and drawbacks of the territorial organization of governance, whether in theoretical or empirical analysis, political consulting, or political decision-making. In a world marked by continuing economic and political integration, which at the same time generates resistance in many people who fear losing their livelihood or their identity, it is imperative to inquire more systematically into the potential effects of the territorial division of power on peace, freedom, democracy, economic wealth and social security.

The book focuses on the following questions:

1　What difference does federalism make to policy-making and political performance, as compared with non-federal systems?[2]
2　Does the type of federalism make a difference, and if so, to what extent?
3　Are there specific vulnerabilities[3] of federal states that affect their steering capacities, and if so, under what conditions can these vulnerabilities be overcome?

The role of the state in policy-making and policy outcomes has long been a central topic of research in political science. After focusing on the significance of variables such as the partisan complexion of government, the party system, and the distribution of power between labour and non-labour parties, scholars have increasingly moved institutional and cultural variables to the centre of attention (e.g. Evans et al. 1985; Scharpf et al. 1976; Schmidt 1998). When it comes to determining the reason for different political outcomes, federalism is a promising candidate in the eyes of one school of thought, while another school of thought suggests that federalism makes no particular difference in terms of public policy (Riker 1975: 143; Lane and Ersson 1996: 112–13).

Studies on federalism have analysed the advantages and drawbacks of federal states as compared to non-federal ones, using both normative theory and empirical research. Among the advantages attributed to federalism is that it attempts to reconcile people's wish for general freedom with their need for (domestic and external) security by making the government big enough to provide security but preventing it from pursuing prescriptive outcomes or imposing 'best' solutions (Madison 1993; Morley 1981). Another advantage, public choice economists argue, is that federalism provides the citizens, apart from their votes, with an additional means of making politicians responsive to their preferences (Brennan and Buchanan 1980). Because of the institutional competition between governments in a federation, it is argued, citizens can threaten to abandon their state and pay taxes elsewhere, thereby adding 'exit' to 'voice' (Hirschman 1970). Other advantages of federalism are that it provides more room for experiment and innovation than a non-federal state (Derthick 1992: 674), and that it boosts economic development by giving the market more judicial security and more room to manoeuvre than unitary states (Weingast 1995). Furthermore, federalism is thought to strengthen not only the market with respect to the state, but also solidarity, since people are more inclined to help each other in smaller entities where ties of solidarity can develop than in big entities (Bohley 1992: 52; Höffe 1999: 149). When a state passes from colonial rule to independence or from a communist system to a more democratic and capitalist system, federalism is said to be the best possible option to prevent the state from falling apart and to avoid ethno-nationalist bloodshed (Stepan 1999). Finally, federalism is labelled an evolutionary progress, because it provides a differentiated decision-making structure as a match for the governance needs of modern complex societies (Mayntz 1995).

Listed as disadvantages of federalism are, among others, its alleged inefficiencies, the political wastage of multiplying parliaments and politicians, and the constraints it imposes on national governments in implementing their political projects, because the lower political units can make choices of their own, or because they can obstruct the federal government's plans using their rights of co-decision in the second chamber. For example, in the United States as well as in Australia, federalism has been blamed for placing special barriers on redistributive policies for individuals and places. In Canada, on the other hand, federalism is said to have created social systems that are in part inefficient, non-transparent and reform-resistant, because they were built not only to assist people in special cases of need, but to meet a second goal, that of competitive state-building (Banting 1987). In Germany, federalism has been neutral with regard to the creation of an extensive welfare state, and a motor for equalizing regional disparities in public services and infrastructure. However, this only worked in times of economic growth. Since redistribution between places and structural reforms appeared on the agenda, federalism has been blamed for being a major obstacle for change (Scharpf et al. 1976).

The theoretical assumptions and empirical findings about the 'federal effect' on public policy do not only vary widely but also contradict each other. Can federalism serve the needs of poor, politically unstable states with a heterogeneous population the same way as it provides sophisticated forms of decision-making for wealthy constitutional democracies? Can federalism foster competition and solidarity alike?

More systematic cross-national research on the effects of the territorial organization of the state is needed in order to answer these questions. The road map for these studies has been clarified with 'new institutionalism'. Of course, the study of political institutions is an old topic in political science, which is what Klaus von Beyme (1997: 15) – author of the contribution on Russia in this book – had in mind when he called himself a 'paleo institutionalist', an ironic term that may be truly used in the sense of 'old institutionalism' when we think of the political scientists who wrote about federalism in the 1930s and 1940s, and whose definitions and analyses are still cited today, such as Carl J. Friedrich (1968) and K.C. Wheare (1963). New institutionalism, as opposed to the classic research on institutions, explores not only constitutional arrangements but also formal and informal rules, norms of action and effective behaviour. It does not exclusively analyse the political sphere, but also the interface between politics and economics. The key variables of political institutionalism are institutions and actors, together with their perceptions of a situation, the choices available to them, and their strategies. The choices are assumed to be made under conditions of bounded rationality. In contrast to the rational choice model of *homo oeconomicus*, political institutionalism conceives of actors' preferences as culturally formed and contingent. The same applies to institutions. Finally, institutions are regarded not only as restricting but also as enabling determinants of political decisions (Scharpf 1997; Schmidt 1992).

A possible way of analysing the effect of federalism on public policy and policy outcomes is comparing largely the same policy areas in both federal and non-federal states (Pierson 1995; Braun 2000). This book opts for another strategy, using different analytical approaches, from cross-national studies to single case studies, and exploring different themes in several countries. The cross-national studies focus on democracies with highly developed economies, a choice that is justified because the potential effect of federalism on state activity and economic performance should mainly be measured among most similar cases. The single case studies, however, seek to avoid a strong Western and European orientation by including not only Canada, Australia, Switzerland, Germany and Spain, but also Russia, a case that is not a highly industrialized country and a stable democracy, and India, the world's largest democracy and largest federal system.

I shall now consider the three key questions of the book in turn.

Does federalism matter?

Is there a difference between federal and non-federal states in policy-making and political performance, and if so, to what extent does federalism make a difference? Some scholars are convinced that there is not much to be said in favour of a 'federalism-makes-a-difference' hypothesis. Federalism is found to be obsolete (Laski 1939), trivial (Riker 1975), or naturally inferior to a non-federal system (Crisp 1978). But if federalism is only a 'standard of style' that differs somewhat from the style of unitary states, as Riker (1975: 144) puts it, and if the central government in a federal state has always the legal authority to do what it wants to do (ibid.), why are there any differences at all in the political outcomes of federal and non-federal states?

There is considerable evidence that there are different policy outcomes worth noting. Drawing on historical evidence, Weingast (1995: 25) argues that federalism, by creating credible restrictions on governmental policy choice, provided the basis for the rule of law and hence the political under-pinnings of economic freedom. Comparative statistical analyses found that both the public sector and the welfare state tend to be smaller in federal than in non-federal states (Cameron 1978; Castles and McKinlay 1979; Schmidt 1996), and that the rates of inflation tend to be lower in federal than in unitary states (Busch 1993; Lijphart 1999: 272). In social policy, a comparative study of the United States of America and Canada has shown that federalism played an important role, in the first case hindering social policy activities of the central government, and in the second case fostering them. The role of federalism thus seems to depend on the characteristics of a particular federal system and its interaction with other major institutions of government, as well as the distribution of power in society (Pierson 1995).

Federalism also seems to have a price, as it benefits those who can use constituent governments to enforce minority policies (Riker 1975: 154) and punishes those who live in states and localities with sparse fiscal resources (Peterson 1995: 189). Furthermore, federalism has a strong tendency to end up in gridlock (Scharpf 1997: 143).

Does the type of federalism make a difference?

Although it is a common claim in federalist studies that federal systems differ significantly from each other (see, for example, Abromeit 1993), comparative analyses of political institutions have raised doubt as to whether federalism exists at all, given that on the one hand formally federal constitutions coexist with centralized structures of decision-making and tax-raising, while on the other hand there are states that are both unitary and decentralized. These mixed types seem to blur the differences between federal and unitary state organizations. It is therefore important to define federalism before going on to inquire about the potential effects of different models of federalism on public policy.

The difference between federal and non-federal states

The basic characteristic of federalism is a *guaranteed* division of power between central and regional governments. Vertical diffentiation of powers exists in federal Switzerland and Germany as well as in unitary Denmark, Finland and Sweden, as measures of fiscal decentralization show (OECD 1998), but none of the unitary states come under Riker's definition of federalism: 'Federalism is a political organization in which the activities of government are divided between regional governments and central government in such a way that each kind of government has some activities on which it makes final decision' (Riker 1975: 101). In the unitary states of Sweden and Denmark, some scholars claim there is a 'nordic way of fiscal federalism' (Rattso 1998), on the grounds that municipalities provide public services and receive financial aid by the government. The existence of these political subunits, however, is not protected by the constitution. It depends on the will of the government *and* of the citizens. Their dis-satisfaction with local public sector services might lead to local authorities losing their character of political institutions, and gradually being replaced by service companies (Lotz 1998: 19). None of this is possible in states which conform to the first characteristic of federalism, as defined by Elazar (1987: 42): the 'desire or will to be federal on the part of the polity involved. Adopting and maintaining a constitution is . . . the first and foremost means of expressing that will.'

A second basic characteristic of federalism is seen in *decentralization*. It is generally assumed that 'the fundamental purpose of guaranteeing a division of power is to ensure that a substantial portion of power will be exercised at the regional level or, to put it more succinctly, that the purpose of noncentralization of power is decentralization of power' (Lijphart 1999: 187). This element, however, would exclude Germany as a federal system, which is why Wheare (1963) did not list it as a federal state. The Federal Republic of Germany, although marked by a high degree of fiscal decentral-ization,[4] allows for relatively little policy discretion at the level of con-stituent states. A largely centralized power of tax legislation, a strong system of joint taxes and regional fiscal equalizsation, together with intense formal and informal intergovernmental collaboration, have resulted in largely uniform policy results across the republic. But in spite of the relatively small degree of autonomy left for the constituent states (which were compensated for this loss of competences through co-decision rights in the second chamber), Germany figures on all of the more recent comparative studies of political institutions as federal (Lane and Ersson 1996; Lijphart 1999; Schmidt 1997).

Therefore, decentralization of power as a criterion for federalism must be complemented with another feature: the way the political sub-units of a central state coordinate their policies among themselves and with the central government, in short the form of 'joint decision-making'. It is not only vertical differentiation that distinguishes federal from unitary systems, but the degree of autonomy of the constituent parts and their forms of co-ordination (see also Schultze 1998: 187). Both characteristics vary between federal systems in a way that can be deduced from two models, collaborative federalism and arm's length federalism (see below).

In addition to these primary characteristics – a guaranteed division of powers, the degree of autonomy of constituent states, and their forms of co-ordination – there are secondary characteristics of federalism, which are generally assumed to be a bicameral legislature with a strong federal chamber to represent the constituent regions, a written constitution that is difficult to amend, and a supreme court or special constitutional court that can protect the constitution by means of its power of judicial review (Lijphart 1999: 187).

If it is true that, as Lane (1996: 105) argues, 'perhaps the difference between a federal system and a unitary system simply boils down to the fact that in a federal system the state or provincial governments are more unambiguously the representatives of self-determination', this should still make a lot of difference in the performance of democracies. Seen from the perspective of new institutionalism, a set of political rules like federalism – dividing political power among different tiers of government and introducing new territorial actors (the constituent units) organized along territorial lines – suggests important political consequences. It has been stated that policies capable of generating legitimacy in the population, such as public social provision or promotion of regional development, can be an object of 'competitive state-building' (Banting 1987; Pierson and Leibfried 1998: 32). While governments care about policy control *independent* of policy content, citizens and social interest groups may care about the locus of policy control precisely because it *influences* policy content (Pierson 1995: 455). In a *quasi*-federal polity like the European Union (Bach 1999: 11; Pinder 1993: 47), governments engage in a 'regulatory competition' to make European regulations resemble their respective national policy solutions (Héritier et al. 1994), seeking to minimize the costs of adaptation and to avoid paying again for 'sunk costs' (Pierson 1996: 145).

Types of federalism

The political institutions of federalism are more than a constitutional arrangement. They are also a complex balance of many social interests that has been sanctioned by institutions (Lehmbruch 1998: 184). Federal arrangements can be tailored to give collaboration between the government tiers priority over their autonomy, if social integration and equivalent living standards over the country are the goal. Vice versa, autonomy of the constituent units will be enshrined in federal institutions if self-determination and diversity are the aims of federalism. These normative decisions of the elites will bring forth two ideal types of federalism. In the first case, political institutions will motivate territorial actors to collaborate by dividing the powers between them functionally and providing for tasks to be accomplished jointly. In the second case, powers will be distributed according to policy areas, and powers will be separated ('dual federalism' or 'interstate federalism'). This second type of federalism characterizes Switzerland, Canada and the United States. The former type – also called intrastate or executive federalism – is to be found in Austria and in Germany with their high degree of joint decision making. The two types of federalism can be mainly distinguished by the role of the second chamber and the structure of fiscal federalism. In intrastate federalism, the constituent units influence federal legislation through the vote of their governments' representatives in the second chamber; in dual or interstate federalism, this task is performed by representatives selected through popular elections. Fiscal federalism in intrastate federalism is characterized by a joint tax system, equal tax rates, and vertical and hoizontal fiscal equalization. 'Dual' federal systems have competing and separate tax-raising powers and variable tax fees. The degree of variation between the two types of federalism is limited, though, because institutional competition between territorial units is restricted by externalities and destructive outbidding ('race to the bottom') (Apolte 1999). This is why joint decision systems are a common feature of all modern federations, varying only in number, duration, character (compulsory or voluntary), and quality of their results (decisions can be binding, or allow for opting out and unilateral action). The denominations of the two types of federal systems used here are *collaborative federalism* and *'arm's length federalism'* (Kincaid 1991), in order to stress their respective main features and to express that it is not only structures but also the norms of the territorial actors that determine how federalism works.

The United States of America provides an example of arm's length federalism, while Germany represents a typical case of collaborative federalism. There are also mixed systems of intergovernmental relations, like Australia and Canada. While in Australia fiscal policy is made by some intergovernmental machinery which reflects 'the brute power' (*Painter* in this volume) of the central government, there are voluntary forms of co-ordination between the states in some sectoral policies. A third, more collaborative mode of co-ordination has evolved where decentralized decision-making caused too much diversity for resolving problems in an increasingly interdependent and complex world. In Canada, as in Australia, parliamentary governments share overlapping functions, and are forced to co-operate while seeking to preserve their jurisdictions (Banting 1987). States therefore prefer informal co-ordination with opt-out possiblities rather than formal co-ordination when the default clause will not be the chance for independent action but some former (unsatisfactory) status quo that may benefit only a minority.

This difference is decisive according to the theory of joint decision-making (Scharpf et al. 1976). In collaborative federalism, the central government can steer its legislative projects through both chambers – federal parliament and assembly of the constituent states – only with the consent of the majority of the constituent states. In practice, this means the central goverment must win over each of the constituent states, because the latter demand *equal treatment* (Scharpf 1988). The theory of joint decision-making holds that this package of rules leads to a poor outcome in material policy, but subsists for two reasons: the real need of co-ordinating decentralized policies, and the advantages joint decision-making entails for territorial political actors.

The material policy outcome of joint decision systems is said to systematically miss the goals of political problem solution, because the only decisions feasible under these circumstances are for the constituent states to produce more or less of a particular public good or negative externality, like owner flats or environmental pollution. Political solutions that require a *varying* treatment or *varying* activities of the constituent states, however, are difficult to impose because the prospective losers can veto them, which means that redistribution other than with additional financial means is nearly impossible, as are complex territorial interactions to implement innovative and comprehensive solutions, e.g. in structural policy, transport, education, energy or housing policy. Though the decision system generates a tendency to underperformance, the authors of the joint decision theory argue, it is not abolished mainly for two reasons. Positive and negative externalities of decentralized policy-making must be avoided through co-ordination, and the actors involved have a twofold gain out of this structure. Regional and national politicians can win more autonomy *vis-à-vis* both the voter-citizens and their respective parliaments. As package-deals are negotiated between the executives, parliaments do not have much choice other than to approve the whole package, in order not to endanger the solutions found. The citizens' demands for more public services can be more easily rejected by the executives, who can argue that they would love to meet the demands if only the other tiers of government would join in the effort.

This joint decision theory – which has been extended to the European Community (Scharpf 1988) – has been very influential in the debate on federalism. It received many comments and criticism.[5] An alternative theoretical approach holds that the political consequences of joint decision-making in collaborative federalism are not rigidity and underperformance but on the contrary flexible and parsimonious adaptation to new challenges. This 'theory of dynamic federalism' (Benz 1985; Hesse and Benz 1990) postulates that the territorial division of powers is a dynamic system which cannot – as suggested in theories of fiscal federalism – be optimized, entrusting each tier of government with a particular task (Oates 1972). In contrast, the theory of dynamic federalism argues, the distribution of powers between the levels of government varies constantly, according to the respective needs of a society, and their perception by the public and the territorial actors, as well as their preferences. A federal reform as demanded by the defendants of the theory of joint decision-making – to reduce the amount of joint decision-making by giving the constituent states more autonomy and diminishing federal grants-in-aid – misses the point, the authors of 'dynamic federalism' say. Not a new and supposedly ideal distribution of tasks in federalism is required, but a capacity for the system and its actors to learn and respond to new challenges. Changes can then be made according to the situation in each policy area, incremental and informally if possible, in order to avoid the costs of reform. When institutional reform is indispensable, the system should be ready for it by permanently making an 'institutional policy'. In a comparative study of four countries, Hesse and Benz (1990: 223) come to the conclusion that Germany's collaborative federalism is more open to respond to new problems than the arm's length federalism of the United States, the British 'Westminster model' of the unitary state, or the French decentralized unitary state.

The above discussion allows the second key question of this volume to be formulated more precisely as follows: is there a difference between real federal systems that correspond to the ideal types of collaborative federalism and arm's length federalism, and if so, which type of federal organization is better in problem-solving? How do the different types of federalism compare to non-federal states, as far as political performance is concerned?

Are there particular vulnerabilities of federal and non-federal systems?

Federal and unitary systems can be compared, for example, with respect to the efficiency and effectiveness of their decision-making, and to their democratic accountability.

For the first criterion, the economic theory of decision-making has developed a yardstick measure. According to this theory, federal systems have higher costs of consent than non-federal systems. This is because the costs to reach a decision – in terms of preparation, reaching agreement, and implementation – are believed to rise with the number of actors involved (Buchanan and Tullock 1965). Decision costs are highest when the unanimity rule is applied. The economic theory of decision-making distinguishes two types of costs: first, external costs, defined as the dis-advantages experienced by members of a collectivity who do not benefit at all (or not in the same way as the rest of the members) from a collective decision not made by unanimity; second, interdependency costs, which are defined as the sum of decision costs and external costs. Interdependence costs provide a criterion for establishing optimal rules of decision-making: they are met when the costs of interdependence are minimized. The two components of interdependency costs – decision costs and external costs – move in an opposite direction. The more decisions deviate from the unan-imity rule, the higher are the external costs and the lower the decision costs.

According to this theory, it can be hypothesized that (centralized) unitary systems generate lower decision costs but higher external costs. The implementation of laws may thus cause more problems than in federal states. Democratic accountability in the 'Westminster' model of democracy is high, under two conditions (Lijphart 1999: 31–2). First, the exclusion of the minority by the governing majority is mitigated, if today's minority can become the majority in the next election instead of being condemned to permanent opposition. Second, if the society is relatively homogeneous and the major parties are not far apart in their policy outlooks, voters' interests are also served by a government they have not elected.

Federal systems, in contrast, tend to have high decision costs and low external costs. In highly fragmented political systems whose lower govern-ment levels enjoy considerable autonomy, co-ordination may be difficult to achieve at all, because actors are mostly faced with so-called *mixed motive games* in which the preferences of players are partly harmonious and partly in conflict. These games or 'actor constellations' (Scharpf 1997: 69–79) have been analysed giving them names like 'assurance', 'battle of the sexes', 'prisoner's dilemma', and 'chicken'. The failure to achieve co-ordination can obstruct the common good considerably, as demonstrated by the case of Australia where it took over a hundred years for territorial actors to agree on a standard gauge railway system that directly linked all mainland Australian state capitals (*Painter* in this volume). In collaborative federal-ism, co-ordination is easier to achieve, given the interdependence of the territorial units and the institutional provisions. However, co-operation among (in principle) equals tends to generate other difficulties, like reaching agreement on controversial policies. The political actors in an arm's length federalism can be made accountable for their decisions by their voters. This is much more difficult in collaborative federalism, because it tends to obscure responsibilities for decisions and for expenditure.

It is likely that neither of the two principles of state organization – federal and unitary – holds the promise to be the ideal solution for governing modern democracies. It is probably sound to assume that the best form of organization for a given state varies with the context in which the state operates, such as the degree of heterogeneity of society, the level of economic development, the historical origin of the state, and the regime type. Notwithstanding, if there are characteristic weaknesses and advantages that can be attributed to each of the political frameworks of the state, it should be possible to find out how the respective vulnerabilities of both systems can be overcome. One of the purposes of this book is precisely to contribute to this task.

Plan of the book

The book is made up of three parts. The first examines the role of federalism in countries that have passed from a non-democratic polity to democratization and are of multinational composition. Does federalism contribute to strengthening democracy and avoiding ethno-national bloodshed, or, asked more modestly, does federalism work at all? Klaus von Beyme explores this question for Russia, Subrata K. Mitra for India, and Mireia Grau i Creus for Spain. The second part contains four case studies dealing with the effect of federalism on policy-making in advanced Western democracies. Here, the emphasis lies on evaluating how complex issues are resolved in complex federations, as well as on the typical performance of arm's length federalism and collaborative federalism, for it is assumed that both types of federal polities will present strengths and weaknesses of their own. Ute Wachendorfer-Schmidt analyses Germany's collaborative federalism and Klaus Armingeon discusses the Swiss case which presents features of both the federal system of the United States of America and the German federal system. Martin Painter depicts Australia as an arm's length polity under change, and Stephen G. Tomblin sees Canada as an arm's length polity resistant to change. The third part is dedicated to comparative statistical analyses of federal and non-federal systems, contrasting also centralized with non-centralized states. Francis G. Castles analyses the effects of fiscal decentralization on economic performance, Hans Keman examines policy performance in four types of 'state formats', and Thomas D. Lancaster and Alexander M. Hicks inquire into the impact of federalism and neo-corporatism on economic performance.

The book has deliberately chosen to give more or less equal attention to the role of federalism in consolidating democracies that have been emerging from non-democratic rule after the Second World War, to the working of federalism in stable and rich Western democracies, and to the comparative statistical analysis of policy performance in federal and non-federal states. The non-Western federal or not-yet federal systems deserve a close look, because they have grown in the last century, outnumbering the six federal systems existing in 1900 by far, so that today's 19 federations are mostly economically weak, politically unstable, and under authoritarian or quasi-democratic rule (Wachendorfer-Schmidt 2000). The experience of India, the world's largest democracy and largest federation, and of Russia, a big and unstable country in transition, may well offer lessons for other federations to follow.

Klaus von Beyme starts the first part with a brilliant analysis of federalism in Russia. The author, a renowned expert in the field, wrote his first book on this same topic thirty-six years ago, suggested by Carl Joachim Friedrich, an advocate of federalism. Beyme's verdict then was that there was no federalism in the Soviet Union. Today, his conclusion is slightly more encouraging. Von Beyme states that there is centrifugal regionalism but not yet a federal system in Russia, as there is no functioning system of centre–periphery relations with a stable legal base, efficiently supervised by the Constitutional Court and a working system of financial support. Furthermore, the fact that there is no federal party state contributes to the lack of influence of the regions in the parliamentary chambers in Moscow. Why federalism does not (yet) work in Russia is explained by the failure of the political centre to build strong federal institutions. Russia had to tackle social and ethnic diversity by granting autonomy to the subunits and by offering the minorities a fair chance in the electoral system. Yet the institutional mix chosen favoured disintegration rather than integration, the author states. With elements of both majoritarian and proportional electoral formulas, and distributing various degrees of autonomy to the regions, Russia's system is somewhere in between the way territorial conflicts have been solved in Austria, Germany and the United States, and the solutions of decentralization and devolution in Spain and the United Kingdom. A consistent federal policy, von Beyme argues, was beyond the power of the central government, because its power had withered away in the conflict between parliamentarization, presidentialization and confederal-ization, and between the three men Gorbachev, Yeltsin and Ryzhkov.

India's federalism was a success for national integration and democracy, as we learn from *Subrata K. Mitra*. He investigates the 'Indian puzzle' stated in the following question: with India's multi-ethnic society, structural asymmetry of constitutional units, mass illiteracy and poverty, and the task of state formation and nation-building, why does federalism even in a broader sense survive in India at all? Mitra focuses first on the constraints of the federal process in India, which give the states a precarious juridical position and strengthen the central government. Mitra then analyses the development of the federal process since independence, distinguishing three phases. After an authoritarian interlude when Indira Gandhi declared a state of emergency, reducing India to a unitary state under authoritarian leadership, the system reverted to the earlier stage of co-operation between the centre and the states. On the basis of a 1996 survey of the Indian electorate, Mitra states that the Indian public has a reasonably high level of trust in all three levels of the federal system. The success story of federalism against all odds is then explained in a neo-institutionalist way, which treats the rules of the federal game not as given but also as part of the game. A prominent place in the explanation is given to the role and impact of political parties. They 'socialize' champions of local and regional interests who become born-again nationalists following the logic of the Indian political process. Mitra concludes that against an adversary like the ethno-nationalist, a genuine and imaginative federal process is the best coping mechanism. This can only work, however, when a federal deal can be struck with a specific group of actors. If the actors themselves are fragmented and some of them are not part of the negotiations at all, like the Kashmiri rebels, the model is no longer effective in producing a legitimate federal solution.

Mireia Grau i Creus' analysis of intergovernmental relations in Spain concludes the case studies of the first part. She argues that Spain is not a fully developed federation, because such a polity presupposes a degree of self-government of the subnational units which make up the state, and a degree of participation of these units in the federal policy process. The first characteristic is only insatisfactorily met, because the powers of the *comunidades* vary considerably and are still subject to negotiations with the Madrid government. Ethno-nationalism prevents the Spanish constitution from acquiring the form it normally has in a federal state, making final decisions about the distribution of powers, because the *comunidades históricas* are in a favourable position to receive even more powers from the central government, which depends on the support of nationalist parties in the parliament of Madrid (see Wendland 1997: 178). Grau i Creus concentrates her analysis on the second characteristic of federalism, on the participation of the *Comunidades* in the national policy process. Drawing on her empirical research in the Ministerio de Administraciones Públicas (MAP), she shows that intergovernmental relations are weak and fragmented. The *comunidades* do not have the right to participate in central state policy-making, nor has the central government succeeded in establishing meaningful joint decision systems, because the *comunidades* defend their own powers and are supported in this policy by the Constitutional Court. The task of co-ordination is therefore fulfilled not by the territorial actors but by the political parties which provide a centralist counter-balance.

The second part begins with an extreme case of collaborative federalism, generally criticised for its slow and deficient policy responses to new challenges, being confronted with a need for extension, for handing over parts of its sovereignty, and for channelling large sums from the old territory to the new one, all simultaneously. *Ute Wachendorfer-Schmidt* shows how Germany's federalism managed to do all this, making only small adaptations in federal institutions and decision-making routines. This outcome is positive, as compared to the predictions made in the theory of interlocking politics (Scharpf et al. 1976; Scharpf 1988). The author finds as an explanation for this unexpected flexibility two factors which oil the intergovernmental machinery. One is pressure from political actors not belonging to the federal decision system, like party politicians or the Bundesverfassungsgericht (Federal Constitutional Court), who – in demanding an appropriate political solution to a problem – force the territorial actors to subordinate their institutional self-interest and bring about a solution. The other mechanism consists of shifting the costs for a political decision to third parties not involved in the intergovernmental decision system. Among the victims of this cost-shifting are self-governed organizations like municipalities or universities, and also future generations. Therefore, collaborative federalism does not always block quick and innovative decisions, yet its political solutions come at a high price in the long run. The federal system works in such a way that it privileges the satisfaction of demands made in the present, neglecting the interests of future generations and the future of society in general.

Klaus Armingeon analyses Swiss federalism in comparative perspective. His starting point is that the Swiss federation shares important traits with the federalism of the United States, as Swiss cantons enjoy discretionary powers comparable to the states of the USA; and there are also similarities with the German model of federalism, because Swiss cantons are strongly interlocked with federal agencies. According to the major findings of research on federalism, the Swiss type is therefore prone to the deficiencies of both models, forming the 'worst of all possible worlds'. Yet Armingeon demonstrates that this is not the case. Using as criteria for evaluation the goals frequently assigned to federalism, the author discusses the deficiencies of Swiss federalism, such as lack of transparency and efficiency, and weighs them against its achievements. He states that Swiss federalism has been successful concerning the core goals of federalism, e.g. constraint on central government, sustainability, policy innovation, integration and preservation of socio-cultural and political differences. The favourable result is explained by three groups of arguments: Swiss federalism is a system of loose coupling and therefore less prone to deadlock; actors in the intergovernmental decision-making operate according to the same logic of negotiation and compromise; and their c-ooperative solidarity is enhanced by several institutions and structural characteristics, such as direct democracy.

Martin Painter presents Australia as a mixed type of a federal system, with elements of collaborative federalism yet a certain arm's length distinctiveness of state governments. The author notes a long-term shift from an unfettered, arm's length type of co-ordination, to closer intergovernmental collaboration. During the 1980s and 1990s, ventures in closer collaboration among the central government and the states increased, a trend pushed by the central government in order to get economic and regulatory reform through. Painter concludes that Australia overcame the problems of unfettered co-ordination, yet used collaborative mechanisms only sparingly and flexibly. This, Painter argues, spared the country *one* of the two drawbacks attributed to joint decision systems, namely the danger of gridlock. The other disadvantage, though, could not be avoided. Australia's polity has become more of an 'executive federalism', with the parliaments only rubber-stamping agreements negotiated among the state governments and the central government.

Another mixed type of federalism is Canada, even though the relations between the provincial governments and the central government are more adversarial than in Australia, and the very 'moral foundations' of federalism are being questioned, to underpin the demand for a new federal bargain, on behalf of ethnic self-determination or of economic efficiency (LaSelva 1996; Robinson and Simeon 1994). *Stephen G. Tomblin* analyses the restraints that Canada's federalism poses on regional integration. As in Europe, economic integration in North America makes boundaries more porous and exerts pressure on the regions to compete. However, regional integration between Canada and the United States has been a source of conflict like the Quebec question in Canada. Tomblin demonstrates from the example of the poor Canadian Atlantic provinces and the New England states how attempts at regional integration have produced only modest results. This was due, to some extent, to the different government structures in Canada and in the United States. An even greater obstacle for regional integration, Tomblin argues, are the territorial and jurisdictional interests of the premiers of the Atlantic provinces. Tomblin's message should be heard in Europe and in Germany, particularly because competitive and decentralized federalism is seen as an asset for change on this side of the Atlantic.

Part 3 about the comparative political economy of federalism and decentralization is opened by *Francis G. Castles*. In a cross-national analysis of post-war economic performance in 21 nations of the Organization for Economic Co-operation and Development (OECD), Castles finds no evidence for a direct link between federalism and economic outcomes in the post-war period, but shows that decentralized fiscal arrangements have been associated with reduced inflationary pressures and with higher rates of post-war economic growth. As far as post-war labour market performance is concerned, no evidence is presented to connect it with either political or fiscal decentralization. According to this study, decentralization of the fisc, not political decentralization, is the crucial institutional parameter for higher growth and more effective inflation control. The author warns, however, against using this result for practical political decisions, and calls for further theoretical and empirical investigation.

Hans Keman objects to the claim implicitly made in many federalist studies that federalism is a superior form of the democratic state. He argues, first, that federal states may have unitary features and vice versa, and second, that unitary states may have alternative institutional provisions for checking the power of the executive. Assessing 18 democracies in terms of their federal–unitary organization ('right to decide') and centralization–decentralization ('right to act'), Keman describes four clusters, with six federal and six unitary states proper (federal-decentral and unitary-central), and six states with mixed forms (federal-central and unitary-decentral). In his comparative cross-national analysis, Keman finds that the 'real' federal cases tend to have a smaller government than others and produce higher levels of affluence and less 'misery'. He makes the point, however, that the organization of the state is only *one* factor among others with respect to material performance.

In a pooled time-series analysis of 18 OECD countries, *Thomas D. Lancaster* and *Alexander M. Hicks* find that federalism tends to improve macro-economic outcomes like investment, income growth, unemployment and inflation. On the other hand, federal states are found to have a tendency to inhibit redistributive social policies. While these findings are perfectly in line with previous analyses (see above), Lancaster and Hicks show by adding tripartite neo-corporatism as a second independent variable that the combination of the two variables produces mixed results. While federalism as an institutional arrangement stands for decentralization and market-preservation, neo-corporatism as an economic policy-making style emphasizes centralization at the national level. The study by Lancaster and Hicks reminds us that federalism interacts with other formal and informal arrangements for decision-making in a political system.

The line of inquiry pursued in this book owes much to the discussions and papers given at a workshop entitled 'Does federalism matter?', held during the joint session of workshops of the European Consortium of Political Research in Warwick in March 1998, as well as to debates in conferences of the German Association for Political Science (Deutsche Vereinigung für Politische Wissenschaft), particularly its section 'Analysis of the public sector and public administration'.[6] It also draws on discussions in the Faculté des sciences sociales et politiques of the Institute for Political Science of Lausanne university, and the Institute for Political Science of Heidelberg University. I am grateful to all these institutions for the opportunities they provided for discussion and scientific exchange. I also thank the political scientists, country experts, and experts on federalism for their helpful comments and interesting papers given. I thank the students of Heidelberg University for their interest in this topic and their questions and comments that opened new angles on it. And many thanks to Tobias Ostheim for his technical support in the final edition of this book.

Notes

1 In 1994, the 19 federations amounted only to 9.8 per cent of the 193 sovereign states, ruling over 36 per cent of world population. See *Fischer Weltalmanach* (1997) *Zahlen-Daten-Fakten '98*, Frankfurt: Fischer, 31–47 (author's calculation).

2 Political performance relates to the degree to which the political system generates appropriate solutions to problems of political guidance. Solutions can be judged by the following factors: (1) efficiency or period of time needed for the political system to respond to a problem that can and should be resolved by the state; (2) effectiveness or material outcome (to what extent does a policy resolve fundamental problems of political guidance and coordination?); (3) capacity for institutional reform or procedural changes (appropriate decisions and their implementation may require that the rules of decision-making and of implementation be adapted; to this end, it may be sufficient simply to modify the

rules and procedures currently used, but institutional reform may also be necessary). See Wachendorfer-Schmidt (1999: 14).

3 Vulnerabilities refer to the typical weaknesses that are attributed to federal or non-federal patterns of state organizations, respectively. Federal systems allegedly have problems of co-ordination which they can only overcome at a price of having problems implementing controversial policies. Non-federal systems, according to the economic theory of decision-making processes, seem to have higher costs of consent than non-federal states have.

4 In 1996 the federal government's tax share was 47.8 per cent, the *Länder* received a portion of total tax revenues of 39.8 per cent, and the communities of 12.4 per cent (OECD 1997: 79).

5 See, for example, Pollack (1994).

6 Some recent workshops focused on the theory and practice of federalism, organized by the 'Analysis of the public sector and public administration' section of the German Association for Political Science. See, for example, 'Föderalismusforschung: Bestandsaufnahme und theoretische Perspektiven', Bundeswehrunversität Hamburg, 4–6 February, 1999; as well as 'Wie problemlösungsfähig ist die EU? Regieren im europäischen Mehrebenensystem', 29–31 October 1999, Technische Universität, München. Another workshop that focused on the effects of European integration on domestic politics and policy outcomes in the EU member states brought together scholars who are engaged in a line of research supported by the Deutsche Forschungsgemeinschaft (German Research Foundation), on governance in the European Union. The workshop was held on 13–14 July 1998 in Mannheim and was titled 'Demokratisches Regieren jenseits des Staates'. All these debates demonstrate how federalism and federal arrangements between nation states are at the leading edge of interest in political science and public law.

References

Abromeit, H. (1993) *Interessenvermittlung zwischen Konkurrenz und Konkordanz*, Opladen: Leske & Budrich.

Apolte, T. (1999) *Die ökonomische Konstitution eines föderalen Systems*, Tübingen: Mohr Siebeck.

Bach, M. (1999) *Die Bürokratisierung Europas. Verwaltungseliten, Experten und politische Legitimation in Europa*, Frankfurt–New York: Campus.

Banting, K.G. (1987) *The Welfare State and Canadian Federalism*, Kingston and Montreal: McGill-Queen's University Press.

Benz, A. (1985) *Föderalismus als dynamisches System. Zentralisierung und Dezentralisierung im föderativen Staat*, Opladen: Westdeutscher Verlag.

von Beyme, K. (1991) *Theorie der Politik im 20. Jahrhundert*, Frankfurt am Main: Suhrkamp.

—— (1997) *Der Gesetzgeber. Der Bundestag als Entscheidungszentrum*, Opladen: Westdeutscher Verlag.

Bohley, P. (1992) 'Chancen und Gefährdungen des Föderalismus', in K. Bohr (ed.), *Föderalismus. Demokratische Struktur für Deutschland und Europa*, München: Beck, 31–84.

Braun, D. (ed.) (2000) *Public Policy and Federalism*, Aldershot: Ashgate.

Brennan, G. and Buchanan, J.M. (1980) *The Power to Tax: Analytical Foundations of a Fiscal Constitution*, Cambridge: Cambridge University Press.

Buchanan, J.M. and Tullock, G. (1965) *The Calculus of Consent: Logical Foundations of Constitutional Democracy*, Ann Arbor: University of Michigan Press.

Busch, A. (1993) 'The Politics of Price Stability: Why German-Speaking Nations are Different', in F.G. Castles (ed.) *Families of Nations: Patterns of Public Policy in Western Democracies*, Aldershot: Dartmouth, 35–92.

Cameron, D. (1978) 'The Expansion of the Public Economy: A Comparative Analysis', *American Political Science Review* 72, 4: 1243–61.

Castles, F.G. and McKinlay, R. (1979) 'Does Politics Matter? An Analysis of the Public Welfare Commitment in Advanced Democratic States', *European Journal of Political Research* 7: 169–86.

Crisp, L.F. (1978) *Australian National Government*, 4th edn, Melbourne: Longman Cheshire.

Derthick, M. (1992) 'Up-to-Date in Kansas City: Reflections on American Federalism', *Political Science and Politics* 25, 4: 671–5.

Elazar, D.J. (1987) *Exploring Federalism*, Tuscaloosa: University of Alabama Press.

Evans, P., Rueschemeyer, D. and Skocpol, T. (eds) (1985) *Bringing the State Back In*, Cambridge: Cambridge University Press.

Friedrich, C.J. (1968) *Trends of Federalism in Theory and Practice*, New York: F.A. Praeger.

Hamilton, A., Madison, J. and Jay, J. (1993) *Die Federalist Papers*, Darmstadt: Wissenschaftliche Buchgesellschaft (American edition 1787/88).

Héritier, A. et al. (1994) *Die Veränderung von Staatlichkeit in Europa*, Opladen: Leske & Budrich.

Hesse, J.J. and Benz, A. (1990) *Die Modernisierung der Staatsorganisation. Institutionspolitik im internationalen Vergleich: USA, Großbritannien, Frankreich, Bundesrepublik Deutschland*, Baden-Baden: Nomos.

Hirschman, A.O. (1970) *Exit, Voice, and Loyalty: Responses to Decline in Firms, Organizations, and States*, Cambridge, MA: Harvard University Press.

Höffe, O. (1999) *Demokratie im Zeitalter der Globalisierung*, München: Beck.

Kincaid, J. (1991) 'The Competitive Challenge to Cooperative Federalism: A Theory of Federal Democracy', in D.A. Kenyon and J. Kincaid (eds), *Competition Among States and Local Governments: Efficiency and Equity in American Federalism*, Washington, DC: Urban Institute.

Lane, E. (1996) *Constitutions and Political Theory*, Manchester and New York: Manchester University Press.

Lane, J.-E. and Ersson, S. (1996) *European Politics. An Introduction*, London: Sage Publications.

Laski, H.J. (1939) 'The Obsolescence of Federalism', *New Republic*, 3 May: 367–9.

Lehmbruch, G. (1998) *Parteienwettbewerb im Bundesstaat*, 2nd edn, Opladen: Westdeutscher Verlag.

Lijphart, A. (1999) *Patterns of Democracy: Government Forms and Performance in Thirty-Six Countries*, New Haven and London: Yale University Press.

Lotz, J. (1998) 'Local Government Reforms in the Nordic Countries, Theory and Practice', in J. Rattso (ed.), *Fiscal Federalism and State-Local Finance*, Cheltenham: Edward Elgar: 19–28.

Madison, J. (1993) 'Federalist No.51', in A. Hamilton, J. Madison, and J. Jay, *Die Federalist Papers*, Darmstadt: Wissenschaftliche Buchgesellschaft, 319–23 (American edition 1787/88).

Mayntz, R. (1995) 'Föderalismus und die Gesellschaft der Gegenwart', in K. Bentele, B. Reissert and R. Schettkat (eds), *Die Reformfähigkeit von Industrie-*

gesellschaften (Festschrift für Fritz W. Scharpf zum 60. Geburtstag), Frankfurt and New York: Campus, 131–44.

Morley, F. (1981) *Freedom and Federalism*, 2nd edn, Indianapolis: Liberty Fund.

Nohlen, D. and Kasapovic, M. (1996) *Wahlsysteme und Systemwechsel in Osteuropa*, Opladen: Leske & Budrich.

Oates, W.E. (1972) *Fiscal Federalism*, New York: Harcourt.

OECD (1997) *Revenue Statistics of OECD Member Countries*, Paris.

—— (1998) *Economic Surveys 1997–1998: Germany*, Paris.

Ostrom, E. (1986) 'A Method of Institutional Analysis', in F.X. Kaufmann et al. (eds), *Guidance Control and Evaluation in the Public Sector*, New York: Walter de Gruyter.

Peterson, P.E. (1995) *The Price of Federalism*, Washington, DC: Brookings Institution.

Pierson, P. (1995) 'Fragmented Welfare States: Federal Institutions and the Development of Social Policy', *Governance* 8, 4, October: 449–78.

—— (1996) 'The Path to European Integration. A Historical Institutionalist Analysis', *Comparative Political Studies* 29, 2, April 123–63.

Pierson, P. and Leibfried, S. (1998) 'Mehrebenen-Politik und die Entwicklung des "Sozialen Europa"', in S. Leibfried and P. Pierson (eds), *Standort Europa. Sozialpolitik zwischen Nationalstaat und Europäischer Integration*, Frankfurt am Main: Suhrkamp, 11–57.

Pinder, J. (1993) 'The New European Federalism: The Idea and the Achievements', in M. Burgess and A.-G. Gagnon (eds), *Comparative Federalism and Federation*, Toronto: University of Toronto Press.

Pollack, M.A. (1994) 'Creeping Competence: The Expanding Agenda of the European Community', *Journal of Public Policy* 14, 2: 95–145.

Rattso, J. (ed.) (1998) *Fiscal Federalism and State–Local Finance: The Scandinavian Perspective*, Cheltenham and Northampton, MA: Edward Elgar.

Riker, W.H. (1975) 'Federalism', in F.J. Greenstein and N. Polsby (eds) *Handbook of Political Science, Vol. 5: Governmental Institutions and Processes*, Reading, MA: Addison-Wesley, 93–172.

Robinson, I. and Simeon, R. (1994) 'The Dynamics of Canadian Federalism', in J.P Bickerton and A.-G. Gagnon (eds), *Canadian Politics*, 2nd edn, Ontario: Broadview Press, 366–88.

Scharpf, F.W. (1988) 'The Joint Decision Trap: Lessons from German Federalism and European Integration' *Public Administration* 66, Autumn: 239–78.

—— (1994) *Optionen des Föderalismus in Deutschland und Europa*, Frankfurt and New York: Campus.

—— (1997) *Games Real Actors Play: Actor-Centered Institutionalism in Policy Research*, Boulder, CO: Westview Press.

Scharpf, F.W., Reissert, B. and Schnabel, F. (1976) *Politikverflechtung: Theorie und Empirie des kooperativen Föderalismus in der Bundesrebublik*, Kronberg: Scriptor.

Schmidt, M.G. (1992) *Regieren in der Bundesrepublik Deutschland*, Opladen: Leske & Budrich.

—— (1996) 'When Parties Matter: A Review of the Possibilities and Limits of Partisan Influence on Public Policy', *European Journal of Political Research* 30: 155–83.

—— (1997) *Demokratietheorien*, 2nd edn, Opladen: Leske & Budrich.

—— (1998) *Sozialpolitik in Deutschland. Historische Entwicklung und internationaler Vergleich*, Opladen: Leske & Budrich.

Schultze, R.O. (1998) 'Föderalismus', in D. Nohlen, R.-O. Schultze and S.S. Schüttemeyer (eds) *Lexikon der Politik Band 7, Politische Begriffe*, München: H.C. Beck, 186–8.

Stepan, A. (1999) 'Federalism and Democracy: Beyond the U.S. Model', *Journal of Democracy* 10, 4: 19–34.

Wachendorfer-Schmidt, U. (1999) 'Der Preis des Föderalismus in Deutschland', *Politische Vierteljahresschrift* 40, 1: 3–39.

—— (2000) 'Zukunftsschancen des Föderalismus', in H.-D. Klingemann and F. Neidhardt (eds), *Die Zukunft der Demokratie*, Berlin: Wissenschaftszentrum Berlin für Sozialforschung.

Weingast, B. (1995) 'The Economic Role of Political Institutions: Market-Preserving Federalism and Economic Development', *Journal of Law, Economics, and Organization* 11, 1: 1–31.

Wendland, K. (1997) *Spanien auf dem Weg zum Bundesstaat? Entstehung und Entwicklung der Autonomen Gemeinschaften*, Baden-Baden: Nomos.

Wheare, K.D. (1963) *Federal Government*, 4th edn, London: Oxford University Press.

Part I

Federalism, democracy and ethno-national conflict

1　Federalism in Russia

Klaus von Beyme

Soviet legacy and Russian options of constitutional engineering

Pre-Communist Russia had no tradition in federalism. Conservatives have always complained that Czarist Russia copied the French revolutionary system of departments. Lenin took the article on 'national self-determination' in his party programme seriously enough to introduce federalism. His hierarchy of 'Union republics', autonomous Republics and national districts (*kraj*) could have been a fair solution if the whole structure of Soviet federalism had developed beyond 'sham federalism' – distorted by the pillars of centralization such as the party, the secret service and the prokuratua (cf. von Beyme 1965; Kux 1990). Whereas the German federal units were meant to combine 'historical and cultural community' with 'economic efficiency' (Basic Law, Article 29), both criteria were lacking in the Russian federation. After the independence of the greater ethnic units of the former 15 Union Republics there were few historical units left, except some ethnic former 'autonomous republics' which claimed sovereign statehood after 1991. Unfortunately, most of the 89 federal units are not economically efficient areas either.

As in Germany – where the combination of the two criteria for a modernized federal system are not realized in many cases – the federal units were created by accident: in Germany by the allied powers, in Russia by Soviet planners who designed the former districts. All attempts to create economically feasible units – such as Khrushchev's attempt to organize 105 *Sovnarkhozy* (regional economic councils) – were doomed to failure (von Beyme 1988: 69ff.). Marx and Engels had accepted federalism only in the case of ethnic diversity. Lenin therefore proved to be a good Marxist when he chose ethnic criteria as his rationale in creating federal units. Stalin later added other criteria. But the federal system with four tiers was not even fully adapted to the ethnic criterion in order to avoid complaints of those ethnic groups which did not get a territory of their own. The most militant unit within the Russian Federation which has no outside borderline – Tatarstan – has only 30 per cent of the Tatars living in this area. The ethnic 'nations' which gave their name to an area (titular nationality) only constitute more than 50 per cent of the population in eight republics. Russians are the majority even in most areas defined in terms of ethnicity.

Russia started as a separatist state. A quite unusual procedure happened in June 1990. Democrats under Yeltsin and the Communists agreed on a declaration on the independence of Russia in the Congress of People's Deputies. That such a move would happen was as unlikely as a common decision of the Conservatives and the Social Democrats in the Imperial Diet in late 1918 to leave the German Empire and to constitute a 'Prussian Federation' in Northern Germany. The Russian decision was supported by almost half of the people asked in a survey whether the Russian Republic should consider independence (43 per cent, Simon 1999: 10). But the underlying assumption was that the framework of the Union territory would be preserved. Russian sovereignty was not wanted *per se* but was rather an instrument of the Yeltsin camp to outmanoeuvre Gorbachev. The Community of Independent States (CIS) founded in December 1991 was a last attempt to limit the parade of declarations of sovereignty which characterized the main activities in most Union Republics.

The new state which nobody really wanted was ethnically more homogenous than the old Soviet Union: 83 per cent of the population were ethnic Russians (Rossijskij statisticheskij ezhegodnik, Moscow 1997: 74). For the rest of the ethnic minorities the non-ethnic term '*Rossijskij*' was invented. For English speakers the term '*Rossian*' has been proposed, but not accepted (Tishkov 1995). In German this was translatable as '*Russländisch*'. Most Russians never felt comfortable with this terminology. The constitution of 1993 illustrated the problem that old imperial claims to a 'Greater Russia' beyond Russian ethnic borders were lurking in the formulation of Article 1.2, which stated that the terms 'Russian Federation' and 'Russia' are identical.

Of the 23 borders within the CIS only three are not disputed in ethnic terms. In a speech in front of the 'Allrussian Assembly for questions of the development of federal relations' in January 1999, Primakov admitted that there continue to exist 30 disputes about boundaries among the federal subunits within the Russian Federation (quoted from Schneider 1999: 24).

Irredentist feelings are widespread among Russians. It is almost a miracle that so far no Russian Garibaldi has landed with military leagues to liberate the Russians on the Crimean Peninsula who constitute about 70 per cent of the population in this Ukrainian territory though Russian parliaments since 1992 have declared several times that the Crimea is 'Russian'. A rather odd historical accident transformed the peninsula into Ukrainian territory when party leader Khrushchev, a Ukrainian, gave the Crimea to the Ukraine as a kind of birthday present to celebrate the Russian–Ukrainian reunification. In spite of a large exodus of Russians from the former Union Republic, Russians still comprise 17 per cent of the Ukraine's population. Another official euphemism was coined in order to emphasise the special situation of a former empire: these Russians are living in the 'near foreign countries'. More than 11 million Russians live in the Ukraine and more than 6 million in Kazakhstan. That there is no organised irredenta movement is not only due to political apathy. Deep in their hearts, many Russians think that the actual division of territories will not be the last word of history. Only militant chauvinists and Eurasians are discussing irredentist feelings quite openly. Belarus so far is the only former Union Republic which is preparing an '*Anschluss*' in a new type of confederation. The nationalist separation of Ukraine is a nuisance to many Russians who think of the three Slavic peoples in the former Soviet Union as constituting 'one nation'. Russian identity historically first took shape in Kiev. No wonder that many Russians do not accept that the 'Ukrainians want to throw the Russians out of their Russian cradle'. The Yeltsin construct of a macro-identity which popularized a 'Rossian' (*rossijskij*) nation is losing ground according to the surveys. The majority of Russians define themselves as 'Russian', almost 13 per cent as 'Soviet Citizens' (Avramova 1998: 23; Simon 1999: 19).

The transformation of post-Communist systems was most difficult in multi-ethnic states. None of the three multi-ethnic states – the Soviet Union, Czechoslovakia and Yugoslavia – survived the collapse of communism. But the successor states are still far from being ethnically homogeneous. The transformational elites sought to tackle social and ethnic diversity in two ways:

- by granting autonomy to the subunits;
- by offering a fair chance in the electoral system for the minorities, which meant that majoritarian electoral systems were not feasible.

The institutional mix which was the outcome of East European 'constitutional engineering' in the period of transition was normally some kind of subsystem's autonomy and proportional electoral law. The Marxists continued to favour a 'winner-takes-all' formula as long as they counted on a majority. But even in Russia, concessions to the democratic movement led to a compromise in the 'parallel electoral system' combining elements of proportional and majoritarian electoral laws – sometimes mistakenly evaluated as a copy of the German electoral system (Ordeshook and Shvetsova 1997: 38). This choice, which in Russia at the local level came closer to a majoritarian system (Nohlen and Kasapovic 1996: 34ff.), strengthened the autonomy of many local leaders who became more independent of the centre than they ever were under Communist rule. Thus the institutional mix chosen in Russia favoured disintegration rather than integration. Combining electoral formula (majoritarian or proportional) and distributing various degrees of autonomy (equal or unequal rights for the federal units), Russia claimed to be close to the institutional mix of Austria and Germany. But a careful examination shows that Russia is located somewhere in the centre of the matrix (see Figure 1.1). Russia

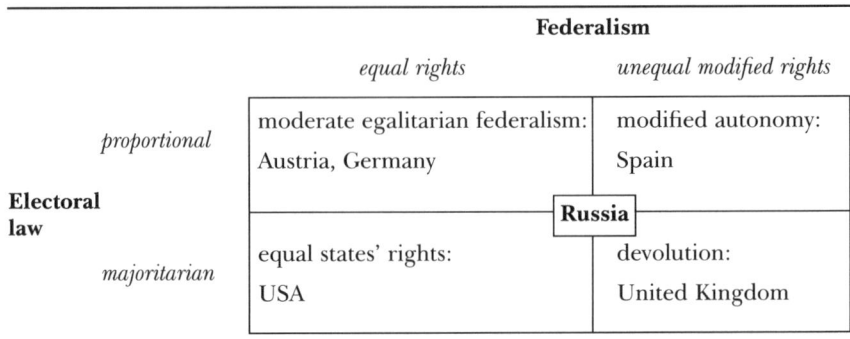

Figure 1.1 Autonomy to solve territorial conflicts.

combined in an awkward way German, American and Spanish elements in its formula for solving conflicts. In this respect it resembles the Indian Federation (Traut 1995: 118).

A priority of statehood for the federation implies that the constituting power of territorial units is not at the grass-roots. The attempt to constitute a Ural republic around Sverdlovsk was not recognized by the federal government (1993). Only the separation of Chechnya and Inghushetia (1991) was accepted by Moscow. Chechnya's attempt to change its status into independence caused even then a long bloody civil war.

The lack of a consistent federal policy was the consequence of a power-struggle in the centre. Three processes came to the fore in the period of disintegration of the Soviet Union. *Parliamentarization* was meant to limit executive power. When Yeltsin was in power it blocked his power in the name of conservative majorities under Chairman Khazbulatov. *Presidentialization* was the answer to this tendency to develop a 'government by assembly'. In this confrontation Yeltsin had to call on the federal units to get support against a hostile parliamentary majority.

Parliamentarization and presidentialization were followed by a third process: *federalization.* In March 1990 the presidential council was dissolved and was substituted by a deliberating body under the same name of 'Federal Council'. In December 1990 the new body received powers which made those of the Congress of People's Deputies redundant. All the republican presidents of 20 autonomous republics which had been partly elevated to the status of a 'Union Republic' were represented. The delegates of eight autonomous republics and ten autonomous national districts were allowed to participate only in questions which directly concerned their territories.

Gorbachev failed to opt early enough for a confederation of states in order to save the Soviet Union. The president lost himself in tactical manoeuvres without a clear concept. He claimed not to have ordered the intervention in the Baltic States, which is likely, and he pretended not even to know about the intervention, which is most unlikely. But the failure of this roll-back policy in the progress of confederalization gave Yeltsin more chances to gain profile as a reformer. Gorbachev was doomed to end as a kind of 'Kerenskij of the perestroika period'. The power to act on the Union level had withered away in the three conflicts between parliamentarization, presidentialization and confederalization, and between the three men Gorbachev, Yeltsin and Ryzhkov. No institution-building according to an overarching concept was possible on the Union level.

After Yeltsin's successful coup in autumn 1993 the wave of regionalization was interrupted for a moment: those governors who had sided with Yeltsin's enemies in parliament were dismissed and the regional and local soviets in many subunits were dissolved (Shlapentokh et al. 1997: 116ff.).

Russia tried to prepare a Federal Treaty when Gorbachev's government was still negotiating for a new Union Treaty for the Soviet Union. The first draft had been rejected by the autonomous republics in January 1991 when the Soviet Union still seemed to function. In March 1992 the Federal Treaty was signed by all the republics except Chechnya and Tatarstan. In the latter case of a territory surrounded by Russian lands this did not aim completely at separation but was used to negotiate special benefits for Tatarstan. The Federal Treaty quickly lost its importance. But the constitution was not implemented either. Sometimes it was too vague to give clear guidance. Judicial review by the Constitutional Court was still very limited (Abrossimova 1995).

The tradition of bilateralism was also started before the end of the Soviet Union. Only the Post-Communists under Zyuganov and Zhirinovskij's-right wing extremists – misnamed as 'Liberal Democrats' – were energetic in opposing the bilateral agreements under Yeltsin (Filippov and Shvetsova 1999: 72–3). Kaliningrad (former Koenigsberg) and other territories negotiated the status of a 'free trade zone'. Tyva has developed separatist tendencies. The Kosaks have since 1993 increasingly campaigned for the status of an autonomous Kosak Republic (Mick 1994: 614). Since Yeltsin did well in the 1993 elections in some of these 'ethnocracies', his policy was said to have paid – at least in the short term.

The by-product of this kind of tolerance towards the regional autonomies was the interruption of the democratization process. Moscow was helpless against the new dictatorship in the Kalmykian Republic, where under Ilyumshinov as president the regional parliament and the parties were dissolved and the rights of the trade unions were seriously reduced. In some regions the governors scheduled elections against the will of the central government. Though Yeltsin had nominated many of the governors not all of them proved to be reliable clients of the president. The initiative of the area of Sverdlovsk to form a Ural Republic in 1993 showed that the administrative units are not willing to serve as a *'clerus minor'* when they are as industrialised and well-to-do as the Ural district. Siberian patriotism and further autonomy for the Far East are widely discussed in the Russian press.

This upgrading is, however, likely only if several units merge in larger entities. But this is not to be expected in most cases because the local elites try to keep their power.

The relationship between democratization and regionalization in the regions is unclear. Until 1996, only the 21 republics had the right to vote for the chairman. In 1996 49 regions also got the right to install the administrative leader by popular vote. On the one hand, this gave democratic legitimation to the representatives of the subunits in the Federal Council, which consists of many governors, chairmen and chairmen of the regional parliaments. On the other hand, it made the regional chief executive more independent of Moscow. In the 'delegated regional democracies' which sprang up in the southern areas, democratic elections are not tantamount to democracy. Some of these leaders – most drastically in the Kalmyk Republic – developed a kind of new populist dictatorship on the basis of ethnic populism for the masses and clientelist relations with the elites (Simon 1999: 26–7).

Asymmetrical federalism and bilateral bargaining between centre and federal units

The Russian constitution of 1993 is contradictory: on the one hand, the equal rights of all the federal units towards the central power are underlined (Article 5.4); on the other hand, republics with statehood and constitutions differ from districts and autonomous areas which have only a 'statute' and some legislation of their own (Article 5.2). These three groups of federal units can be briefly outlined as follows.

The first group of republics with non-Russian titular nationality has increased from 16 (1989) to 21 (1993). In some cases this proliferation was due to separation (Chechnya and Ingushetia became two republics). In most cases it was due to an upgrading of former autonomous areas (*okruga*, e.g. Altai and others). Only this group has the right to bilingualism in state institutions.

Not all the oddities of inherited Soviet territorial divisions are ill-intended Stalinist manipulations. Stalin gave the status of a republic to border areas such as Karelia and later downgraded the Finnish-speaking territory when it lost its value as an 'irredenta' for the reintegration of Finland. Karelia contained less Karelians than the Tatar autonomous republic which originally had a lower status than Karelia. But in most cases the problem is ethnic heterogeneity, which does not allow for logical ethnic borderlines. Chechnya, Chuvashya and Tyva were the only ethnic republics which had a majority of the titular nation according to the last census held in 1989 (Kirkow 1995: 1019). The most difficult problem is that in Eastern Europe ethnic groups live in territories according to a model of 'interwoven tapestry' and not clearly 'separated like fields on a chess-board' as we find predominantly in Western Europe.

The second group is considered as an entity on the *national-territorial level*. To this group belong the ten non-Russian titular nations which had only a national district (*okrug*) under Soviet rule. The Jewish district of Birobidzhan is one of them.

The third group is located on the hierarchy of regions on the *administrative-territorial level*, and contains the bulk of the units: 49 districts (*oblasti*), six regions (*kraya*) and the two major cities of Moscow and St Petersburg.

Article 65 of the constitution which enumerates them does not underline the hierarchical position of the three groups. In most cases the former Soviet territorial division was preserved. As in East Germany a systematic territorial reform was impossible. Contrary to East Germany the local elites had a considerable continuity in power and were not interested in losing their power base by territorial reorganization. The clear legal hierarchy of the 'federal subjects' as the Russians call them, does not reflect, however, the actual power and autonomy of the entities. Moscow has legally a third-class status, but financially it is pre-eminent among the 89 units. The legal status so far is less important than the economic situation of a region.

The centralizing power of presidential decrees (*ukazy*) does not respect the rights and equality of federal subjects. According to Article 88 of the constitution, the president has the right to declare a state of emergency, but he or she must inform the Federal Council and the Duma. Yeltsin did not respect this when he dispatched troops to Chechnya in order to 'restore constitutional order'. Article 102.1.b even asks for the approval of a presidential decree in a case of martial law. But the ukaz of intervention was one of hundreds of 'secret decrees' issued by the president (Parrish 1998: 95).

The Constitutional Court did not prove to be an effective counterweight against the abuses of Yeltsin's *ukazokratiya*. Yeltsin's *ukazy* concerning the reform of local authorities were considered as being binding for the regions and districts but only 'recommendations' for the republics (Bell 1998: 146). This difference clearly violated the equality of the federal subjects.

The constitution tried to suggest more equality of the units than the Federal Treaty (Kazansev 1994). But the Treaty was soon a forgotten document when Yeltsin had stabilized his rule by a constitution. The equality of the federal subjects was also violated in many cases where a unit with vested rights was at the same time a part of a larger unit with some autonomy.

The constitution emphasizes the priority of federal law over the whole Russian territory and claims 'sovereignty' correctly only for the Federation. This did not prevent Tatarstan and Chechnya from declaring their own sovereignty. Violations of the constitution occur on both sides. Nobody prevented the then 19 out of 20 republics from inserting articles into their constitutions which clearly contradict the federal constitution (Schneider 1999: 9).

On the whole, the republics still more frequently exceeded their competences than the president. Yeltsin was in the position of Goethe's sorcerer:

he was not able to get rid of the spectres he had called upon. In his struggle for power he originally encouraged the units to enlarge their powers. As Louis-Philippe said to the bourgeois who supported his revolution in 1830: 'enrichissez-vous', Yeltsin encouraged the regions to 'Take as much sovereignty as you can swallow! For the remainder agree to hand it over to the Russian Federation' (quoted in Götz and Halbach 1994: 30).

The inconsistencies of the federal 'system' in Russia thus can be explained by three factors:

- the remainders of Marxist ideology and Soviet territorial structure;
- the conflicts between the two levels of power – Soviet Union and Russia – and later, when this issue was settled by the end of 1991, the conflict between two powers in the centre which made it possible that the federal units played a far greater role than envisaged;
- the continuously miserable economic situation in Russia which strengthens the financial egotism of all the layers of the federal 'system'.

Note that inverted commas are used to qualify the term 'system' here: there is a federal device but not yet a working federal system, similar to the central decision-making system where there are parties but not yet a party system with a consistent influence on federal policy-making.

One of the main reasons for the centrifugal tendencies in the federal 'system' is the lack of a nation-wide party system. The governors of the regions in the Federal Council no longer strengthen the power of the president as do so many heads of the French 'departments' and communes in the French parliament. In 1993, 67 constituencies voted non-partisan representatives who combined their efforts in a group 'New regional policy'. Many of them were rather ambassadors of their regions to Moscow rather than true representatives. The parties and lists were frequently Moscow-centred. This aroused suspicion in the regions. Russian parliamentarianism is characterized by a double volatility:

- volatility of electoral votes because the parties are not consolidated;
- volatility of the elected deputies who frequently change their parliamentary group.

Some 142 independent deputies and members of 18 minor groups were initially without recognition as a parliamentary group – which requires 35 members. This caused an enormous migration between the groups in the first parliamentary period between 1993 and 1995. Later this movement slowed down. Only 'Yabloko' and Zhirinovskij's 'Liberal Democrats', an extreme right-wing group in spite of the innocuous name, remained basically unchanged in their size. The Communists lend deputies to their satellite groups, such as the Agrarians and Women – a kind of 'communist multi-party-system' (Oleshchyk and Pavlenko 1997: 16). A formally democratic election thus ended up in clientelistic intransparency.

This does not mean that there are no parties present in the regions. But they are still more unprogrammatic and focused upon a leader than the nation-wide groups which were reduced to the Communists, the Liberal Democrats of Zhirinovskij and Yabloko. Parties are much stronger in Moscow and Petersburg than in most regions (Luchterhandt 1998: 214ff.).

Since there is no federal party state which develops nation-wide parties as a link between the regional governments and the central government – as moderates the conflicts in Germany or Canada – Russian regionalism recently tried to compensate for this by building new parties from below: the 'Voice of Russia' fighting for less state regulation (since February 1999) and 'Whole Russia' (since May 1999) which does not aim at a federal electoral list of candidates but concentrates on streamlining the regional lists which support the parliamentary group of Russian regions in the Duma under the leadership of Vladimir Medvedev. Thus the regionaliz-ation of the political system is strengthened by the deficiencies of the three-quarter-presidential system developed under Yeltsin. The president tried to imitate de Gaulle's stance above arty politics, but he did not appreciate that French presidents normally try to keep permanent contact with 'their' party, even if they refuse – like de Gaulle – to serve as a party leader.

Two processes were noteworthy in the development of the regions, both the consequence of staggering economic development:

- an indigenization of the regional elites;
- a 'commercialization' of the regional elites.

As in the former Union Republics which became independent after 1991, many leaders were not completely in command of the local language. The first Tatar leader was said to be a Bashkir and many leaders discovered their ethnic heart not so much for deep-rooted cultural and linguistic reasons but because the centre was no longer able to guarantee the welfare of the regions. The regional leadership had to develop strategies for eco-nomic survival of their own. Economic deficits rather than genuine ethnic strife caused the collapse of the Soviet Union as well as the centripetal forces of regionalization in the Russian Federation. The indigenization (*korenizatsiya*) of the regional elites is considerable. In Tatarstan the ethnic Tatars got 85 per cent of important positions though they constituted less than half of the population (Galymajov 1998).

The power struggle between central and regional governments was aggravated by the second transition: transition to a market economy. Usually the old nomenclature elites were – at least rhetorically – more open to democracy than to capitalism. In the regions sometimes the opposite was the case. Local elites favoured privatization because they had a chance to appropriate parts of the state property (Hanson 1994: 1ff.). Patron–client relations sprang up in the centre as well as in the regions. But in the regions the interlacing of economic and political elites was still further developed than in the centre – at least as long as there was a minimum of political administration under Primakov. His weak followers in the office of the prime minister, however, rather tended to develop into marionettes of financial clans and Mafia groups. The only difference was that local bosses sometimes were able to develop a kind of regional dictatorship, as Huey Long's dynasty once did in the American South. In the regions up to 80 per cent of the former nomenclature elites are still in office (Magomedov 1994: 74). Only in those areas where a substantial elite circulation took place was the readiness of the elites to support democratic reforms increasing. In the power struggle between the levels, the old Soviet '*Kto kogo?*' (who against whom) was still valid. The struggle for competences was not really policy-oriented, but rather a struggle for who is to govern in the regions (Friedgut and Hahn 1994: 231; Kirkow 1995: 1008).

Politics was increasingly linked with business. Lapina (1998) differentiated various models: *patronage* prevails among the national republics (Tatarstan, Bashkortostan) and the Russian areas with communist orientation, such as Ulyanovsk and Krasnodar. In this model, strict control over the enterprises is common. In regions which underwent democratic reforms, a model of *partnership* with a dialogue of political and economic elites was developed (St Petersburg, Novgorod, Nishnyi Novgorod). A model of *struggle of everybody against everybody* prevails in poor areas with weak political leadership where regions are completely dependent on resources from the centre (Kirov). A fourth model was called '*privatization of power*' where groups of entrepreneurs control the political decisions. This model prevails in poor as well as in some rich areas (Kalmyk Republic, Chakassiya, Tyumen). The permanent economic crisis strengthened the weight of the governors. The new local dictators were frequently accused of corruption and abuse of power (Shklyar 1999; Schneider 1999: 14).

The economic predicaments of Russian federalism and regionalism took legal shape in a new kind of bilateralism which was rare in the history of federalism. The Russian federal 'system' remained asymmetric. The system was so hazardous that it has been dubbed 'roulette federalism'. The deficits of a consistent legal framework are already visible in the fact that 19 out of 21 republican constitutions contain articles which contradict the federal constitution. These deviations result from a 'confederalist' conception of centre–periphery relations. Competences of the centre are frequently conceded only by 'agreement with the regions' (Basygina 1998: 247–8).

The irrational system under conditions of consolidation might have been reshaped into a consistent system by policies in the centre. But the development did not go in the direction of *centripetal* but rather *centrifugal* developments. Between 1994 and 1998 more than half of the subunits (46 out of 89) negotiated 'power-sharing treaties' with the federal government in order to obtain special economic and political rights. Some regions pay no taxes. Others such as Moscow transfer about 60 per cent of the tax revenues to the centre. Some of these treaties are simply unconstitutional.

Attempts to unify regulations by law have been blocked by the leaders represented in the Federal Council, the upper house of parliament (December 1997). The tradition of bilateralism had already been established by Gorbachev for political reasons and under Yeltsin developed in an economic direction in order to cushion the shock of a transition to market economy which affected some regions more severely than others (Filippov and Shvetsova 1999: 62).

In questions of vital regional interests the federal chamber of consolidated federal democracies normally reaches a compromise based on the views of most of the subunits, even across the party cleavages. This mechanism does not work in the Russian Federation. The Federal Council has legislative rights but it is unable to create a common interest of the regions because more than half of its members were installed by the president until 1996 or represented governors who were dependent on Yeltsin. The Federal Council has declined to a kind of 'stock market' for presidential favours and privileges (Kirkow 1995).

Even the *Duma* did not play a major role. The power bargaining is predominantly a bargain between bureaucracies, no longer party bureaucracy, but federal and regional bureaucracies. This type of decision-making is not open to reform initiatives. It rather serves to preserve the status quo of power relations.

The spreading of 'intergovernmental decision-making' (*Politikverflechtung*) has created similar tendencies in some consolidated democracies, unless they preserved a clear division of competences. But this intergovernmental decision-making – though not very transparent – is still subjected to certain rules which are absent in Russia. Russia shows many traits of a delegated democracy. Participation from below is better developed than the legal and constitutional state and the rights of the citizens as well as those of collective entities.

All the experts in and outside Russia agree: there are too many subunits. The irrational structure of Soviet territorial division should be overcome. Also consolidated federations such as the German Federal Republic time and again discuss the reduction of subunits in order to overcome the inconsistencies of financing regional government. Ex-prime minister Primakov opened a new debate in the 'Allrussian Assembly for questions of the development of federal relations' in January 1999. He did not support further strengthening of the administration of the regions, but development of 'interregional economic associations', which had formed spontaneously up to 1994 to overcome the economic crisis. The idea of interregional associations is not new. The Soviet Union in the 1980s proposed three macro-zones and subdivided them into eight *meso-regions* (von Beyme 1988: 33). On the smaller Russian territory again eight regional associations were created: North-West, Volga–Vyatka, Central, Central black soil zone, North-Caucasia – with the exception of Chechnya – Ural, West and East Siberia and finally Far East (Bell 1998: 316–17). The problem of these associations is a double one: on the one hand, the associations contain very different interests from various regions and are hardly reducible to mere economic questions; on the other hand, only the three eastern regions, plus Ural, have sufficient potential and roots in the population in order to develop into a forthcoming new federal subunit. If this was to happen, as is sometimes discussed in reform groups, the danger might be that powerful areas such as Far East might aim at further independence and undermine in the long run the Russian Federation (Lyashevskaya 1995: 297–8).

Economic constraints and financial chaos

The combination of bilateral bargaining strategies with economic diversification was intended to mitigate the economic and social inequalities of the regime, which had also existed in the old Soviet Union – in spite of an equalizing wage policy and an equalizing system of social security provisions. The removal of the old equalizing policies in the name of deregulation and liberalization has increased the financial needs of the regions. In 1993, 54 federal units needed subsidies. Only seven units were rich enough to balance their budget. In 1997, more than 50 per cent of all taxes to the federal budget were paid by 10 out of 89 regions. Moscow alone paid 22 per cent, where 82 per cent of the joint ventures combined with foreign investments were concentrated. The percentage of donors went down from 25 (1994) to 8 (1998) (Filippov and Shvetsova 1999: 76).

In order to contribute to the financial survival of most units, the central government had to resort to individual arrangements. Being permanently under economic pressure, Yeltsin's governments were unable to work out a generalized scheme for the transfers to the regimes. But we should not forget that even a fairly well-functioning system like the German one has federal additional transfers besides the general horizontal and vertical burden-sharing schemes in order to meet special urgent needs.

Tax evasion is not only common on the enterprise level. It is practised quite open by the regions. In 1992, 20 federal subjects fixed the tax transfers to Moscow without agreement of the central government. One year later 30 units followed this example. Some taxes, such as tax on income from manufacturing are highly monopolized. Only the electric company GASPROM payed 30 per cent of this tax (Schneider 1999: 16). This practice seems to be justified because the central government frequently did not pay the civil service. The regional governments took over this task and in exchange can count on the loyalty of the state employees more than the federal government (Bell 1998: 280). The Soviet Union counted on *redistribution from above*. The Russian Federation developed the dysfunctional practices of *redistribution from below*. The contradictions of the system confused the competences. On the one hand the subunits exceeded their powers and created fiscal policies, privatization policies and economic strategies of their own. On the other hand Yeltsin from August 1991 to 1996 tried to nominate the governors and created a system of personal clientelism (Bell 1998). The 'common tasks' which, according to Article 72 of the constitution, have blurred the borders of responsibilities within the federal system of the Federal Republic of Germany are also existent in Russia. As in other federations, the centre tries to regulate the guidelines of policies, but to leave the financial responsibilities to the subunits. No wonder that these try to evade the federal tax system wherever this is possible. Even completely legal behaviour has its detrimental sides: the policies are determined by fiscal possibilities, which does not lead to economic efficiency. Most spectacular attempts to delegate financial responsibilities to the federal units happened in Siberia and Far East when the central government stopped paying the military (Leppingwell et al. 1994: 7). Fiscal favours done by the federal units are normally transformed into bargaining for more investments by the central ministries in the respective area (Wallich 1994: 107). The unsatisfactory distribution of powers in the Russian federal system is due to the fact that neither the Union Treaty nor the constitution has regulated in detail the financial burden-sharing and the administrative competences.

The asymmetries of Russian federalism were quite obvious in the process of privatization. On the one hand some local elites pushed towards managerial privatization. But in their other transformational strategies they remained rather conservative. Many regulations of prices were introduced or reintroduced. The old policy of subsidies for the enterprises by regional governments were revived. Regional governments thus became frequently captives of their most important producers. They bargain subsidies and price regulations for guarantees that unemployment will not rise because of lay-offs by the industrial plants. The official unemployment rate of 11 per cent (1998) is hardly trusted by the experts. But it could be worse if a 'gradualist laggard' like Russia did not try to keep the unemployment below average in the post-Communist countries by bilateral negotiations between local governments and local industries. The bargaining strategies have an indirect impact on the bargaining between centre and periphery.

The negotiations between local governments and local industries so far lack transparency. There are, of course, pressure groups of economic entrepreneurs and trade unions. But they operate without a stable basis. Also lacking in Russia is a system of collective bargaining, which in consolidated democracies contributes to diminishing wild-cat strikes and riots – still common in Russia.

The egotism of regions is proliferating and does not stop at those competences which in all federations are clearly located at the level of central government, such as foreign trade. Tatarstan and Bashkortostan – not to speak of Chechnya – aim at complete independence in foreign trade and have started to negotiate bilateral treaties with foreign countries. Tatarstan in 1994 illegally decreed tax-free opportunities for foreign investment on its territory (Bell 1998: 160). Sometimes the initiative for privileges came from above. By presidential decrees, Kaliningrad was exempted from paying tolls for ten years, a privilege which the area also lost by presidential *ukaz*.

Regional ambitions in foreign policy occasionally counteract the central foreign policy in Moscow. Even security policy is affected, when Lebed as governor of Krasnoyarsk paid the soldiers of his regions and asked for permanent authority over the security forces in his area (*Nezavisimaya Gazeta*, 28 July 1998; Schneider 1999: 23).

Privatization policy was another striking example of increasing asymmetries. The constitution (Article 9 and 72d) remained quite unclear which level was entitled to which kind of property. Only a decision of the Supreme Soviet and later an *ukaz* of the president specified the division of resources. Already before the end of the Soviet Union privatization was initiated and entrusted to a state committee (Gosudarstvennyi komitet pro upravleniyu gosudarstvennym imushchestvom, abbreviated as GKI) which was created in July 1990. Branches of this institution were installed in all the regions and on the local level – with the exception of Chechnya. This body was sometimes compared with the German trusteeship institution (Treuhand). But the ownership was handed over to property funds. The GKI had only supervisory functions. The property funds were regionalized and under the jurisdiction of the legislative assemblies of the respective area. In some regions the co-operation of the funds with the GKI branch was never working (Slider 1994: 370).

In order to buy support for the privatization policy the central government delegated the right to administrate the process of privatization to the federal units and even left a certain share of the revenues to the regions. In June 1993, four regions, among them St Petersburg, Sverdlovsk and Nishnyi Novgorod, were rewarded for their quick support by being granted the privilege to privatize transport, communication and the arms industry, which normally were exempted from privatization (Bell 1998: 181).

Regionalization did not even stop at former centralized hierarchically organized industries such as the arms industry. But regional competences which diminished central influence were counterbalanced by the increasing dependence of regional governments on the centre's economic elites.

The fiscal relations of centre and periphery demonstrate some serious deficiencies of Russian federalism: the subunits are financially under-privileged. Most of the income of the regions comes from *shares of the national taxes*. The most important regional tax is the profit tax. It is lower than in developed market societies. This source of income is extremely dependent on the cycles of economic development and increases the regional imbalance in the budget. Rich areas such as Moscow, Bashkortostan and Tatarstan benefit from the regional nature of this tax, whereas the poorer regions would prefer to see it as a national, redistributed tax (Bell 1998: 325). Income tax is likely to remain a national domain. Its maximum is 35 per cent in Russia and 53 per cent in Germany. Nevertheless this tax is detrimental to medium-size wage-earners and small businesses.

The value added tax (VAT) has no exceptions in the Russian Federation. All goods are taxed at a unified rate of 20 per cent. The regions may impose retail taxes (up to 5 per cent of prices, excluding only basic food such as milk and bread) (Stroev et al. 1999: 341). Special consumption taxes amount to 35–40 per cent of the income of the regions.

All scholars of Russian federalism agree that the financial base of the regions should be strengthened. This is necessary also to reduce tax evasion. The equivalent of $12 billion is transferred every year from Russia to foreign banks. Collective tax evasion is also unilaterally organized by regional government.

Conclusion

When this author wrote his first book (1964), suggested by Carl Joachim Friedrich, a prominent advocate of federalism in the world, he had to deliver a manuscript with the conclusion: there is no authentic federalism in the Soviet Union. The conclusions about federalism in Russia are slightly more positive.

Nevertheless, the conclusion is appalling. There is centrifugal regionalism but not yet a federal system, e.g. a functioning system of centre–periphery relations with a stable legal base, efficiently supervised by the Constitutional Court and a working system of financial support. There is no federal party state and this contributes to a lack of influence of the regions in the parliamentary chambers in Moscow.

The Russian Federation is the product of the disintegration of the Soviet Union, a country in an economic and political morass. The declaration of sovereignty by Russia was a mistake in the light of the complete disintegration of the Soviet Union. Further disintegration even of Russia – comprising only slightly more than half of the Soviet population – is frequently discussed abroad and feared in Russia. Further centrifugal developments cannot be excluded if economic problems are not ameliorated in the foreseeable future.

The reduction of inflation and the reappearance of some growth (1998: 2 per cent) led to optimistic slogans such as 'the worst is over'. But during the economic crisis of 1998 regionalization was increasing. The illegal acts of local leaders are increasingly supported by two-thirds of the regional population when 'deviant political behaviour' is suspected to be in the interest of the region (Simon 1999: 5). The Kalmyk 'dictator' Ilymushov announced in 1998 that his region would consider itself only as an 'associated territory' if Moscow did not accept his republic's financial demands (Mark 1998). One should not overrate this rhetoric of separation. Only some non-Russian regions at the borders of the Federation, such as Chechnya or Tyva, may have a chance to separate completely. Most Russians still have large reserves of a sense of national identity.

Federalism in the West in its emphasis on 'concurrent majorities' instead of 'numerical majority' (John Calhoun) may also have undemocratic aspects. On the one hand, there is an impact of democratization from the federation on the less democratic subunits – as in some American states in the deep South. On the other hand, federalism can facilitate regional deviant behaviour. In the Russian Federation 'electoral dictatorships' have developed in at least six republics from Bashkortostan to Udmurtiya (Ross 1999: 27). This does not mean, however, that in the Russian regions democracy is always more than 'delegated'.

References

Abrassimova, Jelena B. (1995) 'Probleme der Organisation und des Funktionierens der Judikative in föderativen Staaten (Erfahrung Rußlands und Deutschlands)', in: J.C. Traut (ed.), *Verfassung und Föderalismus Rußlands im internationalen Vergleich*. Baden-Baden: Nomos.

Avramova, E.M. (1998) 'Formirovanie novoj rossijskoj makroidentichnosti', *Obshchestvennye nauki i sovremennost'* 4: 23–9.

Basygina, Irina M. (1998) 'Der asymmetrische Föderalismus. Zur besonderen Rolle der Republiken in der Russischen Föderation', *Osteuropa* 48, 3: 230–52.

Bell, C. (1998) *Der fiskalische Föderalismus in der Rußländischen Föderation*, Baden-Baden: Nomos.

von Beyme, K. (1965) 'Federal Theory and Party Reality in the Soviet Union', *Public Policy* 395–412.

—— (1988) *Reformpolitik und sozialer Wandel in der Sowjetunion (1970–1988)*, Baden-Baden: Nomos

Filippov, M. and Shvetsova, O. (1999) 'Asymmetric Bilateral Bargaining in the New Russian Federation', *Communist and Post-Communist Studies* 32, 1: 61–76.

Friedgut, T.H. and Hahn, J.W. (eds) (1994) *Local Power and Post-Soviet Politics*, London: Sharpe.

Galymojov, R.R. (1998) 'Politicheskie elity rossijskikh respublik', *Polis* 2: 108–15.

Götz, R. and Halbach, U. (1994) *Politisches Lexikon Rußland: die nationalen Republiken und Gebietseinheiten der Rußländischen Föderation*, München: Beck.

Hanson, P. (1994) *Regions, Local Power and Economic Change*, London: Chatham House.

Kazansev, M. (1994) 'Rechtliche Probleme der Wechselbeziehung zwischen der russischen Verfassung und dem Föderationsvertrag', *Osteuropa Recht* 4: 383–92.

Kirkow, P. (1995) 'Roulette zwischen Zentrum und Regionen. Rußlands asymmetrischer Föderalismus', *Osteuropa* 45, 1: 1004–20.

Koroskowkin, W. (1996) 'Zur finanziellen Situation der russischen Regionen', *Berichte des BIOsT* 39.

Kux, S. (1990) *Soviet Federalism: A Comparative Perspective*, Boulder: Westview.

Lapina, N. (1998) 'Business und Macht in Russland', *Berichte des BIOsT* 41.

Leppingwell, J.W.R. et al. (1994) 'Russia. A Troubled Future', *RFE/RL Research Report* 3, 4: 1–12.

Luchterhandt, G. (1998) *Parteien in der russischen Provinz*, Bremen: Temmen.

Lyashevskaya, M. (1995) 'Russia's Inter-Regional Associations. A New Form of State Life', in: K. Segbers and S. De Spiegeleire (eds), *Post-Soviet Puzzles: Mapping the Political Economy of the Former Soviet Union. Vol. 2: Emerging Geopolitical and Territorial Units*, Baden-Baden: Nomos, 284–96.

Magomedov, A. (1994) 'Politicheskie elity rossijskoj provintsii', *MEiMO* 4: 72–9.

Mark, R. (1998) 'Die Republik Kalmyckien (Chalmg Tangtsch)', *Berichte des BIOsT* 35.

Mick, C. (1994) 'Probleme des Föderalismus in Russland', *Osteuropa* 44, 7: 611–29.

Nohlen, D. and Kasapovic, M. (1996) *Wahlsysteme und Systemwechsel in Osteuropa*, Opladen: Leske & Budrich.

Oleshchyk, V.A. and Pavlenko, V.B. (1997) *Politicheskaya Rossiya god 1997. Partii, bloki, lidery*, Moscow: Izdatel'stvo Moskva.

Ordeshook, P.C. and Shvetsova, O. (1997) 'Federalism and Constitutional Design', *Journal of Democracy* 8, 1: 27–42.

Parrish, S. (1998) 'Presidential Decree Authority in Russia 1991–95', in J.M. Carey and M.S. Shugart (eds), *Executive Decree Authority*, Cambridge: Cambridge University Press, 62–103.

Ross, K. (1999) 'Federalizm i demokratizatsiya v Rossii', *Polis* 3: 16–29.

Schneider, E. (1999) 'Probleme des Föderalismus in Russland', *Berichte des BIOst* 24.

Schwanitz, S. (1998) *Rußlands Regionen als neue Machtzentren. Föderale und regionale Entscheidungsstrukturen am Beispiel der Privatisierung des Rüstungssektors*, Baden-Baden: Nomos.

Shklyar, N. (1999) 'Economic Crisis Strengthens Governors', *Russian Regional Report* 4, 1.

Shlapentokh, P. et al. (1997) *From Submission to Rebellion. The Provinces versus the Center in Russia*, Boulder: Westview.

Simon, G. (1999): 'Rußländische Nation – Fiktion oder Rettung für Russland', *Bericht des BIOst* 11.

Slider, D. (1994) 'Privatization in Russia's Regions', *Post-Soviet Affairs* 10, 4: 367–96.

Stroev, E.S. et al. (1999) *Russia and Eurasia at the Crossroads: Experience and Problems of Reforms in the Commonwealth of Independent States*, Berlin and New York: Springer.

Tishkov, V. (1995) 'What is Russia?', *Security Dialogue* 26, 1: 41–54.

Traut, J.C. (ed.) (1995) *Verfassung und Föderalismus Rußlands im internationalen Vergleich*, Baden-Baden: Nomos.

Wallich, C. (1994) *Russia and the Challenge of Fiscal Federalism*, Washington: World Bank.

2 The nation, state and the federal process in India

Subrata K. Mitra

Introduction: the problem stated

With a clear, constitutionally guaranteed division of power between the central government and the constituent states,[1] effectively policed by an independent Supreme Court; separate, direct elections to the central and regional governments monitored by an independent Election Commission; and the capacity of the political process to sustain a dynamic balance between the jurisdictions of the two sets of governments, India exhibits many of the features of federalism. But India's membership of this exclusive club remains a matter of some dispute.[2] The Indians themselves, as the findings of a national survey[3] conducted in 1996 discussed later in this chapter show, do not appear to share these doubts about the existence and effectiveness of a federal government, along with regional and local governments. The political evidence with regard to the characteristics of a federal process (Watts 1998)[4] are present and appear to support the conjectures based on the survey data. But scholarly scepticism persists nevertheless and surfaces as part of a larger question: with her multi-ethnic society, structural asymmetry of constituent units, mass illiteracy and poverty, and the uphill task of state-formation and nation-building, why does federalism even in a broader sense survive in India at all?[5] The main objective of this chapter is to highlight an important facet of this complex question by focusing on the role of the federal process in facilitating India's transition from a poor, traditional society, with mass illiteracy, and political heterogeneity reflecting the complex nature of territorial divisions under British rule to its present form in a relatively short time.[6]

India started its perilous and uncertain journey towards independent nationhood in 1947, at the end of a century and a half of British colonial rule. Unlike the majority of post-colonial states that set off on the same quest with India, after five decades, India still retains the basic structure of its constitution and its territory intact. Though contested in Kashmir, Punjab and the North-East by subnationalist movements and at the heart of India itself by a darker shade of Hinduism, the Indian nation is well-poised to stride into the next millenium in the company of the nations of older, more established states. The economy, which has grown modestly since independence, has turned around sharply since the early 1990s in its pace. In 1991, the Indian state embarked on yet another major venture of downsizing through a series of fiscal policies intended at the liberalization of the economy, privatization and integration with the international market economy. These facts set India aside as the odd one out among post-colonial states. Among poor countries, facing the dual challenge of simultaneous democratization and industrialization, and state-formation and nation-building, India's reputation as a 'puzzle'[7] is well-established. This chapter seeks to contribute to this debate by focusing on the federal process in India.

Since the indiscriminate use of the concepts of federalism, federal systems and the federal process might lead to confusion, following Watts (1998) the terms will be defined at the outset. Federalism is a normative category, implying the opposite of unitary rule, embodying the normative ideal of a division of substantive areas over which power is exercised between two sets of governments. A federal system is the constitutional arrangement that gives federalism its institutional form. The federal process is the ensemble of legislative and policy matters that relate the federal system to the dynamics of everyday political life. This chapter describes the features of India's federal system and process, and seeks to explain their effectiveness in terms of their symbiosis with the projects of nation-building and state-formation in India. This is done through a brief presentation of the basic structure of federalism in India along with its historical antecedents and political constraints. It next discusses the main role that the federal system and process have played in transforming a mere collection of rudderless former princely states, set free to follow their destiny by their British 'allies' at the end of colonial rule, and the Indian provinces, into an effective 'Union of States'.[8] Besides, the chapter will also make references to how the flexibility of the federal process has made it possible for the state in India to accommodate ethno-national movements in the form of new regions, thus gradually increasing both the number of states and the governability of the Union. Finally, the chapter refers to the vertical expansion of the federal structure, to which a third tier was recently added through the inclusion of India's half million villages in a gigantic experiment of self-rule, with constitutionally mandated authority and financial autonomy and an obligatory minimum of 30 per cent of seats for women. This has turned the federal process into a major source of legitimization and democratization of power in India. But, as the example of Kashmir indicates, this success story has its limitations, for the juxtaposition of religion and geo-politics defines the limits of the integrative potential of federalism in India.

Indian federalism in comparative and historical perspective

Seen against the impressive record of durability of its Western counterparts, the federal system of India at first appears like an unlikely member of the

club. Compared to the relatively longer existence of the four key federal
states, namely the United States (1789), Switzerland (1848), Canada (1867)
and Australia (1901), their racial homogeneity, and high literacy and
standards of living considered necessary for the sophisticated power-
sharing that a federal system requires, India presents a set of apparently
insurmountable obstacles against a likely federal solution. Wheare, reflecting this reservation, describes the Indian case as '. . . a quasi-federation – a
unitary state with subsidiary federal features rather than a federal state with
subsidiary unitary features'.[9]

Even while they were debating the basic structure of India's government, the members of the Constituent Assembly of India were aware of the
departure from the American norm with regard to Indian federalism.
Their approach was both functional and pragmatic. In the opinion of
several leading participants in the debate, Austin remarks, 'India had
unique problems, problems that could not be solved by recourse to theory
because federalism was not a definite concept and lacked a stable
meaning'. As such, Austin suggests, the framers of the constitution felt free
to pick and choose and see 'what would suit the genius of the nation best'.
(Austin 1966: 186). One of the main imperatives of the moment was the
problem of law and order resulting from the partition of British India into
India and Pakistan, causing an enormous amount of carnage, looting and
rape, producing in the process half a million deaths and 15 million
refugees. With these shocking events in the background, many in the
country were of the opinion that public order required a firm control over
national politics from the centre. In addition, there was a strong socialist
lobby in the Assembly which favoured centralized planning and central
leadership to transform Indian society based on caste hierarchy and
inequality into a modernized democracy. Dr Ambedkar, a formidable force
in the Constituent Assembly, who was born an untouchable and had
vigorously campaigned for social justice, summed up these sentiments in
his description of the constitution as '. . . a federal constitution in as much
as it establishes what may be called a dual polity . . . [which] will consist of
the Union at the centre and the States at the periphery, each endowed
with sovereign powers to be exercised in the field assigned to them
respectively by the constitution'. 'The constitution', said Ambedkar,
'avoided the tight mold of federalism in which the American was caught,
and could be both unitary and federal according to the requirements of
time and circumstances'.[10]

In the event, independent India, rather like the Mogul and British
rulers, sought to blend strong central control with local initiative. This has
elicited oblique praise from two foreign commentators who have highlighted
the unique attributes of the Indian constitution with regards to the nature
of centre–state relations to which it gave rise. Thus, C.H. Alexandrowicz
observes in his *Constitutional Development in India* that 'The constitution of
India is neither purely federal nor purely unitary but is a combination of

both. It is a union or a composite state of a novel type. It enshrines the principle that in spite of federalism the national interest ought to be paramount.'[11] And Paul Appleby (1953: 51) adds: 'No other large and important national government is so dependent as India on theoretically subordinate but actually rather distinct units responsible to a different political control, for so much of the administration of what are recognized as national programmes of great importance to the nation.' However, the celebrated Indian commentator D.D. Basu (1985: 50) strikes a differing note by holding that India's constitution is 'basically federal, but of course with striking unitary features'.

The basic conditions of effective federalism: the institutionalist view

The scholarly disputes with regard to the character of India's federalism are quite understandable in view of the various provisions that constitute the basis of Indian federalism. While these articles appear at first glance to meet the basic requirements of federalism, a number of additional provisions hold up the potential of diluting their effects in reality and transforming the system instead into a unitary system. The main conditions of federalism from the institutionalist point of view are mainly four. First, there should be two sets of governments, each with its independent spheres of administrative and legislative competence; second, each set of governments should have independent tax bases; third, there should be a written constitution from which each side derives its legislative power; and finally, in case of conflict, there should be a system of independent judicial courts to arbitrate between the centre and the constituent units.

The Indian constitution provides for a clear division of powers between the central government (referred to in Indian usage as the Union government) and the state governments, both directly elected through elections, respectively to the national Parliament and State Assemblies, in the seventh schedule. The Union controls the 'central list' consisting of areas which involve inter-state relations, national security and foreign affairs. Subjects of primary interest to the regions, called the 'State list', are under the jurisdiction of the states. The 'concurrent list' holds subjects of overlapping interest like land reform laws, or issues relating to the cultural or religious minorities where both centre and state can make laws with the understanding that in case of conflict the central laws will take precedence. Subjects not specifically mentioned in the constitution, called the residuary subjects, come under central jurisdiction. Each list also mentions where the two governments can raise income through taxation. In case of a conflict of jurisdiction, the centre or the state or any individual of India can move the Supreme Court to have the point of law authoritatively interpreted. But doubts about the authenticity of Indian federalism arise from the constraints placed upon it by a number of provisions.

Constraints on the federal process in India

The precarious juridical position that the Indian constitution accords to the constituent states of the Union must appear startling to the federalist. Not only did the construction of the Union not follow from a decision by a group of independent political units to shed bits of their sovereignty out of mutual interest and create a federal state. The Union and the states were a simultaneous creation of the Constituent Assembly in which the provinces did not have any special representation. Further, the central government gradually dissolved the political character of the units that existed at the time of independence and started creating new units. The process has continued unabated, facilitated by the fact that the consent of states is not required for alteration of the names or boundaries of the states.

Even though in normal times the states have the exclusive power to make laws in the areas allocated to them (which are far less numerous than those given to the centre anyway), the central Parliament has an extraordinary power of legislation on state subjects in the national interest when authorized by the Rajya Sabha, the Upper House of the Parliament, to do so (Article 249). The Rajya Sabha, which is designed to be the states' representative at the centre, is far from the co-equal to the Lok Sabha, the Lower House. It has far fewer legislative functions, particularly with regard to finance. Traditionally, the prime minister and other important members of the national cabinet are members of the Lok Sabha. In view of its size, which is roughly half of that of the Lok Sabha, it runs the risk of being outvoted in a joint session which is what is prescribed in case of a serious difference of opinion between the two houses. Nor does the composition of the Rajya Sabha reflect the courtesy and dignity that is accorded to all members of a federation which are treated as equals, for the number of seats allocated to the states, in spite of the weighting added to the smaller members of the Union, still reflects the inequality that flows from the fact that the population of Uttar Pradesh is about 125 million compared to three million for tiny Nagaland.

There are other points that continue to question the trust of those who believe in states' rights. The governor of each state, head of the state under the constitution and the ceremonial head that the parliamentary democracy requires, is an appointee of the president of India, acting under the advice of the prime minister. The governors of India, invariably political appointees of the ruling party at the centre, have continued to act as the eyes and ears of the centre. Their role becomes crucial should no majority party or coalition emerge from the election, in which case the governor has actively to seek out a viable government. Besides, should the state develop problems with the majoritarian base of the government due to defection or splits, or if law and order declines precipitously, the governor's report becomes the basis of the declaration of president's rule. The period of emergency government (Articles 352, 356, 360) holds the federal character of the division of powers under temporary abeyance.

The state of emergency is no paper tiger. The national emergency of 1975–77 deeply scarred India's democratic and federal record. Proclaimed by the president under Article 352, it can in principle reduce India to a unitary state with an authoritarian government. If the president is satisfied that the security of India or any part of India is threatened, whether by war, or external aggression or armed rebellion, the emergency provisions are applicable to the whole of India or any part (Article 352). Article 353 specifies the implications of emergency. Two of these are relevant to federalism. During the state of emergency 'the executive power of the Union shall extend to the giving of directions to any State or as to the manner in which the executive power thereof is to be exercised'. Further, 'the power of Parliament to make laws with respect to any matter shall include power to make laws conferring powers and imposing durites, or authorising the conferring of powers and the imposition of durites, upon the Union or officers and authorities of the Union as respects that matter, notwithstanding that it is one which is not enumerated in the Union List'. The constitution provides safeguards against the abuse of this provision. Thus, the President may act only at the written recommendation of the cabinet and the proclamation of emergency needs to be approved by the Parliament. Still, the experience of 1975 remains a reminder of the potential threat. In smaller doses, the same purpose is served by the emergency at the state level, declared by the president at the recommend-ation of the governor (a central appointee and not, as in the United States, a political leader elected by the people of the state) under Article 356. So far as federalism is concerned, the negative implications of this article became clear as early as 1957 when the elected communist government of Kerala was dismissed by the Congress-ruled central government. Article 356 authorizes the president to dismiss the government of a state and dissolve or suspend the legislature of the state when he receives a report from the state governor, or in any other way, that 'the government of the state cannot be carried on in accordance with the provisions of the Con-stitution', and he may 'assume all or any of the powers' vested in the government of the state. Once again, safeguards such as approval of the Parliament are provided for but the abuse of this power under Indira Gandhi, which drastically reduced the autonomy of the States, is a reminder of the potential threat to federalism from this angle.

Even under normal circumstances the central government possesses superior financial powers because the more lucrative sources of revenue like import or export duties, income tax and corporate tax are allocated to the centre. The revenue of the states, on the other hand, constitute a shrinking base because, under the pressure of populism, most states have done away with or drastically reduced the taxation on land, education, health and welfare. The Union government alone is empowered to regulate the money supply, contract foreign loans, charge income tax, or collect import and export duties. Part of this income is of course redistributed among states, on the basis of the advice of the independent Finance Commission. But the impression that is created is one of profligate states, and careful and sophisticated central financial management. The superior financial powers of the centre are further reinforced by other functions relating to financial management that are allocated to the centre. For it is the central leadership which appoints the Planning Commission which used to set the priorities for the national government, to allocate resources to the states and to act as a clearing house. Even the sheer presence of the All India Services at the helm of affairs is a reminder of the juridical inferior position of the states because the members of the central services, even as they administer the economic and social lives of the regions, are answerable to the central government for their service conditions, and have significantly higher status, salary and career prospects than the officers in the state administrative services.

Finally, the problem of structural asymmetry, implying a great difference in the size of the members of a federation, is a key feature of the Indian federation. In terms of their presence in the Lok Sabha, for example, the contingent from Uttar Pradesh, with 85 Members of the Parliament, is a much more significant presence than tiny Tripura with just two. With just a few exceptions, nearly all of the prime ministers of India and many important members of the central cabinet have come from Uttar Pradesh. Watts (1998) mentions India along with Spain, Belgium, Malaysia and Russia as a federation that shows the presence of structural asymmetry either in its constitution or in political practices. Drawing on the work of Tarlton (1965), who first drew attention to the phenomenon of structural asymmetry in federations, Watts shows how 'political asymmetry, arising from the impact of cultural, economic, demographic and social conditions [could affect] the relative power and influence of different constituent units, as well as their relations with each other and with federative institution' (Watts 1998: 123). The dominance of Pakistan politics by Punjab, or the great sense of insecurity that the Tamil minority of Sri Lanka feels because of the dominance of the Sinhala majority both in terms of numbers and area are enough evidence of the potential consequences of structural asymmetry in terms of compromising the federal quality of the Union.

Three phases of the development of the federal process since independence

The Fathers of the Indian constitution, as we have seen above, were keen on federalism as a functional instrument for the creation of an Indian nation and a strong, cohesive state. The leaders of the post-colonial state were besieged by threats to India's security both from outside and inside, and faced the challenge of development by having chosen centralized economic planning as an optimal method to reach that objective. Thus, both for constitutional and political reasons, the case for federalism in

India appears to have been seriously compromised from the outset. In fact, such was the apprehension of 'fissiparous tendencies' and 'balkanization' among the informed observers that the professional predictions for the future of India as a democracy and a federation were pretty grim. The leading voice was that of the American journalist Selig Harrison:

> India's struggle for national survival is a struggle against herself. As a civilization and as an integrated cultural whole, India has shown a power of survival rivalled only by China. But multilingual India's separate territories have failed as consistently as Europe's to hold together as a political unity. . . . Nowhere do so many linguistically differentiated peoples, all of them so self-aware, all numbered in millions and tens of millions, confront each other within a single national body politic. The prospect that 'anarchy', 'fascism', and 'totalitarian small nationalities' will each torture this body politic, at one time or another in the decades ahead, is a measure not of some endemic Indian incapacity but of the challenge built into Indian nationalism.
>
> (Harrison 1960: 3–4)

Jawaharlal Nehru – India's first Prime Minister (1947–64), who led it through two crucial wars, the first, against Pakistan (1948–1949) over Kashmir, being inconclusive, and the second (1962), against China, being disastrous – appears to have thought otherwise. He took democracy seriously enough to face the enormously expanded Indian electorate (in 1952, in the first general election held, both to the national Parliament and the provincial Assemblies), providing for full and free participation in the election for all Indians, significantly including the Hindu nationalists, one of whose members assassinated Mahatma Gandhi, the Father of the Nation, and the communists who had just staged an armed revolution in Telengana in South India. He took the chief ministers (all of whom with rare exceptions were members of the Congress, the party to which Nehru belonged and of which he was for part of this period the president and, all of this period, leader of the parliamentary party) seriously enough to write to each of them every month, in an effort to keep them informed of the state of the nation and the world, and to solicit their opinion in an effort to build a national consensus.[12] The Indian National Congress, which had already embraced the federal principle back in the 1920s by organizing itself on the basis of Provincial Congress Committees based on the linguistic regions, institutionalized the principle of consultation, accommodation and consensus through a delicate balancing of the factions within the 'Congress System' (Kothari 1970), the co-optation of local and regional leaders in the national power structure (Lijphart 1996), and the system of sending out Congress 'observers' from the centre to mediate between warring factions in the provinces, thus simultaneously ensuring the legitimacy of the provincial power structure in running its own affairs, and the role of central mediation.

The fourth general election (1967), which drastically reduced the over-whelming strength of the Congress party in the national Parliament to a simple majority and saw half of the states moving out of Congress control into the hands of opposition parties or coalitions, caused a radical change in the nature of centre–state relations. No longer could an imperious Congress prime minister afford to 'dictate' to a loyal Congress chief minister. But, even as the tone became more contentious, the essential principles of accommodation and consultation held between the crucial 1967–69 period of transition. The Congress-dominated centre started cohabiting with opposition parties at the regional level before the French put the word into wider political science vocabulary. The balance was lost once the Congress party split (1969) and Indira Gandhi, her party reduced to a minority in the Parliament, took to the strategy of radical rhetoric and authoritarian leadership. However, after the authoritarian interlude of 1975–77, which, in both law and fact reduced India's federal system to pretty much a unitary state, the system reverted to the earlier stage of co-operation between the centre and the states. That balance has acquired a steady state during the alternating rules of the Congress party and the Janata coalitions, and endures up to the present day. The Hindu nationalist Bharatiya Janata party which leads the current ruling coalition, has been solicitous in its adherence to the norms in centre–state relations established by its predecessors, including such hallowed principles of the Indian Union as the three-language formula, in spite of its advocacy of Hindi as India's national language during the long years in the opposition.

Perception of the federal process in India

While it can be argued that the Indian political elite has demonstrated its trust in the Indian Union through participation in its electoral and everyday politics, the question, raised by Harrison (1960) and Moore (1966), about the acceptance of the democratic and federal rule of the polity by ordinary people still remains. To measure the trust of the electorate in the political system at the central, regional and local levels, three separate questions were asked in the 1996 national survey of the Indian electorate. The first was: 'How much trust/confidence do you have in the central government – a great deal, somewhat or no trust at all?' The same question was then asked in relation to state government and to local government. The answers, presented in Table 2.1, show a reasonably high level of trust in all three levels of the system.

Further analysis of these findings and their distribution over some selected regions reveal interesting patterns. Two new variables were constructed by isolating those who repose their trust in all three levels of the political system, and those who trust both the centre and the regional government, and the latter variable was compared with similar findings from a survey conducted in 1971. The findings are presented in Table 2.2.

Table 2.1 Trust in local/state/central government (%)

	Great Deal	*Somewhat*	*Not At All*
Local government	39.0	37.8	23.2
State government	37.2	43.6	19.2
Central government	35.2	42.5	22.3

Source: Centre for the Study of Developing Societies (Delhi), National Election Studies 1996.

Table 2.2 Confidence in local/state/central government (%)

State	*(1)* *(1996)* *Central+state+local*	*(2)* *(1996)* *Central+state*	*(3)* *(1971)* *Central+state*
Bihar (1947)	10.1	16.9	12.0
Gujarat (1961)	11.4	13.5	7.5
Maharashtra (1961)	13.8	20.8	18.5
Punjab (1966)	5.1	9.2	9.6
Tamil Nadu (1947)	11.1	20.8	24.2
West Bengal (1947)	17.2	22.5	9.3
Six states average	12.4	18.8	14.6
INDIA	16.2	24.3	14.4

Source: Centre for the Study of Developing Societies (Delhi), National Election Studies 1971 and 1996.
Notes: (1) How much trust/confidence do you have in the central government and in the state government and in the local government/panchayat/ municipality? – great deal.
(2) How much trust/confidence do you have in the central government and in the state government? – great deal.
(3) Do you have more faith and confidence in the national government in Delhi or the government of (name of the state)? – both.

We do not have comparable data from long-established federations, and as such we are not in a position to undertake a spatial comparison. However, the data presented in Table 2.2 make it possible to undertake a time–space comparison within India itself. The first column presents the percentage of people who have a 'great deal of trust' in the government at all three levels of the political system. The second column reports the percentage of people having a great deal of trust at both the central and the regional levels. Column three presents the same information from the survey of 1971. The last line reports the national figures and the penultimate line the average figures for six states chosen for spatial comparison. The states represent the diverse world of federalism in terms of the chronology of their creation, history of separatist movements, poverty and literacy, and geographical location.

The shared trust in different levels of the political system is the main conjecture that we need to examine in the light of the evidence presented in Table 2.2. On the whole, compared to 1971, the shared trust in both centre and region has gone up from 14.4 to 24.3 per cent for the country as a whole. Tamil Nadu, which has experienced intense anti-North, anti-Hindi and on occasions anti-Indian Tamil movements, was at the top of the league in 1971, indicating, for its time, the ability of India's federal process to turn anti-Indian tendencies into a successful marriage of region and nation. While the figure still remains high, it has come down somewhat in 1996, perhaps reflecting the changing equations of power both in Tamil Nadu and Delhi, each under the dominance of different Tamil factions. West Bengal, with a strong, leftist, anti-Delhi opposition, had a comparatively low score in 1971. However, with a solid and continuous rule of the Marxist-led left government in West Bengal, the former anti-centre tendencies have given way to an attitude of co-operation, taking the figures from 9.3 to 22.5 per cent. Punjab, the last state to be created in our sample, is a state that has been rocked by a militant Sikh movement for the creation of a separate, sovereign state of Khalistan. A combination of accommodation and repression has pacified Punjab but the indicator of joint trust is less than a third of the national average.

A neo-institutionalist explanation of the Indian puzzle

The supportive empirical evidence about the functioning of the federal process that one gets from the opinion data presented in Tables 2.1 and 2.2, and the negative predictions of Harrison (1960) and Wheare (1964), suggest that India's federal system constitutes a puzzle. One is entitled to ask: if it 'works' why does it work? Drawing on the works of Friedrich (1968), Riker (1975), Dikshit (1975), Watts (1981), Elazar (1987, 1994), Pinder (1993), Buchanan (1995) and Hesse and Wright (1996), Watts (1998: 128) suggests four general conditions to explain why federal processes work. The first and foremost of course is 'elite accommodation'. Next, reflecting the democratic trends of our times, comes 'public involvement' though it may 'complicate the patterns of negotiation for the establishment of a federal system' (Watts 1998: 128). An atmosphere of 'competition and collusion' between inter-governmental agencies is mentioned as a third condition (Watts 1998: 130). In the fourth place, drawing on Riker (1975), Watts mentions 'the role and impact of political parties, including their number, their character, and the relations among federal, state and local branches' as helpful in explaining the dynamism of federal processes (Watts 1998: 130).

Looking at the pattern of elite recruitment employed by the Congress party during the period of its hegemony (1952–67) where local and regional talent rose to prominence by rising within the party organization and moving horizontally to government, and the subsequent practice which saw new, upwardly mobile social groups enter the electoral arena directly in the form of political parties organized under their own names, one could see a steady expansion of the social base of leadership in India. That satisfies the first two of the conditions mentioned by Watts. The competition among Indian states for scarce resources such as river waters, where the centre often plays the role of the mediator, involving bureaucrats and political leaders from competing regions, is a good example of the third condition at work. Finally, just as regional parties emerge as champions of special and exclusive interests, the next career ladder of these leaders which is aimed at Delhi encourages them to place the region in the larger context of the nation. Eventually, as members of national coalitions of regional parties, they start striking the posture of national leaders, ready to bargain and conciliate conflicting regional interests. Thus, even as the Congress as the one dominant party has declined, the multi-party system that replaced it has produced the same institutionalized method of regional conflict resolution within a national framework.

Looking at the social origins of these 'new regionalists' – champions of local and regional interests who become born-again nationalists following the logic of the Indian political process – helps identify the dynamic process that sustains the federal system in India. These 'new regionalists' (who should be distinguished from the old regionalists, given to striking non-negotiable, primordial stances during the period of Congress dominance) are likely to be upwardly mobile educated males, the erstwhile 'bullock capitalists' who have now graduated beyond exclusive reliance on agriculture to other avenues increasingly opening up in the countryside thanks to the plethora of new programmes being introduced by the government as well as non-governmental agencies. They are into agri-business, small-time contracts, acting as brokers for outsiders seeking access to ministers, officials, local markets. These 'new regionalists' are busy in the construction of India's centre from the periphery.

One point that comes across clearly from the analysis of their attitudes towards divisive issues like Kashmir is that the average regionalist is unlikely to be the 'my region, right or wrong' variety. As we have seen, their attitudes towards centre–region issues are not specific only to their region but to the general way in which they would like regional issues to be solved. The point is borne out by the following newspaper report of a statement by Parkash Singh Badal, made on the 75th birth anniversary of the Akali Dal:

> 'Shiromoni Akali Dal is a symbol of the aspirations and hopes of Punjab. The Dal has always struggled for human rights, Punjab, Punjabi and the rights of Sikhs. For this the Akali Dal has made innumerable sacrifices.' He went on to add, 'we are committed to peace and shall not allow it to be disturbed at any cost. We have full faith in constitutional methods. We shall curb corruption and shall strive to give a clean government . . . when today we are celebrating our 75th anniversary we reaffirm our commitment to our goals.' He then confirmed the resolve of the Akali Dal to 'rejoin the national mainstream',

'now regional parties and national parties who believe in internal
autonomy for States are coming together. Akali Dal is very keen to co-
operate with them.'[13]

To sum up, the data from Lok Sabha electoral results and the survey
findings strongly indicate the presence of a keen awareness of region as an
important level of the Indian political system. That the region is present in
a distinctive way does not of course suggest that it is exclusive, or that
'regionalists' necessarily pit the region and nation as polar opposites,
separated by a chasm of distrust and conflict of loyalties. While the survey
data support the existence of the two as separate and distinct entities on
the basis of popular perceptions, the relationship of the two emerges as
much more complex than is commonly supposed. The bark of regional
chauvinists is louder than their bite: political scientists measuring the
depth of national integration can accept the separatist rhetoric of the
regional leader as indicator of the imminent dissolution of national unity
only at their peril.

But what about the regional chauvinists that Harrison (1960) warned us
about? Subsequent political developments in India have shown them to be,
to use the language of Paul Brass (1991), 'instrumentalists'. The 'regionalists' emerge from the further analysis of our survey data as a significant
section of the Indian electorate which has had the benefit of greater
education, is upwardly mobile and confident in its ability to negotiate its
way through the economy and the policy process. It has a tendency to back
the best agent available to promote the regional interest in a given arena.
Thus, when a credible regional party is available, the 'regionalists' prefer it
to its nationalist competitors. But they are unwilling to do so mechanically
or uncritically.

The existence of regionalists in the mass electorate provides the popular
base for the formation of regional parties. From the point of view of social
forces concentrated in a specific part of the country, control of the regional
government appears as both a desirable and achievable goal, and an effective method of reaching the objectives important to regional movements
such as use of mother tongue as official language, cultural hegemony,
control over the practice of faith in everyday life, religious property, law
and order, agricultural and developmental subsidies and various forms of
state administered welfare.

Having established themselves in their regions, regionalists have, in this
new phase of Indian politics that we have now entered, set their sights at
constructing the kind of nation that would be appropriate to the new
scheme of things. Increasingly, rather than remaining content with their
own region, they are stretching out their hands, and – using their alliances
with similar forces from outside – beginning to define the nature of the
national community in their own way. Recent experience in different parts
of the country has demonstrated that the pursuit of these goals can not

only coexist with similar aspirations elsewhere; regional movements can, in fact, reinforce one another by pooling their political resources. Hence the unprecedented scenes of regional leaders from one part of India campaigning for regional parties in other parts of the country in local and regional elections in addition to elections to the Lok Sabha. The Congress system encapsulated the expressions of local and regional interests and symbols at lower levels of the system; the new element in Indian politics makes these processes of consultation a systematic way of bringing out bits of India's outlying areas and peoples, and weaves them into different ways of defining what the nation is about and who has the legitimate right to speak in its name.

The political process of the 1990s shows the internalization of federal norms in the game plans of local and regional political leaders. Rather than taking a mechanical, anti-Delhi stance as their only *raison d'être*, the new breed of ambitious, upwardly mobile leaders of India have learnt to play by the rules even while they challenge them and thus have developed for themselves a new, federal space in which the nation and the region can coexist. This neo-institutionalist explanation, so called because it treats the rule of the federal game not as given but also as part of the game (and thus, essentially heuristic in nature), explains the effectiveness and vibrancy of the federal process in India. But, as Mitra and Lewis (1996) show, the integrative power of this model is at its best in Tamil Nadu where a federal 'deal' can be struck with a specific group of actors, such as the Dravida Munetra Kazagam (DMK), a leading Tamil political party. But when the actors themselves are fragmented and some of the distant actors are not a part of the negotiation (as in Kashmir), the model is no longer very effective in producing a legitimate, federal solution.

Conclusion

Nothing symbolizes the duality of contemporary political life more acutely than the ethno-nationalists, with their assertion of an exclusive territorial identity on the one hand and desire to be a part of the international community on the other. Their chosen instruments of struggle, the kalashnikov and the satellite phone, the cyanide pill and the colourful flags, may not be a match for the tanks and war planes of the central state in conventional warfare, but then more often than not it is the political dissidents who chose the time and place of armed conflict and the medium of international publicity, and therein find their room to manoeuvre against overwhelming force. Against such an adversary, a genuine and imaginative federal process, as we learn from the case of Tamil Nadu and recently India's Northeast, is the best coping mechanism that the central state can devise in its response to such demands for political autonomy and cultural self-expression.

With remarkable prescience, the framers of the Indian constitution have equipped the Indian state to respond to the demands for autonomy through the double mechanism of individual and group rights. During the first phase of India's constitutional development, some of these instruments were useful in empowering political majorities below the level of the national state through the effective enactment of provincial administrations. The second phase of constitutional development through the states reorganization of 1957, which created linguistically homogeneous states and counterbalanced the likely chauvinism through the promotion of the three-language formula, requiring the use of Hindi, English and the regional language, made it possible to institutionalize the multicultural nature of the Indian state. One can see the wisdom behind the Indian policy when one contrasts this with parallel developments in Pakistan and Sri Lanka during the same period, with the former unable and unwilling to accommodate the Bengali language movement in East Pakistan leading to the violent end of the federation, and the latter, thanks to the 'Sinhala only policy' that virtually reduced the Tamil minority to second-class citizenship, eventually subsiding into the civil war in which the country is engulfed today. In its third phase, the same process of constitutional development of federalism in the 1990s, India has witnessed the deepening of the principle of power-sharing by the statutory power now accorded to village councils.

These normative developments of the federal principle and their adaptation to India's cultural and historical context has been ably complemented by the political process. During the critical years of transition from British rule and the consolidation of popular democracy in India, the Congress party provided the link between the modern state and the traditional society. Congress rule both at the centre and in the states provided informal channels of communication and balancing of national, regional and sectional interests. The politics of coalitions that has replaced Congress hegemony has given a public articulation to the process of the integration of the local and regional for the purpose of launching a new debate on the nature of the nation and for identifying the variable boundaries of the nation and region. In consequence, looking for regional allies has now become an imperative for all national parties.

The new group of highly visible and effective regional leaders of India, drawing on their power bases in the states, often consisting of people from India's periphery (in terms of religion, elite caste-status or geographic distance from the centre), are able to generate a different construction of the nation-state that is better suited to the spirit of our times. When speaking in the national mode, the regionalists do not count out the need to be well-informed and decisive in defence of the security and integrity of the nation. But in terms of actual policies of the state, the regionalists are much more willing and (in view of their social base) able to listen to the minorities, to regions with historical grievances, to sections of the society that entered the post-independence politics with unsolved, pre-independence (in some cases, pre-modern) grievances. It is thanks to these 'regionalists' that the emerging multi-party democracy of India is not merely an anomic battle for power and short-term gain but the releasing of pent-up creativity and visions that provide a fertile and cohesive backdrop to the realignment of social forces. Far from being its antithesis, region has actually emerged as the nursery of the nation.

Indian experience holds an important lesson for the normative content of federalism. By complementing the perception of the electorate with that of local and regional leaders, we would be able to specify the regionaliz-ation conjecture in theoretical and comparative terms. The research on region and nation in India can then join similar projects elsewhere. We can thus unite the fragmented discourse on nation-building, divided on the lines of Western and non-Western societies, a division imposed and legitimated by orientalist prejudices whose time is now past. One can now formulate the problematic in terms of a common research agenda: is national identity in India, like in Germany or France, like a Matruska doll – such that, once we strip off the upper layers, one begins to discern a series of identities, carefully constructed by the political actor in a manner that optimizes his or her chances of achieving a life of affluence and dignity, in a secure environment?

The constitutional, legislative and policy instruments that India has drawn upon to reach the positive outcomes with regard to the development of federalism have an important implication for the comparative analysis of the federal process. Whereas old institutionalists such as Wheare (1964) prescribed a given set of institutions as the necessary and sufficient basis of a federal state, neo-institutionalists (one thinks of Watts 1998 though he does not use the appelation) show the importance of being pragmatic in devising the institutions appropriate to specific cultural, religious and historical contexts. The creation of sub-regional states like Gorkhaland, as a result of protracted negotiations between the Congress government of New Delhi, the communist government of Bengal and the Gorkha leadership is in every sense a genuine and unprecedented innovation, guided by the heuristic notion of power-sharing and solid, political common sense. The rules of the federal system, rather than being exogenous to the federal process, have become endogenous to it.

Finally, the horizontal and vertical expansion of the federal process has brought greater legitimacy to the Indian state and cohesion to the Indian nation. Rather than high theory, the process has been based on a series of *ad hoc* decisions, sometimes against the advice of the specialists who have made the conventional arguments based on the imperatives of modernization and the logic of economic viability. While a functioning political system can afford to ignore the technical advice of the specialist only at its peril, in its limited way, the Indian experience with the unprecedented and uncon-ventional expansion of the federal principle also teaches us to be wary of the 'Orientalist' prejudices of specialists which often make them underestimate the political intelligence and capacity of those considered inferior on the grounds of their race, class, caste, gender or language.

Notes

1 Following Indian usage, the constituent units of the Indian federation will be called States and state will refer to the central state.
2 Watts, in his comprehensive study of federal systems (1998: 121), counts 23 states as full federal states but one senses a certain reluctance to admit India as a full member of this club. 'India and Malaysia, marked by deep-rooted multi-lingual, multicultural and multiracial diversity, have nevertheless managed to cohere for half and a third of a century respectively, but are at a critical phase in their development' (Watts, 1998: 118).
3 The national opinion survey, in the course of which a sample of ten thousand men and women, representing the Indian electorate, was interviewed by trained investigators from the Centre for the Study of Developing Societies during May–June 1996, on the basis of a questionnaire designed by the Lokchintan, a group of scholars based at various Indian research institutes and universities. Financial assistance for this project was provided by the Konrad Adenauer Foundation, the Indian Council for Social Science Research and *The Hindu* (Delhi).
4 Following the usage of Watts (1998: 117), federal process is used in this chapter as a descriptive category which refers to the presence of a 'broad genus of federal arrangements' in a political system. These characteristics, which could in principle be composed into a scale, are drawn from the definition of a federation as 'a compound polity combining constituent units and a general government, each possessing powers delegated to it by the people through a constitution, each empowered to deal directly with the citizens in the exercise of a significant portion of its legislative, administrative and taxing powers, and each directly elected by its citizens' (Watts 1998: 121).
5 Wheare (1964) is the main source of such contestation of India's federal status. Watts (1998: 131) mentions India's multi-ethnicity as a possible factor in why federalism might be difficult to sustain. Indian writing on the theme (Bose, 1986) pleads for more decentralization but such arguments are based on the fact that a federation already exists and has the necessary capacity to decentralize even further.
6 See Mitra (1996), and Mitra and Singh (1999), which reports the findings of a national survey conducted in 1996.
7 Indian exceptionalism has produced a rich crop of explanations. See Moore (1966). One of the most recent and most challenging is Lijphart (1996)
8 Article 1, Constitution of India, describes the Indian federation as follows: 'India that is Bharat shall be a Union of States'.
9 K.C. Wheare, Federal Government (1951: 28), cited in Basu (1985: 58).
10 *Constituent Assembly Debates* VII, I, 33–4, cited in Austin (1966: 188).
11 Cited in Basu (1986: 59).
12 These letters are now available in the form of four volumes (Nehru 1985), which are a veritable treasure trove on the politics of the early post-independence decades.
13 B K Chum, 'Akali Dal Goes for Mainstream Politics', *Deccan Herald*, 27 February 1996.

References

Appleby, P. (1953) *Public Administration in India: Report of a Survey*, New Delhi: Government of India.
Austin, G. (1966) *The Indian Constitution: Cornerstone of a Nation*, Bombay: Oxford University Press.

Basu, D.D. (1985) *Introduction to the Constitution of India*, New Delhi: Prentice-Hall.
Bose, T.C. (ed.) (1986) *Indian Federalism: Problems and Issues*, Calcutta: K. P. Bagchi & Co.
Brass, P. (1991) *Ethnicity and Nationalism*, Delhi: Sage.
Buchanan, J.M. (1995) 'Federalism as an Ideal Political Order and an Objective for Constitutional Reform', *Publius Journal of Federalism* 25, 2: 19–27.
Dikshit, R.D. (1975) *The Political Geography of Federalism*, New York: MacMillan India.
Elazar, D.J. (1987) *Exploring Federalism*, Tuscaloosa: University of Alabama Press.
—— (1994) *Federalism and the Way to Peace*, Kingston, Ontario, Canada: Institute in Intergovernmental Relations, Queen's University.
Friedrich, C.J. (1968) *Trends of Federalism in Theory and Practice*, New York: Praeger.
The Government of India, *The Constitution of India*, Delhi: 1991. See in particular the seventh schedule.
Harrison, S. (1960) *India: The Most Dangerous Decades*, Princeton: Princeton University Press.
Hesse, J.J. and Wright, V. (eds) (1996) *Federalizing Europe? The Costs, Benefits and Conditions of Federal Political Systems*, Oxford: Oxford University Press.
Kothari, R. (1970) *Politics in India*, New Delhi: Orient Longman.
Lijphart, A. (1996) 'The Puzzle of Indian Democracy: A Consociational Interpretation', *American Political Science Review* 90, 2: 258–68.
Mitra, S.K. (1996) 'India', in G. Almond and G. Bingham Powell Jr. (eds), *Comparative Politics Today*, 6th edn, New York: HarperCollins.
Mitra, S.K. and Lewis, A. (eds) (1996) *Subnational Movements in South Asia*, Boulder, CO: Westview Press.
Mitra, S.K. and Singh, V.B. (1999) *Democracy and Social Change in India*, Delhi: Sage.
Moore, B. (1966) *Social Origins of Dictatorship and Democracy: Lord and Peasant in the Making of the Modern World*, Boston: Beacon Press.
Nehru, J. (1985) *Letters to Chief Ministers, 1947–1964*, Delhi: Oxford University Press.
Pinder, J. (1993) 'The New European Federalism: The Idea and the Achievements', in M. Burgess and A.-G. Gagnon (eds), *Comparative Federalism and Federation: Competing Traditions and Future Directions*, Hemel Hempstead: Harvester Wheatsheaf.
Riker, W. (1975) 'Federalism', in F.I. Greenstein and N.W. Polsby (eds), *Handbook of Political Science, Vol. 5: Governmental Institutions and Processes*, Reading, MA: Addison-Wesley, 93–172.
Tarlton, C.D. (1965) 'Symmetry and Asymmetry as Elements of Federalism: A Theoretical Speculation', *Journal of Politics* 27, 4: 861–74.
Watts, R.L. (1981) 'Federalism, Regionalism and Political Integration', in D. Cameron (ed.), *Regionalism and Supranationalism*, Montreal: Institute for Research into Public Policy, 3–19.
—— (1998) 'Federalism, Federal Political Systems and Federations', *Annual Review of Political Science* 1: 117–37.
Wheare, K.C. (1964.) *Federal Government*, 4th edn, New York: Oxford University Press.

3   Spain: incomplete federalism[1]

Mireia Grau i Creus

Introduction

The development of the *Estado de las Autonomías* has taken Spain towards a federal system of governance to such an extent that it is nowadays common to describe the country as 'quasi-federal or federal-like', or as a state 'moving towards federal arrangements' (Agranoff 1993; Agranoff and Ramos Gallarmn 1997; Moreno 1997).

The degree of federalism may in general be measured according to two factors: the degree of self-government of the subnational entities which make up the state; and the degree to which those entities participate in federal policy processes (Moreno 1997: 141). In Spain, although the powers of the *Comunidades Autónomas* (CAs) have increased, their participation in central government policy-making processes is weak and very poorly structured. Accordingly, Spain may not be considered to be a completely federal state.

This chapter examines the participation of the CAs in national policy-making processes. It is divided into five sections. The first aims to identify the type of federalism which characterizes the Spanish institutional setting, by looking at the interaction between central government and the CAs. The second section analyses intergovernmental mechanisms for co-operation in sectoral policies.[2] The third section examines intergovernmental policy outputs, that is, joint programming and *convenios* (agreements between CAs and central administration). The fourth section focuses on the role that state-wide political parties have in the intergovernmental game; it aims to assess the importance of politics in the Spanish intergovernmental process. Finally, the fifth section attempts to draw some conclusions.

The participation of the CAs in central government decision-making and policy-making.

In federal systems, the participation of territorial interests in federal decision-making and policy-making is generally structured in one of two ways: *within* national institutions (intrastate federalism), or through institutions for bargaining *between* national and sub-national governments (interstate federalism) (Simeon 1972). Intrastate institutions rely on the formal representation of subnational interests within national institutions: for example within the executive, through the existence of regional quotas in the composition of the government (as in Belgium); and within the legislature, through the existence of a second chamber. Interstate institutions rely on bargaining amongst political representatives of each level of government, usually in arenas other than formal institutions. One of the clearest examples of this is the Canadian inter-ministerial conferences amongst the provincial governments and the federal government.[3]

The characterization of Spanish institutions as either intrastate or inter-state can be better understood by distinguishing, at a policy-making level, two arenas which involve the interests of both the CAs and the central government. It is in these arenas that the influence and participation of the CAs in central government decision-making processes could be expected to be found.

The first arena concerns the broad policies formulated with the intention of producing an impact on the nature of the state itself (for example, policies which deal with the financing system and the distribution of powers). This is known as the *política autonómica*. Although Spain has a bicameral system where the second chamber, the Senate, is meant to be the territorial chamber, the CAs do not in fact participate in issues related to *política autonómica* through the Senate. The functions of the latter in this respect remain not just incomplete, but ill-defined. Both its subordinated role to Congress and the poor definition of its territorial functions limit its effectiveness as a forum for the participation of the CAs. Reforms have been implemented since 1994, and the establishment of a Committee for the CAs (Comisión General de las Autonomías) has now introduced some changes in the internal workings of the Senate. However, these reforms – and many other proposals for reform – have mostly centred on the *internal* institutional design of the chamber. The *external* institutional design, that which links the Senate to the political system as a whole, has not been considered. Thus, crucial issues, such as the Senate's relationship with Congress and the attitude of nationalist actors towards a territorial forum, remain unresolved.[4]

The second arena concerns sectoral policies, for which the policy process falls mainly within the powers of central government: this includes most public works policies such as infrastructure networks, water policy and telecommunications. Although the Committee of the CAs in the Senate may deal with these issues once they become part of the legislative process, sectoral policies may in practice be dealt with in forums attended by the top political representatives of the CAs and central government: the Sectoral Conferences (*Conferencias Sectoriales*). The participation of the CAs in this arena is, thus, through interstate institutions created by central government. The effectiveness of these Conferences as mechanisms for the participation of the CAs in central government policy-making is, however, very often questioned. I will return to this point in the next section.

Intergovernmental relations in sectoral policies

The establishment of the Sectoral Conferences

The main reason that led central government to create the Sectoral Conferences was its increasing concern over the diversity of policy outputs which could result from the 17 CA administrations working without any co-ordination, either horizontal or vertical. Its goal was therefore to provide, through multilateral forums of discussion chaired by the central administration, a certain standardization of criteria in the policy process.

However, when they were created – in 1981, by the Organic Law for Harmonizing the Process of Autonomy (the Ley Armonizadora del Proceso Autonómico, LOAPA) – the Sectoral Conferences got off to a very conflictual start. The section of LOAPA which created them was challenged by the CAs before the Constitutional Court. They argued that the Conferences would work as a mechanism for central institutions to intervene in the concerns of the CAs. The ruling of the Constitutional Court partially dismissed these claims, but explicitly limited the decision-making power of the Conferences. It held that decisions made within the Conferences could never replace those made by the CAs on issues falling within their powers (ruling 76/1983 (FJ 13) of the Constitutional Court).

In 1992, central government sought to consolidate the Conferences through the Autonomy Agreement concluded by the Partido Socialista Obrero Español (PSOE) and the Partido Popular (PP). In the Agreement, these political parties committed themselves to foster 'co-operative behaviour' amongst the institutions which they controlled (MAP 1996: 143). The emphasis here on co-operative *behaviour* reflects the constraints derived from the ruling of the Constitutional Court, which re-directed the focus of central government towards seeking to influence the styles of interaction: the aim of the Sectoral Conferences was now to smooth conflicts at the intergovernmental level.

At present, 24 Sectoral Conferences have been set up. Figure 3.1 illustrates their gradual establishment from 1982 to 1995. Whilst in 1982 there existed only one (the Council for Fiscal and Financing Policy of the CAs, or Consejo de Política Fiscal y Financiera de las Comunidades Autónomas), seven years later (1989), 17 had been created, at a rate of two a year. This growth could be taken as an indicator of a growth in formal intergovernmental contacts and, as a consequence, in intergovernmental co-operation. This is the perspective adopted by the Ministry of Public Administration (MAP) in its report on the implementation of the 1992 Agreements (MAP 1996).[5]

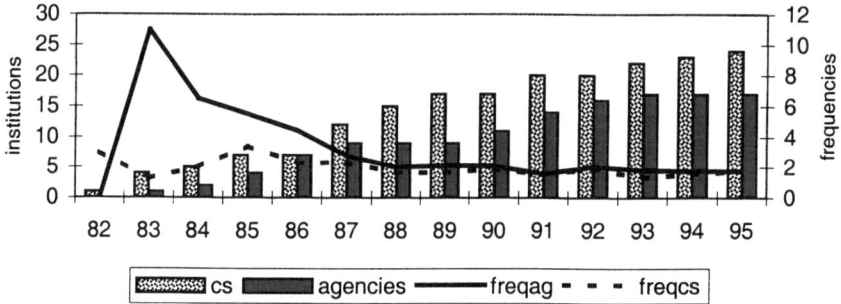

Figure 3.1 Establishment of *Conferencias Sectoriales* and agencies, and average
frequency of the meetings, 1982–1995.

Source: Own elaboration from data of the MAP (1996).

However, the growth of institutions has not been accompanied by a
similar growth of contacts and meetings (see Figure 3.1). The importance
of the establishment of mechanisms for intergovernmental co-operation
seems to be the mere fact of their establishment. Their activities are quite
irregular, and do not seem to be based upon an established agenda. Few of
the Sectoral Conferences meet regularly, or even have a significant number
of meetings; most of them have a poor and irregular level of activity. In this
sense, diversity is perhaps one of the main trends of intergovernmental co-
operation.

There is then little evidence that the growth of these mechanisms has
resulted either in a change of the style of intergovernmental relations, or in
the standardization of policy criteria across the different CAs. To analyse
this point further, we must turn to what is decided, discussed and dealt with
in these intergovernmental forums.

Sectoral Conferences and their impact on the policy process

One of the functions that central institutions gave to the Sectoral Conferences was that of being an instrument to promote a certain degree of
standardization of policy criteria amongst the CAs. Given the diversity in
the functioning of the 24 Conferences, it is difficult to assess whether this
objective has been achieved.

The role of the Conferences in generalizing policy-making processes
does not seem to be their most important feature; rather, it could be said
that they are mechanisms of 'institutional courtesy': that is, the Conferences
are where institutions *inform* others about their plans, activities and proposals. Most of the time, however, only central institutions provide such
information. Although CA institutions could also use the Conferences to
provide information about their respective programmes and activities, in
practice, the Conferences are more like closed 'seminars' where central

institutions set out their policies and CA institutions protest, or seek funding for their own projects. In some constitutional conflicts, the relevant Sectoral Conference has served to narrow the differences between the parties and, as a result, intergovernmental actors have reconsidered their initial position. However, the body which decides whether to appeal or withdraw an official appeal is the Judicial Office of each CA. Whether because of their different political goals, or because of the weak links between the Conferences and the Judicial Office, the result is that decisions on constitutional conflicts taken in the Sectoral Conferences have rarely changed the positions of the CA Judicial Offices.

Thus, the role of the Sectoral Conferences in the policy-making process does not seem to be that of a multilateral forum for joint decision-making. Where there is political agreement, they are used simply as mechanisms to ratify political decisions. And where there is no political agreement, they are rarely used as mechanisms to reach agreements (Nieto 1996). Meetings of the Conferences are not automatically called when there is a need for consensus on a controversial political issue; and when such a meeting is called, there are few incentives to promote negotiation and consensus amongst the parties. Two factors explain this: the decision-making powers of the conferences, and the commitment of the participants.

Decision-making power

Following the ruling of the Constitutional Court (STC 76/1983), decisions taken in the Sectoral Conferences cannot replace decisions taken by the CAs on issues within their competences. This constraint seeks to prevent the Sectoral Conferences from being in effect forums for final political decisions. Given the distribution of powers, final decisions are taken either by central or CA institutions.

This system of sharply separated decision-making has consequences for the mechanisms of intergovernmental co-operation. It is difficult to imagine incentives for co-operation in those Conferences dealing with policy areas that fall mainly under the competences of one side only. And as they cannot be forums for taking final decisions, very little is at stake in the meetings. The CAs jealously guard their constitutional rights to make decisions and so there is no joint decision-making with central government. Only particular political events or personal affinities allow joint decision-making. Moreover, it often proves difficult for the 17 CAs to find a common reason for voluntary co-operation; and even where agreement is achieved, another obstacle appears: the great difficulty of compelling the parties to abide by any such agreement.

Commitments and intergovernmental co-operation

There are no judicial mechanisms to oblige CA institutions to execute any policy for which the CAs alone are responsible; a constitutional procedure is available, but is entirely ignored because of its potential political costs.[6] In order to promote the execution of any intergovernmental agreement reached in the Sectoral Conferences, the MAP designed a quasi-contract, the *Convenio de Conferencia Sectorial*. By this device, agreements reached in the Conferences could result in a single document committing all the parties to that agreement. Up to now, only one of these quasi-contracts has been signed.[7]

At a more technical level, some aspects may be identified as impediments to the development of intergovernmental co-operation:

1 *Co-operation as hierarchical co-ordination*. The pattern of the Conferences responds to a hierarchical perception of intergovernmental relations, since the minister calls the conference, chairs it and sets the agenda. This fosters the atmosphere of 'institutional courtesy' in the forums, as the CAs have only a very passive role in the discussions.[8]

2 *Political and personal dependence*. The organization and proceedings of the Conferences are dealt with by the cabinets of the respective ministers (at both central and CA levels). Therefore any change of personnel usually results in the development of new impasses to the intergovernmental policy of the central ministry concerned. No permanent agencies for intergovernmental co-operation exist within either the central or the CA ministries; co-operation depends very much on the personal attitude of the politicians involved, and on the political mood in general.

3 *Erratic meetings*. Very few of the Conferences are supported by permanent agencies which work regularly between meetings, and which supervise implementation. As Conferences are usually held at very irregular intervals, the issues concerned are tackled very intermittently.

4 *Diversity of administrations*. The sporadic nature of the Conferences is due, very often, to difficulties in fixing a date. The CA governments hold their respective governmental meetings on different days of the week, and since the Conferences do not generate much interest, CA representatives hardly ever miss their own governmental meetings in order to attend. In addition, differences in the organization of the CA governments mean that some of the CA organizations correspond to more than one Conference: this further complicates the setting of agendas and the attendance of politicians.

5 *Excessively wide objectives*. Some of the Conferences deal with very broad policy sectors (such as 'public infrastructures') so finding concrete issues to discuss can be very difficult.

The Conferences are not then mechanisms for joint decision-making. One could argue that in spite of their weak decision-making powers, they could nonetheless work as instruments for considering interests and preparing decisions; but again, whether these forums can actually succeed in this role depends on too many contingent factors. Although, exceptionally, some Conferences seem to be quite efficient as mechanisms of information exchange (for example, Rico[9]) argues that the Intergovernmental Council on Health Matters works as a mechanism for considering different points of view, and the Sectoral Conference for European Affairs seem to be an effective forum for intergovernmental discussion, and for preparing further decisions), the majority of Conferences seem to be dependent on contingent factors, such as the political mood or the personality of ministers. Poor levels of intergovernmental co-operation are achieved by these meetings. Even the MAP, in evaluating the development of mechanisms for co-operation, concludes that 'The institutional establishment of these mechanisms is one thing, the use of these mechanisms and techniques for co-operation, and their stability is quite another. In practice, these mechanisms are subject to changes of direction within the different institutions involved, and, in most cases, are not supported by an appropriate legal base. . . . as a consequence, the question arises of whether there has been a significant development of mechanisms of co-operation, or whether this depends upon changes at political or organizational level' (MAP 1996: 129 – my translation).

From the point of view of central government, the development of mechanisms for multilateral co-operation is necessary for standardizing policy criteria. However, the effects of the institutional setting do not permit the mechanisms which it has created to work in an efficient manner. From the point of view of the CAs, co-operation is often understood simply as an intrusion of central government in their concerns.

This brief analysis of the Sectoral Conferences seeks to illustrate the weaknesses of intergovernmental co-operation in decision-making processes. In the next section, the analysis of the policy outputs reinforces this argument. The MAP refers to the policy outputs of intergovernmental interaction as 'joint programming', and as *convenios*.

The policy outputs of intergovernmental co-operation

Joint programming

By 'joint programming' the MAP means those intergovernmental policy programmes that require the participation of both central and CA institutions. The degree of participation, however, ranges from the initiation and formulation of policy, to the right to be informed about the policy. According to this graduated concept of participation, the MAP has elaborated a typology of 'joint programming':

* Category 1 comprises those policies entirely decided and implemented by central government. There is no participation of the CAs in any stage of the policy process. An example of this is general road planning and all kinds of public works policies covering more than one CA.

- Category 2 comprises those policies decided entirely by central government but where the CAs may be involved in their implementation. In most cases, this concerns a CA which is interested in the implementation of a given policy in its territory, but lacks either the financing or the competences to do so itself.
- Category 3 comprises those policies designed in broad terms by central government but adopted by each individual CA, according to its particular needs. In general, these policies are adopted through a *convenio*, which in fact is a mechanism of financing: it specifies the economic participation of each institution in the implementation of the policy.
- Category 4 comprises those policies designed in broad terms by central government which, by virtue of the constitutional distribution of powers, require implementation by CA institutions. This category is very similar to category 3 but differs from it by the fact that the CAs hold the power of implementation. These policies may be also adopted through *convenios*.
- Category 5 comprises those policies formulated jointly by central government and the CAs. In theory, they result from meetings of Sectoral Conferences. These may can be considered as the 'real' joint programming.
- Category 6 comprises those policies which originated at the European Union (EU) level and which require both the participation of the CAs and of central government in the implementation process.

Following this typology, Table 3.1 shows the distribution of the different categories of joint programming.

Two aspects may be noted. One is the weak role of 'real' joint programming (category 5): only two such programmes have been designed since 1989 (2.7 per cent of the total number of programmes). The other is

Table 3.1 Joint programming in 1989, 1992 and 1995

Category of joint programming	1989	1992	1995	Total
2	9	9 (+0)	12 (+3)	12 (16%)
3	19	36 (+17)	37 (−4+5)	41 (56%)
4	7	9 (+2)	11 (+2)	11 (15%)
5	1	1 (+0)	2 (+1)	2 (2.7%)
6	0	2 (+2)	7 (+5)	7 (9.5%)
Total (columns)	36	57	69	73 (100%)

Source: Compiled with data from MAP (1996).
Note: Data is cumulative, that is, programmes have not been counted twice; in general, these programmes last for more than one ear. The 'Total' column must be read as all the programmes during all the years being considered.

that central government plays a dominant role in policy formulation (categories 2, 3 and 4: category 1 – policies entirely formulated and implemented by central authorities – has been excluded, as there is clearly no joint participation in decision-making here).

Categories 2, 3 and 4 account for the greatest number of programmes (16 per cent, 56 per cent, and 15 per cent respectively, that is, 87 per cent of the total number of programmes since 1989). Most of these programmes are implemented through a series of bilateral *convenios* (that is, one programme may give rise to several *convenios*, each devoted to the implementation of particular aspects of the programme). Although the pattern of the *convenios* used in joint programming tends to be uniform (even if a programme gives rise to several bilateral *convenios* with different CAs, the text of the documents tends to be the same), one cannot assume that all the CAs will participate to the same extent in the practical development of the joint programme. Clearly, agreeing to the general programme, and formulating concrete policies to implement it, are two distinct processes.

An interesting aspect is the increasing development of joint programming resulting from EU directives (category 6). For example, of the seven joint programmes in 1995, four were related to the Common Agricultural Policy, and the other three to the environment at Spanish level.[10] This then raises the question of whether EU policies promote intergovernmental co-operation in Spain. It would seem that, in order to implement EU directives, intergovernmental co-operation is required, but is in practice not achieved very easily. Central government is accountable to the EU for implementation, but where an issue is within the sole competence of the CAs, it has no power to intervene, and there is no legal mechanism by which it can oblige the CA institutions to implement the policy. In the case of the three programmes on environmental issues, central government played a clear co-ordinating role. Given that some CAs had already passed their own laws implementing the EU directives, the secretary of state for the environment adopted the principles of these existing laws as models for further negotiations. She then negotiated with each of the 17 CAs, one by one, over the general criteria which should be followed. These negotiations allowed the CAs without laws to develop them (according to the model), and allowed the CAs with a law to participate in the formulation of the national programme. Eventually, and only when each of the 17 CAs had either a law or a project to create one, central government drafted the national programme.[11]

This example shows that EU policies can promote intergovernmental co-operation, although they cannot do this by themselves: the role of central government as a co-ordinator is also necessary. Nevertheless, given the lack of formal institutions for political negotiations, the ability of central government to play such a role will depend very much on its perspective on intergovernmental relations: a simple hierarchical approach will lead to confrontation with the CAs.

As joint programming is usually implemented through *convenios*, we should now turn to these.

The convenios

The *convenios* may be taken to mean 'agreements between central and CA institutions'. The aim of this section is to see whether, as the MAP states, there is an increase in multilateral *convenios,* and, as a result, a reduced importance of the bilateral *convenios* (MAP 1995). The analysis here is based mainly on data provided by the MAP in its annual reports on the evolution of *convenios* (MAP 1995)

Some aspects of the data treatment in these reports have to be taken carefully into account.[12] In calculating the total number of multilateral *convenios*, the MAP counts each individual adhesion to such agreements. So, for example, of the 424 agreements signed in 1994, 145 are taken as bilateral agreements in that they were signed only by a single CA and central government. This leaves 279 agreements which the MAP considers to be multilateral, in the sense of being signed by more than one CA. However, these 279 agreements are in reality the individual acts by which one particular CA adhered to a general agreement. The conclusion of 43 general agreements resulted in the signature of 279 *convenios*, and of these 43 general agreements, only 11 may be considered truly multilateral, in the sense that they were signed by all 15 eligible CAs;[13] all of the other general agreements merely involved the signature of more than one CA.

Thus, analysing the official data from a perspective different from that of the MAP, shows that although *convenios* are elements of intergovernmental co-operation, they are *bilateral* not multilateral elements. An examination of the economic provisions of these agreements reinforces this point (see Figure 3.2):

According to the MAP (1995: 26), four *convenios* alone account for 46.6 per cent of the total expenditure. These four are all bilateral *convenios* which deal with spending on public works mainly financed by central government.

The concentration of *convenios* in policy areas related to public works, social affairs and culture (see Figure 3.3) reveals an important feature of the *convenios*: they are mechanisms for policy financing. In the case of public works, most of the *convenios* are explicitly mechanisms for the financing of these works. In the case of social affairs and culture (policy areas falling under the competences of the CAs), the general agreements reached in the *convenios* are in practice a means of obtaining grants from central institutions. Figure 3.4 illustrates the participation of central government and each CA in the *convenios*. It can be seen that central government provides the major part of the financing.

Here, according to some officials of the MAP, co-operation between central government and the CAs exists because of the economic dependence

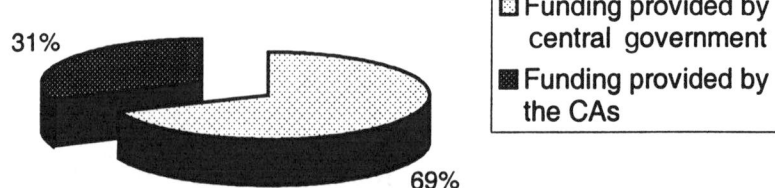

Figure 3.2 Expenditure of the *convenios* in 1994.
Source: MAP (1995).

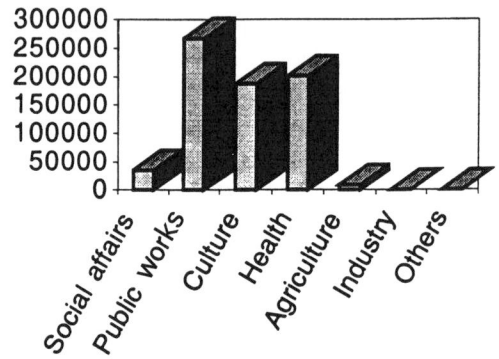

Figure 3.3 Expenditure on *convenios* by ministry (millions of PTAS).
Source: Own elaboration after data from MAP (1995: 27–31; 1996: 80).

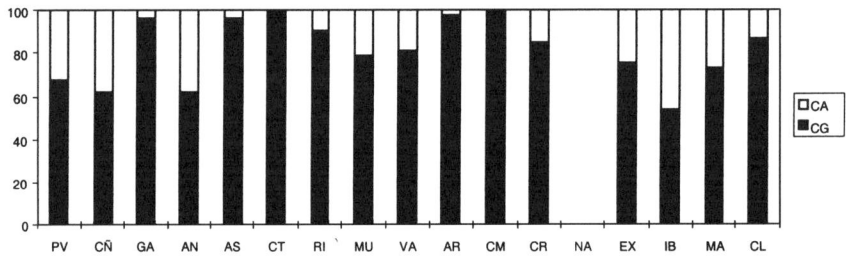

Figure 3.4 Financing participation of central government (CG) and the CAs in the
     convenios.
Source: Own elaboration after data from MAP (1995).
Note: See appendix to this chapter for explanation of abbreviations.

of the CAs on central government. Indeed, the low levels of participation of
Navarra and the Basque Country in the *convenios* (and other, similar
agreements) are due to their different financing system: unlike the other
CAs, these two CAs collect and manage their own taxes. Because of this,
they do not take part in the system of redistribution of funding from the
central institutions.

The changes to the financing system of the CAs, which the Catalan coalition *Convergència i Unió* (CiU) negotiated with central government in 1996, may thus mark the end of the system based mainly on redistribution from central government to the CAs. Because of the importance of grants in the *convenios*, these changes will probably lead to changes in the existing mechanisms for intergovernmental co-operation.

Spanish political parties and the intergovernmental game

The importance of politics in the intergovernmental game, and more specifically of the role which Spanish political parties play in it, has not been fully examined in studies and analyses of the Spanish political system. At most, it is merely stated that 'political forces play a considerable role in shaping the territorial system' (Agranoff 1993: 13), and that intergovernmental relations are closely linked to the political context (Wright 1997: 47). In short, although it seems obvious that politics and political parties do have an impact on the intergovernmental game, there are no in-depth analyses which illustrate why and how.

The aim of this section is then to look at the impact that Spanish political parties have upon intergovernmental policy-making. In order to do so, it is useful to distinguish between three forms of political impact. The first is the *ideological impact* of the parties upon intergovernmental conflicts. The second is the *political patronage* or privileged treatment which the party in office at central level may show to the CAs in exchange for electoral or other political favours. The third is the *political integration* which political parties, through intra-party relations, can provide in intergovernmental policy-making. I will explore each of these three aspects in turn.

Ideological impact

The impact of parties upon the intergovernmental game may be seen in the ideological influence which they have upon the definition and formulation of intergovernmental policies: that is, whether intergovernmental issues take dimensions which relate to the interests of political parties or to the interests of subnational governments. Looking at the influence of the PSOE on the content of policies, Subirats and Gomà (1997) show that the party guidelines have had only a small influence. They argue that the reason for this is that the party apparatus was completely subordinated to the party in central government, so governmental priorities came to influence the party guidelines.[14]

What, then, may be said about the ideological dimension of intergovernmental policies? Are intergovernmental policies discussed from subnational or from partisan perspectives? A subnational perspective would imply that the CAs take institutional positions towards central government policies; that is, notwithstanding the party in control in central government, the governments of the CAs constitute the 'subnational level opposition'. This sub-national perspective would allow for intergovernmental conflicts and agreements independent of the party in office at central and at CA level. By contrast, a partisan perspective would imply that the nature of the intergovernmental game would depend upon the political party in charge of the different governments. One could expect to find agreements between CAs and central government where the parties in government were the same, and conflicts between them where these parties were different.

To date, the intergovernmental game has clearly developed according to a partisan perspective. This is clear in the area of the *política autonómica*, where the issues are discussed by political parties and the positions of the CAs respond, to a large extent, to the resulting political guidelines. One example of this is the debate on the financing system of the CAs. Changes to the financing system began in 1993, when the PSOE formed a minority government with the parliamentary support of the CiU. The PSOE and the CiU negotiated changes in the financing system which in essence increased the transfers which the CAs received from central government. These changes were opposed by the PP. The CAs run by the PP rejected the new system, and some of them brought an appeal before the Constitutional Court. In 1996, the situation was reversed: the PP came to power thanks to the support of nationalist parties, and it negotiated with them further reforms to the financing system which enlarged the CAs tax-raising powers.[15] This time three socialist-controlled CAs appealed to the Constitutional Court over the new changes; meanwhile the CAs governed by the PP were persuaded (by virtue of party discipline) to withdraw the existing appeals.

Thus, the changes to the system which have taken place are due to changes in the political coalitions supporting central government, not to intergovernmental negotiations; and the CA governments have adopted their respective positions towards the financing system according to party political considerations.

Political patronage

The political advantages enjoyed by CAs governed by the same political Party as that in office in central government may be linked to considerations of political patronage and electoral strategies.

Boix (1996) tested the correlation of the public investments in the CAs made by the PSOE central government with different variables, such as the average income per inhabitant of the CAs; the level of competences enjoyed by the CAs; and electoral support for the PSOE within the CAs. He concluded that, although investments were concentrated in the less-developed CAs, political support for the PSOE was one of the variables that most influenced investments by central government. Moreover, the two variables which best explained the location of new public investments between 1982 and 1986 were the level of PSOE membership in the CAs, and the particular influence which certain CA branches of the party (such as those in Andalusia and Extremadura) had on the national party (Boix 1996: 203–46). These findings show that not only ideology but also intra-party relations seem to affect the style of intergovernmental relations. These intra-party relations involve trade-offs for both national and CA branches of the party, which, in turn, have an impact on the relations between the different levels of government run by the same party.

Political integration

The role of parties in the intergovernmental relations may also be seen from a broader perspective: that of the structure of the party system. From this perspective, it can be said that whether parties matter in defining the intergovernmental game depends to a large extent on the subordination (or integration) of the country's political life to national-level politics.[16] This movement can balance out the decentralization and the bilateral trends of the Spanish intergovernmental system.

Here, the level of subordination will be briefly illustrated using some of the distinctions made by Smiley (1980) between 'integrated and confederal party systems'. These distinctions relate to electoral dependence and party symmetry, and party organization.

Electoral dependence and party symmetry

Throughout the last fourteen years, the party elected to government in most of the CAs has been the same as the party elected to central government (see Table 3.2); and the same two parties have been the main competitors in both types of elections (party symmetry, see Table 3.3). Voters have generally supported the same party at CA elections as at general elections,[17] and electoral changes at one level have foreshadowed changes at the other (López Pintor 1994; Pallarés 1994; Pallarés and Font 1995; Crespo 1997).

The political competition between the PP and the PSOE has to a large extent determined intergovernmental relations. These are moulded through the political and electoral competition for central institutions.

Subordination to the central arena has undergone different phases. Yet, as Table 3.2 and Table 3.3 illustrate, the long period of PSOE predominance (1982–96 at central level and 1983–95 at CA level) was neither static nor unidirectional. Electoral changes did occur, although they were more perceptible at central level: the loss of support for the PSOE at CA level occurred gradually between 1983 and 1995. At the same time, some of the CAs became the electoral fiefdoms of the two main parties: Castilla y León and Galicia for the PP, Andalusia, Extremadura and Castilla-La-Mancha for the PSOE. This had consequences for intergovernmental relations: the institutional power of the regional leaders of these CAs should not be

Table 3.2 Parties in central and CA governments 1983–1999

	1983–87	1987–91	1991–96	1996–99	1999*
Party in central government (CG)	PSOE	PSOE	PSOE	PP	PP
CA governments of the same party as that in CG	12	9	9	10	8
CA governments of the main opposition party	3	4	4	3	4
CA governments of nationalist/ regional parties either in coalition or in mono-colour governments	2	3	4	4	5
Others	0	1	0	0	0

Source: Own elaboration after data from Anuario El País (1996, 1997, 1998).
Note: *At the moment of writing (July 1999), CA elections were held on 13 June 1999 except for Catalonia (last elections in 1995), the Basque Country (last elections 1998), Galicia (last elections 1997), and Andalusia (last elections 1996), Ceuta and Melilla are not considered here (nor in Table 3.3).

Table 3.3 Structure of the electoral competition (CA elections)

	1993	1987	1991	1995	1999
CAs where the first and the second parties are the PP and the PSOE	14	12	11	14	13
CAs where either the first or the second party is neither the PP nor the PP	3	5	6	3	4

Source: *Anuario El País* (1996), Wert (1994: 619, 620), and the web site of the CAs (see link at www.map.es) for 1999.)

dismissed in considering the evolution of the styles of intergovernmental relations, for they represent the joining of political parties and institutions.

Party organization

The structure of the PSOE is federal,[18] although the margin of real federalization, and consequently the margin of manoeuvre of the party's regional organizations, is quite different across the CAs. In some of the CAs, the leaders preferred to remain in the shadow of their high-profile national leader, Felipe González; whilst in others they used the CA institutions to advance their own power within the party organization (Méndez Lago 1998).

In the early 1980s, concerns arose over the consequences that the federalisation of the party might have on the party's unity of action. This may be traced through the annual reports of the party (Memoria de Gestión). One result of the process of federalization was the increasing presence of the regional secretaries in the Central Committee of the Party (Ejecutiva Federal). In practice, however, the centrifugal trends which might have resulted from these federal structures were balanced by the fact that the party was in office in central government: Méndez Lago (1998) demonstrated the relevance of the informal but regular meetings held between the president of the government (who was also General Secretary of the PSOE) and the socialist presidents of the CAs.

In the case of the PP, two aspects of the party's organization influence the intergovernmental game: one is its presidential and hierarchical organization; and the other is the fact that the members of the party hierarchy (Comite Ejecutivo Nacional) also hold office in central government.

The presidential and hierarchical organization implies that power is concentrated in the hands of the president of the PP, and collegiate bodies are of minor importance (Wert 1994: 640). This tight form of organization is, in turn, reproduced within the regional branches[19]. The room for manoeuvre within these branches is quite limited. One of the reasons for this is the clear intention of the party leaders to avoid the emergence of strong regional leaders who could question the party's national policies (Burns Marañón 1997: 346). The PP's regional organization is therefore deliberately subordinated to national objectives (Trillo in Burns Marañón 1997: 346). Disagreements between CA and central structures have rarely become public, but that does not mean they do not exist.[20]

The form of the PP's organization, and the fact that almost all the members of the party hierarchy hold office at central level, have resulted in a very limited freedom of movement for the CA branches, whether a particular CA branch is in or out of office. In an integrated party such as the PP there is in any case a shared belief that the national objectives of the party are the political priority for all.[21]

Some conclusions

The analysis of the formal institutions of intergovernmental relations demonstrated their weaknesses and fragmentation. Decision-making processes involving the CAs and central government are practically non-existent. At a sectoral level, central government has unsuccessfully (and without much conviction) sought to promote a model of intergovernmental relations based on a mild multilateralism. This model clashes directly with the reality of the situation: promoted by the constitutional setting and by the political interests of the more active players within the system, bilateral relations are the most relevant trend in the system. Intergovernmental relations are not one game with 18 actors (17 CAs and central government) but 17 games played by two separate actors. This is mainly due to three factors: the constitutional distribution of competences, which allows for separate decision-making processes and consequently promotes bilateral trends; the ineffectiveness of the multilateral forums; and the economic dependence of the CAs upon central government. Thus, the major changes in the financing system for the CAs may be an initial step towards a new system of relations.

At a broader level, related to the *política autonómica*, the CAs do not have a collegiate role in central decision-making processes. Although in principle the Senate is the constitutional institution intended to cover such functions, in practice decision-making on these issues is more related to party guidelines than to institutions. The German federal government would not, for example, consider a road-building project without meeting the *Länder* and agreeing it with them; and in Canada, national policies have become matters of intergovernmental concern (Simeon 1972). In Spain, however, the lack of participation of the CAs in central policy processes has not led to political controversy. The CAs have not expressed any political willingness to create multilateral forums for decision-making with the exception of EU issues. The issue of the participation of the CAs in central policy-making processes has never been defined as a significant problem. One reason for this may relate to the link between intergovernmental relations and politics: that is, to political parties and the electoral competition. The *política autonómica* depends on political coalitions rather than on institutions. This dependency is enhanced by the high level of political integration: political actors focus the political game around central institutions, and in doing so, provide a counter-balance for the decentralization of the intergovernmental system.

Appendix: The Comunidades Autonómas

Andalucía (AN)
Aragón (AR)
Asturias (AS)
Illes Balears (IB)
Castilla y León (CL)
Castilla-La Mancha (CM)
Catalunya (CÑ)
Cantabria (CT)
Canarias (CR)
Extremadura (EX)
Galicia (GA)
Madrid (MA)
Murcia (MU)
Navarra (NA)
País Vasco (PV)
La Rioja (RI)
Comunidad Valenciana (VA)

Notes

1 I would like to thank Mark Jeffery, Rosarie McCarthy and Mónica Méndez Lago for helpful comments and English corrections on earlier versions of this chapter. My special thanks go to José Mª Pérez Medina at the MAP for his insightful comments.

2 This section is based mainly on interviews with senior civil servants in the Ministerio de Administración Pública (MAP), and on information provided by them as part of my PhD research at the European University Institute (Florence) during September–October 1996 and September 1997.

3 For a general overview, see Simeon (1972), and for a comparative perspective between Canada and Germany, see Chandler and Zöllner (1985).

4 For a complete picture of the Senate reforms, see Institut d'Estudis Autonòmics (1996).

5 The role of the MAP in intergovernmental relations is that of privileged observer and adviser. It does not have any authority over either central or CA institutions, but works as a bridge between the two levels of government. Representatives of the MAP may attend the meetings of some Sectoral Conferences as observers.

6 Article 155 envisages intervention by central government where a CA does not observe constitutional principles or its legal obligations. Such intervention requires the agreement of an overall majority in the Senate.

7 Convenio of the Conference on the Planning of the Industrial Development of Small and Medium Firms 1994–1999, 13 April 1994.

8 This passive role is illustrated in the notes taken by the MAP representatives in some meetings. For example, '[the] low level of participation of the CAs in the meeting must be emphasised. Only Madrid, Catalunya, Navarra and Asturias said something. The Basque Country, Aragón and Castilla-León remained in total silence' (my translation).

9 Quoted by Agranoff (1993: 18–19).

10 Plan Nacional de Depuracion de Aguas Residuales Urbanas (EU directive 91/271); Plan Nacional de Residuos Peligrosos (EU directive 91/689); Plan Nacional de Recuperacion de Suelos Contaminados. The three plans were adopted by the Spanish Council of Ministries on 17 February 1995, Boletín Oficial del Estado (BOE) no. 114, 13 May 1995.

11 Interviews in the Ministerio de Obras Públicas, Transportes y Medio Ambiente, March 1996; interview with C. Narbona, former Socialist Secretary of State for the Environment (1993–96), October 1996.

12 This data comes from the complete list of *convenios* in 1994. The list contains a summary of each *convenio*, the names of the CAs which have signed it, and the date on which it was officially published in the BOE. *Bilateral convenios* is taken to mean those *convenios* which have not only been signed by a single CA, but which have also been designed to deal with the particular needs of a single CA. *Multilateral convenios* is taken to mean those *convenios* which are open to all CAs (with the exception of Navarra and the Basque Country – see note); here the number of signatories may range from 2 to 15 CAs. The category of *multilateral convenios* also includes *model convenios* (*modelos de convenio*). These are draft documents which result from joint agreements amongst all the CAs and central government, and which allow for the development of actual *convenios*. However, their influence is limited. Although 15 *model convenios* were agreed in 1994, they did not all lead to actual *convenios*, and nor did all of the CAs sign the actual *convenios* which were developed.

13 Because of their different financing system, the Basque Country and Navarra participate in very few agreements.

14 Note, however, that some authors stress the gradually weakening relationship between the PSOE party apparatus and central government. See Kitschelt (1995); Méndez Lago (1998) and Wert (1994).
15 The new financing system will allow the CAs not just to collect and manage up to 30 per cent of national taxes in their respective CAs, but also to pass legislation in this area.
16 This subordination of political life to national-level politics is not a characteristic of the Spanish political system alone; in Germany, for example, it is also considered that the main political arena is the federal one. See von Beyme and Schmidt (1985); Chandler and Chandler (1987); Döring and Smith (1982).
17 The most significant exception to this is the 'dual behaviour' of the Catalan electorate, who change their votes (or abstention) according to the type of elections. See Montero and Font (1991).
18 The structure of the PSOE is based on territorial organizations coinciding with the CAs.
19 There is a branch of the PP in each CA except Navarra, where the PP is integrated into a regional political party, the Unión del Pueblo Navarro.
20 In 1998, a conflict between the CA president of Asturias and the central party apparatus led to the expulsion of the CA president from the party.
21 See the interviews with J. Aznar, F. Trillo and M. Fraga by Burns Marañón (1997).

References

Agranoff, R. (1993) 'Inter-governmental Politics and Policy: Building Federal Arrangements in Spain', *Regional Politics and Policy* 3, 2: 1–28.

Agranoff, R. and Ramos Gallarmn (1997) 'Toward Federal Democracy in Spain: An Examination of Intergovernmental Relations', *Publius. The Journal of Federalism* 27: 4.

von Beyme, K. and Schmidt, M.G. (eds) (1985) *Policy and Politics in the Federal Republic of Germany*, New York: St Martin's Press.

Boix, C. (1996) *Partidos Políticos, Crecimiento e Igualdad. Estrategias Económicas Conservadoras y Socialdemócratas en la Economía Mundial*, Madrid: Alianza Editorial.

Burns Marañón, T. (1997) *Conversaciones sobre la derecha*, Barcelona: Plaza & Janés.

Chandler, W.M. and Chandler, M.A. (1987) 'Federalism and Political Parties', *European Journal of Political Economy*, Special Issue 1 & 2: 87–109.

Chandler, W.M. and Zöllner, C.W. (1985) *Challenges to Federalism: Policy-Making in Canada and the Federal Republic of Germany*, Kingston, Ontario: Queen's University Press.

Crespo, I. (1997) 'El sistema electoral', in M. Alcántara and A. Martínez (eds), *Política y Gobierno en España*, Ciencia Política 2, Valencia: Tirant lo Blanch.

Döring, H. and Smith, G. (eds) (1982) *Party Government and Political Culture in Western Germany*, London: Macmillan.

El País (1997–9) *Anuario El País 1996, 1997, 1998*, Madrid: El País Aguilar.,

Institut d'Estudis Autonòmics (comp) (1996) *Ante el futuro del Senado*, Barcelona: Generalitat de Catalunya.

Kitschelt, H. (1994) 'Internal politics in social parties', in *The Transformation of European Social Democracy*, Cambridge: Cambridge University Press.

López Pintor, J. (1994) 'El Sistema Político', in Fundación FOESSA, *Informe Sociológico sobre la Situación Social en España*, Madrid: Euramérica.

MAP (1995) *Informe sobre los Convenios de Colaboración entre la Administración del Estado y las Comunidades Autónomas*, Madrid: Secretaría de Estado para las Administraciones Territoriales.

—— (1996) *Puesta en Práctica de los Acuerdos Autonómicos de 1992 y sus Efectos sobre el Estado Autonómico*, Madrid: Secretaría de Estado para las Administraciones Públicas.

Méndez Lago, M. (1998) 'Organising for Victory . . . and Defeat? The Organizational Strategy of the Spanish Workers' Socialist Party (1975–1996)', PhD Dissertation, Florence: European University Institute.

Montero, J.R., and J. Font, J. (1991) 'El voto dual: lealtad y transferencia de votos en las elecciones Autonómicas' in Equip de Sociologia Electoral, *L'Electorat Català a les Eleccions Autonòmiques de 1988: Opinions, Actituts i Comportaments*, Barcelona: Fundació Jaume Bofill.

Moreno, L. (1997) *La Federalización de España*, Madrid: Siglo XXI.

Nieto, A. (1996) *La 'Nueva' Desorganización del Desgobierno*, Barcelona: Ariel.

Pallarès, F. (1994) 'Las elecciones autonómicas en España: 1980–1992', in P. del Castillo (ed.) *Comportamiento Político y Electoral*, Madrid: Centro de Investigaciones Sociológicas.

Pallarès, F. and Font, J. (1995) *The Autonomous Elections in Catalonia (1980–1992)*, Barcelona: Institut de Ciències Polítiques i Socials.

Simeon, R. (1972) *Federal–Provincial Diplomacy: The Making of Recent Policy in Canada*, Toronto: University of Toronto Press.

Smiley, D.V. (1980) *Canada in Question: Federalism in the Eighties*, Toronto: McGraw-Hill Ryerson Ltd.

Subirats, J. and Gomà, R. (1997) 'Las políticas públicas' in M. Alcántara and A. Martínez (eds), *Política y Gobierno en España*, Ciencia Política 2, Valencia: Tirant lo Blanch.

Wert, J.I. (1994) 'La vida interna de los partidos políticos', in Fundación FOESSA, *Informe Sociológico sobre la Situación Social en España*, Madrid: Euramérica.

Wright, V. (1997) 'Relations intergouvernementales et gouvernement régional en Europe: Réflexions d'un sceptique' in P. Le Galès and Ch. Lequesne (eds) *Les Paradoxes Des Régions En Europe*, Paris: La Découverte.

Part II

Federalism and policy-making in advanced democracies

4 Collaborative federalism in Germany

Keeping the system in the eye of the storm

Ute Wachendorfer-Schmidt

Collaborative federalism is most markedly developed in Germany. The constitution divides the powers of the *Länder* (provinces) and the federal government in such a way that none of them can act autonomously. While the federal government is responsible for the bulk of legislation (including tax laws), it is the competency of the *Länder* to implement federal legislation. In order to pass most of its legislation (and all of the important laws), the federal government needs the consent of the second chamber (Bundesrat), composed of the representatives of the *Länder* governments. These, in turn, are supervised in implementing laws by the federal government. The competencies that have remained with the *Länder* governments, mainly in the fields of education, police and culture, are exercised to generate not so much diverse but rather uniform policy outcomes across the federation. To this end, innumerable formal and informal committees have been established to co-ordinate the policies among the *Länder*, and between the *Länder* as a whole and the federal government. These horizontal and vertical joint decision systems (*Politikverflechtung*) have been identified as the main obstacles to flexible and responsive policy-making (Scharpf et al. 1976; Scharpf 1988).

My theme is the role of federalism in the 1990s, when the political system of the Federal Republic was subject to changes that came close to a revolution. How did the governments in Bonn and the *Länder* capitals respond to German unification, European integration, and to political and social problems in the enlarged federation? What is federalism like ten years after unification?

After discussing some essential features of federalism in the old Federal Republic, I will analyse how federalism coped with the challenges of the 1990s. This analysis is divided into three parts, testing the propositions of the theory on joint decision-making (*Politikverflechtungstheorie*) (Scharpf et al. 1976 and Scharpf 1988) for the cases of unification, European integration, and problem solution in other policy fields. Finally I will consider the theoretical implications of the empirical findings, and evaluate the strengths and weaknesses of collaborative federalism.

Federalism in the old republic

Decentralized rule has a long tradition in Germany. For hundreds of years, the traditional princely states and the regional identities of their inhabitants have frustrated any attempt of establishing a centralized power.[1] The Reformation strengthened the autonomy of the estates in the Holy Roman Empire of the German nation even more. The Peace of Westphalia in 1648 consolidated the fragile federal structure of the Empire, making it the basis of a policy of power-balancing in Europe. Therefore it remained a confederation of territorial states with limited sovereignty. The autonomy of the princely states, though, was not really threatened because the *Kaiser* had no executive powers in his own right. After Napoleon's armies had conquered the Empire, the territorial states obtained their full sovereignty, and the manifold forms of corporative self-government and participation in the old order were replaced by the centralist bureaucratic rule of the unitary state of French complexion. The Congress of Vienna (1815) re-affirmed the sovereignty of the bureaucratic princely states, which left a confederation as the only possible form of integration. The German Confederation was a system designed for international peace-keeping and restoration in middle Europe, yet it did not correspond to the liberal-bourgeois ideas of German integration. Among republican groups in Germany, only a radical liberal minority pleaded for a national unitary state, while most of the liberal bourgeoisie hoped that the confederation of princely states could be peacefully transformed into a federation of constitutional monarchies. In 1849 a federal constitution was elaborated, following the models of the United States and Switzerland (whose federal constitution was written nearly simultaneously in 1848). After the revolution of 1848 had failed, however, the liberal bourgeoisie abandoned its plan to establish a modern federal order in Germany.

The plan was realized by Bismarck, if not in the form the liberals had in mind. The Kingdom of Prussia, which until 1863 had blocked all attempts to deepen political integration in Germany for fear of Austria's dominance, from then on took the lead in the integration process. Bismarck formed an alliance with the national liberal movement, in order to found a German federal state without Austria. Under Bismarck's influence, the German Empire of 1871 received a constitution that merged contradicting traditions and principles. In order to comply with the bourgeoisie's desire for parliamentarization and political integration through a directly elected all-German parliament, Bismarck provided for a Reichstag to be elected and endowed with ample legislative competencies to regulate matters of civil law, penal law and business law. On the other hand, he restricted the power of the parliament by reserving all the executive functions to the constituent states. Therefore, the union was not allotted a public administration of its own but depended on the states for the implementation of laws. Where a unified executive was necessary, as in foreign relations and military affairs, it was directed collectively by the state governments in the Bundesrat, the second chamber. In this way, the unitarization of policies in the constituent states was more moderate than it would have been in a federation with an American-type senate; furthermore, the executive – administration, diplomacy and military – was placed beyond the control of the parliament.

The attitude of the opposition parties in the Empire towards federalism was marked by this experience. Left-wing liberals and Social Democrats turned into firm opponents of federalism, which to them meant conservatism. The French-type unitary state became their ideal of a modern state. Only the Catholic opposition party Zentrum took a different view. To the Zentrum, federalism was an instrument of protecting the Catholic ways of life in several constituent states against Prussian-Protestant hegemony. The Catholic opposition against the Prussian element of the federation was given a theoretical basis by the social philosophy of the Catholic church, with its principle of subsidiarity.

After the experience with National-Socialist dictatorship, federalism was seen in the light of the principle of checks and balances Madison had developed in the *Federalist Papers* (Hamilton et al. 1993). This was true at least for the Bavarian federalists and politicians of some other south German *Länder* (Eschenburg and Benz 1983: 476). When the Western allied occupation forces required the newly elected heads of the occupation zones to elaborate a constitution that would be federal in character, only the American government had a particular type of federalism in mind. Yet the dual federalism with a separation of powers along policy fields, not functions, and the senate elected by the population of the constituent states was not what the German federalists wanted, for they preferred the federalism Bismarck had created which would allow them to continue with the practice of decision-making and compromise among the executives, leaving the parliaments behind (Lehmbruch 1998: 81). Apart from tradition and self-interest of the *Länder* heads (who drafted the constitution *before* a federal government was established), the situation in Germany in 1949 did not lend itself to competitive federalism. Regional identities had been weakened by the war and the influx of millions of refugees and displaced persons to the Western occupation zones. And finally, any *Land* that insisted on autonomy would have risked the blame of separatism after the defeat of the Third Reich (Scharpf 1994a: 74).

The allied military governors intervened several times in the process of drafting what the *Länder* heads preferred to call basic law, *Grundgesetz*, in order to show their reservations against founding a state only in the Western part of the country. But no matter how much the American military governor pressed for more autonomy of the states, the constitution finally adopted was a compromise among the unitary ideas of the Social Democrats, the Bismarckian federalism advocated by the Bavarians, and the United States federalism.

Subsequent years have seen a redefinition of this compromise by strengthening the Bismarckian component. Policies were unitarized, first through voluntary co-ordination of the eleven states and city states who wanted to keep the federal government out, particularly in education policy, later through centralization by the federal government, and in 1969 through a reform of the fiscal constitution that aimed at distributing financial resources more evenly among the constituent units. Furthermore, the 1969 reform gave a constitutional basis to the practice of the federal government of supporting poor states bilaterally, in order to enable them to carry out expensive policies, such as agrarian restructuring, coastal infrastructure, promoting weak regional economies, and building universities. For these policy areas, 'joint tasks' were established in the constitution. They gave the Bonn government the right to engage in these areas originally attributed to the *Länder*, on the condition that it would co-finance the respective policies and plan them jointly with the *Länder*. These joint decision systems were empirically analysed by Scharpf, Reissert and Schnabel (1976), who demonstrated that they minimized the federal goverment's capacity to implement reform policies, as consent was only reached when all the participants were treated equally and vested interests were respected.

The proliferation of joint decision systems in all kinds of policy matters came to a halt when the economic situation worsened by the mid-1970s. The *Länder* were unevenly affected by the consequences of structural change and industrial decline, so that a new north–south divide appeared, as the once prosperous north was overtaken by the south (Owen Smith 1994: 44). Federal money to be dished out indiscriminately among the *Länder* became scarce. Moreover, joint planning was no longer considered the ideal solution to many problems, so that it gave way to more decentralized policy-making in the 1980s. The process of decentralization was realized merely through incremental adaptation without amending the constitution, a form of flexibility below the threshold of institutional reform typical of Germany's federalism that was to be used in managing unification ten years later. Besides decentralization, another development loosened the ties of solidarity among the German *Länder*. After years of stagnation and frustration (Scharpf 1988), European integration was intensified. When the European Single Act envisaged the completion of the internal market in 1987, it enhanced competitive orientations at least in the economically stronger states, exacerbating the distributional conflicts among the *Länder*. On the one hand, the *Eurofürsten*,[2] state premiers of rich and populous states such as Baden-Württemberg, Bavaria, and North Rhine-Westphalia, focused on their potential in the European internal market and demanded more autonomy to compete in it. On the other hand, the state premiers of the poorer states complained of growing unemployment rates and high social assistance payments. While the richer states felt they were being exploited paying unduly high financial equalization sums, the poorer states were convinced they did not receive enough financial support to resolve their problems of economic weakness. In 1986 and again in 1992, the Federal Constitutional Court had to rule on the federal financial equalization system. Before the decade was through, the Federal Constitutional Court would have to render judgement on the same topic again (see below). In public debate, the sharpening of interregional distributional conflict gave rise to proposals to redress federalism through constitutional reform, using the American federation as a model, and creating fewer but economically more viable *Länder*.[3] The federalism debate focused on questions of economic efficiency, mirroring the shift in the thinking about the state's role in the economy which replaced Keynesian ideas of planning and demand-management with more supply-side oriented economics. Some critics also pointed to the weaknesses of collaborative federalism with respect to democratic accountability (Scharpf et al. 1976; Abromeit 1992). Federalism was not only criticized, though. It was also praised for its contribution to the achievements of the post-war period: social peace, political stability, economic success and the acceptance of the democratic order on the part of the German population (Gunlicks 1989; Hesse and Renzsch 1990).

The federal system was not the only aspect of the political order to come under criticism. The combination of collaborative federalism with competitive party politics was termed a 'fault line' (Lehmbruch 1998: 9) of the political system. Gerhard Lehmbruch argued that the federal system and party competition obeyed different logics that were mutually exclusive, at least in principle. While federalism was based on negotiating and consensus-building, party competition for power called for confrontation and winner-takes-all strategies. Lehmbruch concluded that either joint decision-making threatened to weaken the democratic legitimacy of the political system, or party competition tended to undermine the capacity of the system to build consensus. This fault line did not appear as long as federal bargaining interacted with a multi-party system and broad coalition governments. In the four decades of the old Federal Republic, however, the party system was condensed into two big parties, the Social Democrats (SPD) and the Christian Democrats (CDU), with their Bavarian 'sister' party CSU, and two smaller parties, the liberal FDP, and the Green Party (represented in the Bundestag since the 1980s). The big parties aimed no longer at all-encompassing government coalitions but at forming the federal government alone, possibly in coalition with the FDP. Party-political polarization also transformed the character of the Bundesrat. Once designed as an unbiased bureaucratic counterweight to the Bundestag, the second chamber often turned into an instrument of opposition against the Bonn government. Party competition combined with collaborative federalism engendered 'antagonistic cooperation' that tended to produce political immobility (Scharpf 1994: 69). The 'state of the grand coalition' (Schmidt 1996a) was born, a polity that can generate significant political change only if both the big political parties agree *and* if the federal government receives the support of the majority of the state premiers. The constitutional mechanism to build this double grand coalition is the intermediation committee (*Vermittlungsausschuss*) in the Bundesrat. In the 1980s, federal chancellor Helmut Kohl, who as a former state premier of Rhineland-Palatinate knew about the problems that bargaining with the *Länder* can create for a Bonn government, sought to neutralize this kind of intergovernmental opposition by building consensus with the CDU/CSU-led *Länder* governments exclusively. This informal co-ordination gave the federal bargaining over interregional financial equalization a party-political twist (Renzsch 1991: 273), which in turn provoked federal constitutional court judgments admonishing the federal government and the richer *Länder* to maintain 'federal solidarity'. The power of the Bundesrat to block federal legislative projects was only temporarily reduced through informalization, though. In 1990/91 the Christian Democrats lost their majority in the second chamber, and in 1997 and 1998 the federal government's plan to pass a tax reform was frustrated by the social-democratic majority of *Länder* representatives in the Bundesrat because this time – as opposed to the tax law the Kohl government had proposed in 1991 and passed with the support of the poor eastern German state of Brandenburg, led by a social-democratic government – the strategy of the opposition party to say 'no' corresponded to the institutional interests of the SPD-led *Länder*, all of whom rejected the federal legislative proposal (Lehmbruch 1998: 169; Zohlnhöfer 1999). Federalism was severely attacked for this outcome, and proposals to cut the Bundesrat's influence down to size proliferated (Grimm 1997; Sachverständigenrat 1997: paragraph 314).

Yet the interplay of federalism and party competition did not as a rule produce political immobility. It has been argued that the federal structure is one of three characteristic features of Germany's political system which have kept the country on a middle course between the Scandinavian welfare state and market-oriented North American capitalism. Together with the co-operative relations between business and labour organizations, and a centrist complexion of governments in the federation and in the *Länder*, federalism created the policy mix typical of the old Federal Republic. The 'policy of the middle way' (Schmidt 2000) gave priority to price stability, aimed at balancing out the goals of economic efficiency and social equality in a 'social market economy', delegated many tasks of social policy to associations (e.g. wage policy to business and labour), and financed an interventionist state policy based mainly on transfer payments through an above-average public expenditure. Were it not for the relatively high rate of unemployment this policy mix generated (see Scharpf 1987), federalism and corporatism in Germany could be named an example of what Lancaster and Hicks (in this volume) have called a possible beneficial combination of state *laissez-faire* and activist government.

When in 1990 East Germans, in their majority attracted to the policy of the middle way, took their chance in joining the Federal Republic, the pillars which had sustained this policy mix had already become cracked, and the political and social costs of maintaining it increased (Schmidt 1999). For federalism, in turn, unification and European integration changed the rules of the game.

Federalism in unified Germany

The big changes of the 1990s were, of course, not programmed, nor were policy responses simulated in scenarios. In a way, unification hit the Federal Republic like a shock, unforeseen and unavoidable. As a consequence of unification and a precondition for its acceptance by the neighbouring states, European integration was deepened in the treaties of Maastricht in 1992 and of Amsterdam in 1997. The competency for an autonomous monetary policy, a cornerstone of the policy of the middle way, was passed over to the European level with the creation of a European Monetary Union, the introduction of the Euro and the establishing of a European Central Bank.

Political and scientific oberservers warned of the potentially disruptive effects that unification and accelerated European integration might have for federalism and its capacity for problem-solving. Centralization seemed unavoidable, an unwelcome perspective because federalism, even though it was being criticized of producing rigid policies and maintaining the status quo, was considered a superior form of governance to the hierarchic unitary state, particularly from the normative point of view and because federal systems were supposed to be in a better position to process local information for decision-making (Scharpf et al. 1976: 37). The only way of avoiding unification- and EU-induced centralization was thought to be a fundamental federal reform which would separate the competencies of federal government and state governments along the line of policy fields, not functions. Likewise, the right to make tax legislation was to be divided between the federal government and the *Länder*, who should also be given back competencies and be enabled to finance part of their activities with tax income of their own. The power of the Bundesrat to block federal legislative projects would be minimized in such a dual federalism. *Länder* that were economically too weak or too small to function on their own should merge with others so that they could compete. If all these reforms had not been made previously, it was for the institutional self-interest and personal interests of the regional political class and regional civil servants, advocates of reform argued. European integration, however, would push the case for reform because the old deal between the territorial actors could no longer work in the European Union. The *Länder* who had ceded competencies to the federal government in exchange for the right to co-determine federal legislation via the Bundesrat could not be rewarded with such a right in the European Union, was the argument. So they could only maintain their influence if they grappled with reform, separating competencies at home and in the European Union (Scharpf 1994b).

None of these reforms were enacted. A shift towards centralization lasted for exactly nine months from the fall of the wall in November 1989 until unification in October 1990. Afterwards, federalism reassumed its traditional position in policy-making in the enlarged Republic. Joint decision systems, far from becoming obsolete in the European Union, were extended to comprise just one more level of decision-making. European integration assimilated joint decision systems through osmosis. The huge financial needs of the newly integrated East German *Länder* were met with minimal adaptations of the interregional financial equalization scheme. Finally, the five East German *Länder* were integrated into the intergovern-mental machinery making only a few changes necessary to maintain the complex balance between territorial actors. Several authors have observed this development with a mix of horror and fascination, labelling Germany's federalism definitively as sclerotic and incapable of self-reform.[4] Others have taken a more moderate view, pointing to the lack of experience with processes such as unification, to the size of the task, to the measure of uncertainty for political decisions to be made. Considering all these problems, federalism had done reasonably well in making decisions one by one and correcting them afterwards, if need be (Czada 1996: 354). Some observers acknowledged the capacity of territorial actors to learn from failures and avoid the joint decision trap (Renzsch 1994). Public adminis-tration was given credit for a high capacity of self-regulation (Seibel 1996).

The next two sections will deal with the main decisions in bringing about and managing German unification and European integration. My aim is an empirical test of the predictions made in the theory of interlocking politics.

The first test case: federalism and German unification

Bringing about unification within nine months after the wall had come down was an achievement hardly to be expected of a 'semi-sovereign state' (Katzenstein 1987). The political process in the Federal Republic changed substantially during this time, with federal procedures of decision-making giving way to spontaneous centralization.

Unification-led centralization

The federal government's role was crucial in paving the way for unification. This required constant adaptation to new policy options, as the historic process unfolded and the main protagonists and opponents of unification defined their interests. The federal government responded to all these contradicting interests, those of the Soviet Union, the Western allies, Germany's European neigbouring countries, the government of the German Democratic Republic, and the East German population, with various policy changes. When the wall came down on 9 November 1989, Chancellor Kohl first assumed the role of an observer. Six weeks later he proposed a confederation between the two German states, and from 19 December on he pursued the goal of unification.[5] The first big step to bring about unification was the promise to integrate the East Germans into the policy of the middle way by offering them the economic, monetary and social union. The treaty on this union was signed between Bonn and East Berlin on 18 May 1990.[6] At this stage of the unification process, federalism in West Germany was practically suspended, with the federal executive making decisions about the future state structure by themselves. The *Länder* heads were informed but not allowed to assist in talks between the two German governments, on the grounds that the negotiations were a matter of exterior policy, the prerogative of the federal government, or purely administrative and technical in character (Dästner 1998: 35).

The constitution prevented the federal government from proceeding this way in the next phase of bringing about unification. Before talks were set up for a second treaty between the governments of Germany (East) and Germany (West), the *Länder* were given access to information *and* were allowed to sit at the negotiation table. The federal government thereby recognized that the planned treaty was about a subject matter it had no authority to decide upon without the *Länder*: the political and legal conditions of unification, that means the very structure of the enlarged German state. For such a treaty to be concluded, the federal government needed the consent of the *Bundesrat*. As the second chamber was dominated by a majority of Social-Democratic-led governments, the Christian-Democratic-Liberal coalition in Bonn needed to forge a twofold grand coalition, between the federal government and the Länder, and (informally) between the big political parties.

This task was met in the typical way Germany's political system bridges the fault line between federal accommodation and party competition from time to time. The state premiers of the *Länder* co-ordinate their policies in a standing commission, with the presidency rotating among the states and city-states. In 1990 it was the turn of North Rhine-Westphalia, the most populous state and a stronghold of the Social Democratic opposition party. Therefore, the director of the North Rhine-Westphalian chancellery of state, Wolfgang Clement (who is now premier of this state), took part in the talks on the unification treaty, representing both the *Länder* and the big opposition party. Together with Wolfgang Schäuble, in charge of the negotiations as the federal minister of the interior, Clement built the informal grand coalition necessary for a treaty that would find acceptance in the *Bundesrat*. All of the remaining ten states and city-states also participated in the talks. Schäuble made it clear to the *Länder* that they would be allowed to attend only at the administrative level (chancelleries of states and senates), not at the level of state premiers. The technical character given to the participation of the *Länder* was meant to secure the federal government's leadership in the talks. Schäuble feared the *Länder* claims for more competencies and power in the federal balance,[7] even though he was conscious of the possibility to play them off against each other. Several state premiers (and, from another perspective, the Social Democratic Party) saw in unification a sort of zero hour, like the one that resulted in the founding of the Federal Republic, and argued for seizing the moment for a general public debate on the state and its constitution (Schäuble 1991: 116). This was what the federal government wanted to prevent at all cost.

Therefore, the federal government asserted its leading role in the unification process, supported by Günter Krause, Schäuble's East German counterpart in the negotiations and head of the Christian Democratic parliamentary group in the democratically elected *Volkskammer* (the East German parliament). The *Länder* largely contented themselves with a supporting role. Their administrative experience, together with the help of their civil servants, was crucial in extending the West German legal and political order rapid and efficiently to East Germany (Dästner 1998). After the conflict about the federal power balance on the West German side had been temporarily suspended, the party political conflict between government coalition and opposition emerged. Yet deadlock was avoided because all those involved in the talks wanted an agreement, and none of them wished to appear as an obstacle to unification which was considered a national project. In the last round of talks between the two German governments, the Social Democratic politicians acted as representatives of East German interests, and demanded and finally received concessions in some conflictual issues, such as abortion law and legal protection for tenants (Dästner 1998: 56; Schäuble 1991: 249).

Managing the consequences of unification – back to federal routines

As soon as the former German Democratic Republic (GDR) acceded to the Basic Law in October 1990, the routines of federal bargaining and interlocking decision-making were reassumed. The balance of power between the federal government and the *Länder* was restored, an outcome that was due mainly to two factors – a federal spirit in the East German population which had long been dominated by centralist elites, as well as the capacity of the old *Länder* to defend their institutional interests against intrusion on the part of the federal government, and against the threat of exploitation by the poor newcomers.

In East Germany, the centralist unitary state was abolished by the democratically elected government of Lothar de Maizière. As demanded by the population, the five *Länder* once founded by the Soviet occupation force, and dissolved by the ruling Social Unity Party (SED) in 1952, were re-established. Five *Länder* were to govern 17 million eastern Germans, a population the size of North Rhine-Westphalia's. West German advocates of federal reform were unhappy about this proliferation of small, economically weak states, pointing to the increase in economic inefficiency it would entail. Yet the political gains of refederalization were obvious. In Saxony, Thuringia, Mecklenburg-Pomerania, Brandenburg, and Saxony-Anhalt, the old political elite was thus quickly replaced by a civil service bound to the rule of law and by democratically elected politicians. The political and legal institutions in eastern Germany were democratically transformed with the bilateral help of the western *Länder* and the federal government, thereby copying the federal structure and permitting adaptations to local needs (Wollmann 1996; Seibel 1996). The genuine interest of East Germans in democratic transition on a federal basis made the transfer of West German institutions to eastern Germany much more responsive to the citizens' needs than transferring institutions in other areas, such as science and health, has been. This is because, in the latter cases, the federal government largely left the task to sectoral alliances of (western) civil servants and associations, while the East Germans lacked effective representation (Lehmbruch 1996: 74). Federalism thus contributed to legitimizing the democratic order in the newly integrated parts of the country, and it contributed to all-German integration (Wolfrum 1995).

Another support for the federal order was the successful striving of the old German *Länder* to maintain the status quo in the federal power balance. On 5 July 1990, a day before talks about the treaty of unification started, the state premiers of the *Länder* and the city-states passed on a message to Chancellor Kohl.[8] It contained the principal views of the western *Länder* on the federal order in unified Germany. The state premiers of the *Länder* declared that they assumed responsibility for unification on an equal footing with the federal government, and therefore were entitled to participate fully in the making of the new federal order. The *Länder* claims addressed three main issues: federal financial relations, legislative competencies and procedures, and foreign relations. In financial relations, the *Länder* made it clear that they did not support integrating the eastern German states into the federal system of financial equalization before the year of 1994/95, when this system was to be reorganized. Even then, extending financial equalization to the territory of the former GDR was only justified in the *Länder*'s view when the great disparities between the two parts of the country had been overcome. With respect to legislative competencies, the *Länder* demanded a more restrictive form of Article 72 Basic Law which authorizes the federal government to make use of its powers in concurrent legislation when necessary for creating uniform standards of living across the federation. The *Länder* suggested replacing the word 'uniform' by the more restrictive condition of 'equivalent' living conditions. Finally, the *Länder* demanded to participate in decision-making on foreign relations when their own powers or interests were affected (see below). Both the demands – excluding the new *Länder* from financial equalization until 1994/95, and constraining potential ambitions of the federal government to use unification for expanding its own legislative powers – were met. Article 72 Basic Law was changed by constitutional amendment on 27 October 1994 , as suggested by the Joint Commission of Bundestag and Bundesrat on Constitutional Reform,[9] together with several other amendments to strengthen the *Länder* position in the federal system (Dittmann 1997: 241). The new *Länder* were not integrated into the financial equalization system until 1994 (see below). Furthermore, ten days before talks on the treaty of unification had even started, the rich and populous *Länder* Bavaria and North Rhine-Westphalia demanded a change in the distribution of votes in the Bundesrat (Küsters 1998: 202). According to the old regulation of Article 51 paragraph 2 Basic Law, all of the new *Länder* except Mecklenburg-Pomerania would have been entitled to four votes because they had more than two million inhabitants. The unification treaty changed this article to the effect that the four most populous states (Baden-Württemberg, Bavaria, Lower Saxony and North Rhine-Westphalia) command now six votes instead of five as before.[10] As the all-German Bundesrat has 68 votes available in total, these four big *Länder* command a tight blocking minority against constitutional amendments (24 votes). The big *Länder* can thus protect themselves against being outvoted by the small ones, which is not true, however, for the wealthy *Länder* who do not possess such a blocking minority.

Financing unification posed three major challenges to unified Germany. First, huge financial resources had to be made available in order to transform the East German economy into a market economy, to repair the degraded environment and the decayed infrastructure in East Germany, and to help the East German population cope with the consequences of transformation through social security provisions. Second, the financial burdens had to be distributed between (mostly West) German citizens in a way that minimized shocks for economic activity and competitiveness, and observed social and intergenerational justice. Third, the costs of unification had to be distributed between the federal goverment, the *Länder*, and the municipalities (which are self-governed and do not directly form part of the networks and institutions of interlocking politics, where they are represented by their respective *Länder*).

The propositions Fritz Scharpf and his colleagues had made in 1976 on the logic of joint decision making predict that raising the money for the eastern German needs is the task most likely to be mastered, because it can be characterized as a problem of level (*Niveauproblem*), demanding simply more activity of a certain kind of all the political units. The second and third challenges are of a sort that collaborative federalism is most unlikely to put up with, given the need to cut into vested interests, to distribute gains and losses, and to co-ordinate action between the political units in such a way that they act different but co-operatively. Distribution problems are expected to be amenable for solution only in a pareto-optimal way, respecting vested interests and meeting new needs with additional means. Interaction problems, whose management causes an uneven distribution of positive and negative effects, and whose exact consequences for each of the political units cannot be known from the beginning, are the most difficult tasks for collaborative federalism (Scharpf et al. 1976: 25–8). With this in mind, we can now assess the contribution of federalism to the solution of the three tasks.

The state treaty establishing economic, monetary and social union set up a German Unity Fund, which was supposed to cover the financial transfers promised by the Federal Republic to the German Democratic Republic for balancing its budget, as well as other financial assistance. The fund amounted to DM 115 billion, to be paid in the period of 1990 to 1994. DM 20 billion were financed by the federal government with cutting subsidies for regions on the inner-German border. The rest was shared by the federal government and the western *Länder*, and to be financed through borrowing.[11] Because of the serious financial problems of what became the new *Länder* of the Federal Republic, the German Unity Fund had to be topped up several times. Together with the privatization agency Treuhandanstalt and the Debt Processing Fund (Kreditabwicklungsfonds), the German Unity Fund represented a new handling of the public budget. Existing supplementary budgets, such as the social insurance branches, were obliged to contribute to the costs of unification, and new supplementary budgets were established for this same goal. Thereby, the dimension of public debt was veiled, and parliamentary control impeded.

In eight years following unification, from 1990 to 1998, the public debt more than doubled, from DM 1,053 billion, to DM 2,285 billion, increasing from 44.9 per cent to 60.4 per cent of gross domestic product (GDP).[12] As a consequence of burdening the social insurance branches with the costs of unification, extra wage costs[13] rose from 35.6 per cent of gross wages in 1990 to 42 per cent in 1997 (Bundesministerium für Arbeit und Sozialordnung 1998).

The unprecedented increase in the public debt and in extra wage costs results from the way in which Germany's interlocking decision system and system of collective bargaining channelled the need to raise huge sums and distribute them among the population and the federal levels. Financing through public borrowing and the social insurance agencies was quick and uncontroversial, because it took place in 'distributional arenas' (Czada 1995: 15) not immediately visible, concerning the intergenerational distribution and the secondary distribution effected through parafisci. Other arenas of secondary distribution – tax policy and social policy – were more difficult to use for financing unification, because they pointed out winners and losers and heightened party competition. The same was true for public services, where price increases, cuts, or privatization contributed to financing the transfers for eastern Germany, but also gave rise to political conflict. Likewise, the arena of primary distribution of income, collective bargaining and labour market policy was resistant to major changes, due to corporatist industrial relations. Finally, federal financial relations were rigid and slow to react, not only because the institutional self-interest of the constituent units was affected but also because of the 'permanent elections' in the *Länder* that made unpopular decisions in parliaments very difficult.

The antecedents of the founding of the German Unity Fund may illustrate this last point. Initially, the federal government intended to finance the transfers destined for the German Democratic Republic as laid down in the State Treaty by changing the inter-jurisdictional distribution of part of the tax revenue. It argued that the *Länder* and the municipalities ought to cede several percentage points of the sales tax to the federal government. The sales tax is the only variable element in the joint tax system introduced by the Grand Coalition in 1969, and it has indeed developed unfavourably for the federal government, whose share decreased from 53 per cent in 1970 to 45.1 per cent in 1988. The federal government wanted to use its additional share of the sales tax claimed from the *Länder* and local governments for financing the East German government. However, a federal law regulating this subject would have required the consent of the Bundesrat which would have been very difficult to achieve because in that case eleven supplementary budgets would have to be approved in the *Länder* parliaments, several of them faced with incoming elections. The federal government chose to opt for the funds solution, and the western *Länder* agreed because they did not wish to risk altering the distribution of the sales tax for a long time to come (Küsters 1998: 150–1).

After a short unification boom, the eastern German economy entered into a recession. In spite of some tax increases introduced in July 1991, the gap between tax receipts and public expenditure widened. The Bundesbank responded to what it saw as inflationary impulses of an expansionary fiscal and wage policy with an increase of the interest rate for the German mark. The restrictive monetary policy dashed the hope for a self-financing economic boom in eastern Germany. From 1993 on, and more so from the mid-1990s, it became clear that the federal government's strategy of financing unification entailed higher costs than originally assumed. Moreover, the two main channels of redistribution – borrowing and burdening social insurance parafisci – became subject to critical public debate, the first because the Maastricht criteria for entering European Monetary Union had focused attention on the public deficit rate, and the second because Germany's high extra wage costs were increasingly seen as a drawback in the competition for investment and jobs.

The result was that during a period of setbacks in economic activity, the federal and *Länder* governments took to expenditure cuts and tax rises. This was done in response to acute fiscal distress, and as a rule came in the form of budget freezes. These, in turn, affected primarily public investment and research and development expenditures, thereby aggravating the weakness of economic growth and investment (Sachverständigenrat 1997: paragraph 323).

Under these circumstances, prospects for resolving the remaining task of financing unification – distributing debts and burdens between the federal government, the *Länder*, and the local authorities – looked dim. However, the federal system managed to deliver a solution. Most experts had expected a major reform of the financial constitution but not the solution finally announced as the 'Solidarity Agreement'. It resulted from the bargaining between the *Länder* governments and the federal government and was laid down in the law on the 'Federal Consolidation Programme' in 1993.[14] The agreement regulated the full integration of eastern Germany into the fiscal constitution, and it did so with only small adaptations of the Basic Law. The incremental adaptation was based on a proposition of the Bavarian government. It rallied the *Länder* – rich and poor, eastern and western – around the demand that the status quo should be maintained in the complex equalization system and that, in order to make this work, the gap between east and west should be narrowed with federal money, coming from eight percentage points of the sales tax hitherto allocated to the federation. The federal minister of finance, Theo Waigel, had originally planned to have it the other way round, but he could not play off the *Länder* against each other, as he had done on former occasions. The federal government thus gave away seven percentage points of its sales tax share to the *Länder*.

The Solidarity Agreement was reached partly because the federal government was prepared to pay in the end. What was more, all the actors in this huge package deal (involving the trade unions and the employers' associations which co-ordinated wage policy) were under strong pressure to come to an agreement, because the Bundesbank had announced it would loosen its tight monetary course if wage policy was moderate and the financial burdens of unification were solidly distributed among the political units of the federal state. Additionally, the unification treaty had set a deadline for a new financial equalization system. If there was no agreement by the end of 1994, the new *Länder* were entitled to full integration into the existing financial equalization system. Another reason for striking a deal was that the territorial actors were bound to implement a ruling of the Federal Constitutional Court. In 1986 and in 1992, the Court had stated that two small west German states, Bremen and Saarland, had run up a budgetary deficit so big that they could not put their budgets back on a sound basis without external support, and that it was the duty of the federal government and the other *Länder* to assist Bremen and the Saarland (Häde 1996: 248). It was therefore the combination of pressure from the Bundesbank, the Federal Constitutional Court, and the Unification Treaty that prevented the joint decision trap from closing (Czada 1995). That the federal and the *Länder* governments found a solution was also due to procedural arrangements, as the federal chancellor intervened on the side of his finance minister to make sure the talks would not fail, and the final agreement was reached in a summit with the heads of the states. The parliaments were informed late and excluded from the decision-making process, which once more documented the executive-based character of Germany's federalism. The pressure on the intergovernmental machinery from outside, and the informalization of decision-making, would not have succeeded had not the actors learnt how to avoid the joint decision trap (Renzsch 1994: 124–7).

In the language of the theory on interlocking politics and contrary to its predictions, federalism resolved the level problem, the distributive problem, and the interaction problem[15] of unification management relatively fast. In several respects, though, the solutions found fell short of other important goals a modern industrial society must fulfil: sustainability and competitiveness. Attempts to correct this problem were made, but budget freezes in order to limit further public borrowing came as emergency measures, cutting down expenditure in investment for research, traffic infrastructure, and education, rather than downsizing consumption as the economic experts had suggested. The next generation will inherit not only a soaring public debt but also a reduced (if not decaying) infrastructure, at least in the western part of the country. As to competitiveness, under the Kohl government extra wage costs continued to rise.[16] It was only under the red–green coalition which took office in September 1998 that a modest intent to reduce contributions for old age insurance was made, using revenues from a new energy tax.

Federalism and European integration

European integration is a much bigger challenge to the fabric of the German nation- state than German unification, for it entails problems of efficiency, democratic accountability, *and* a threat to federalism.

To start with federalism: the state premiers perceived European integration as a threat to the federal structure as laid down in the Basic Law from the mid-1980s on, when the project of completing the internal market advanced by the European Commission's president Jacques Delors resulted in the Single European Act (SEA), which supplemented the Treaty on the European Economic Community. The Bundesrat commented that the SEA had unfavourable consequences for the *Länder* insofar as it affected 'their own jurisdiction as well as their rights of co-decision in the federal legislation as laid down in the constitution'.[17] Consequently, the *Länder* made use of their veto position in federal legislation to demand a say in the federal government's European policy. The *Länder* consented to the SEA only after including in the ratification law that the federal government was obliged to inform the Bundesrat 'as early as possible and comprehensively' about its plans in European policy that might be of interest to the *Länder*. Further, the federal government was to hear the position of the *Länder* on subject matters of their interest dealt with in the European Community, and to consider these positions in the negotiations at European level. If the

planned European regulations affected matters of exclusive *Länder* competence, the federal government could diverge from the *Länder* position only
'for irrebuttable reasons of exterior policy or integration policy', which
needed to be exposed.[18]

The principle of interlocking politics became thus introduced into
foreign affairs. In contrast to earlier arrangements of interlocking politics,
it was not the federal government that intruded into *Länder* competences
but vice versa. The *Länder* consolidated their success when the federal
government needed the Bundesrat's approval of the Maastricht Treaty. The
co-decision rights were now laid down in the constitution under Article 23,
and 'double interlocking politics' (Hrbek 1986) was formally installed.

As a consequence of the SEA, Fritz Scharpf warned of a worst case
scenario coming true: first, the defensive reaction of the German *Länder*
would unleash a nightmare of intranational and European coordination;[19]
second, the completion of the European internal market would definitively
end the constellation that had tamed capitalism, a 'historic symbiosis of
capitalist competition, regulation by the nation-state, and trade union
counter-balance' (Scharpf 1994a: 99). The internal market was equivalent
to a 'revolution from above', as it ended the capacity of the nation-state to
protect national producers against the competition of foreign manufac-
turers. As long as the European integration was accelerated in the
economic dimension but blocked in the political dimension, the role of the
nation-state in regulating capitalism for the sake of social and ecological
protection, could not be replaced by the European Community. A neo-
liberal dream or a nightmare of competitive deregulation, depending on
one's own preferences, had been born (Scharpf 1994a: 101).

What can federalism do when confronted with such changes? For several
authors, the answer lies in a stronger division of powers like in the federal
system of the United States of America. When intrastate arrangements of
interlocking politics can no longer compensate for the loss of state rights,
because the federal government passes on competences to the European
Union, the way back to more autonomy for the *Länder* seems to be
attractive. A fundamental federal reform, it is argued, would allow for a
'new constitutional balance, with the European policy being responsible for
all subject matters that require a uniform regulation, and the German
Länder finding their main tasks in a competitive and distinguishing
structural policy'. The federal government would be the loser of such a new
division of powers, because it would only keep its powers in social policy, its
co-decision rights at European level, and could hope for additional powers
in the culture and media policy merely, as well as in the representation of
national culture (Scharpf 1994b: 91).

Such a scenario corresponds to the postulates of fiscal federalism,
founded by the economic theory of federalism, and empirically confirmed
for the USA by Peterson (1995). According to his findings, the states and
the federal government in the United States divide public policy functions

in such a way among themselves that the outcome is acceptable in terms of general welfare. The states and local governments are responsible for structural policy, while macro-economic regulations, especially social policy, are made at the highest – the national – level. Yet in the European Union it is the other way round. Social policy remains to a large extent with the lower political units, the European member states, whereas structural policy has become an EU-regulated policy field (Wachendorfer-Schmidt 2000).

If joint decision-making is stabilized in the European quasi-federal system, what are the consequences for problem-solving and democratic accountability in such a complex multilevel structure? In Germany, the debate about the consequences of integration – world-wide and European economic integration and European political integration – has been focusing on the 'capacity to govern' (Scharpf 1999). It was largely a discussion on the remaining powers of the national state. The dwindling capacity of the nation-state to resolve social and political problems is strongly connected to the question of democratic rule, because the latter has always been tied to the nation-state. Normative standards of democratic rule are met by the European Union only to a small extent (Bach 1999). As long as the Union's democratic deficit seemed justifiable on the grounds that the Union was a system *sui generis,* the problem could be downplayed. This is no longer the case because the European Union's powers have greatly increased. There is widespread consent that the Union must be democratized, but that a mere legal-institutional solution, like increasing the power of the European Parliament, will not be appropriate. Democratic rule depends on social preconditions, such as a general European public and a European demos capable of debating alternative political solutions and possessing a measure of collective identity strong enough to accept electoral defeats and demands of redistribution. Most scientists agree that such a European public does not exist and cannot be easily created. Where they differ is on the political consequences: should the need for democratic legitimization on the part of the European Union be reduced by going back to mere intergovernmental co-ordination? Can alternative concepts of a democratic public and of part-demoi be found? Does supranational governance create a new model of democracy (Kohler-Koch 1998)?

From the point of view of federalism in Germany, there are some viewpoints to be added to the debate. The double interlocking politics of the European Union in federal member states has rightly attracted criticism because it enhances the democratic deficits of executive federalism, reducing parliaments even more to rubber-stamping the results of intergovernmental bargaining, or obliging them to accept the decisions of the European Commission or the European Court of Justice in subject matters passed on to the Union in the integration treaties. The democratic deficit could be mitigated through a new 'federal bargain', introducing an American-style dual federalism. The danger of subsequent centralization could be minimized by a bipolar power distribution that enumerates not only the powers of the political centre but expressly protects the powers of the lower units. For such a constitutional framework to function, the European Court of Justice would have to rule in favour of subsidiarity, not integration, and the constituent states would have to consider the common good in their decisions (Scharpf 1994c). Such a solution, however, will not come, because it presupposes that all the member states of the Union want a federal state, which is certainly not the case. With the Union's enlargement, the federal bargain is even more difficult to achieve. Sometimes, *Politikverflechtung* is the best that can be obtained (Scharpf 1997: 145), and this seems to be the case with the European Union.

A small comfort in view of these circumstances is that double interlocking systems of decision-making are not impossible to govern. Sometimes, they are even helpful for resolving problems that collaborative federalism alone cannot resolve, as in the case of regional policy. Yet the result of 'European multilevel policy-making' is not always satisfactory from a normative point of view.[20]

Problem solution in other policy fields

Federalism had proved to be flexible and capable of redistribution in the processes of German unification and enhanced European integration. However, not even the theory on interlocking politics would preclude this, given the extraordinary nature of the situation.[21] What about the responsiveness of federalism to political problems in ordinary political life?

Studies of the federal legislative process have shown that the federal parliament (Bundestag), which alone is the legislator according to Article 77 paragraph 1 of the Basic Law,[22] in most cases gets its proposals through. The proportion of legislative proposals approved in the federal parliament but blocked through a veto of the *Bundesrat* oscillated between 0.8 per cent and 2.2 per cent, in the ninth and eleventh election period respectively (Schindler IV 1994: 848). An analysis of 150 key decisions in seven policy fields, over the period from 1949 to 1994, found that the intermediation committee had been active in a third of the cases, mostly in the area of education (von Beyme 1997: 298). It has also been shown that the federal government has considerable room for manoeuvre because of its role as agenda setter for legislation, although the leeway varies with the policy fields (König and Bräuninger 1997).

The findings are reasonable evidence that, in most of the cases, the Bundesrat is not the cause of political immobility as often assumed. Moreover, blockade is sometimes necessary, as not all political decisions are better than non-reform, and not always is state interference necessary to solve a political problem. The question asked here is about the capacity of collaborative federalism to generate appropriate solutions to political and social problems.[23]

This question has guided an empirical test of the theory of interlocking politics and competing theories on the policy outcomes of federalism. It analysed the major decisions and non-decisions in eleven policy fields in unified Germany.[24] The main findings are four. First, federalism has generated appropriate political solutions, as well as political immobility and partial solutions in the 1990s. Second, even Germany's collaborative federalism can react to extraordinary challenges with innovative policies and big redistribution. Third, the fault line between partisan competition and federal accommodation (Lehmbruch 1998) is indeed a potential source of gridlock, but it is not the only one. Fourth, the Federal Republic is capable of responding reasonably adequately to political and social challenges, even when the *Länder* hold powers to veto and co-decide federal legislation. These findings will not be unfamiliar to any impartial observer of German politics.

The explanation of these findings will be new, however. On the one hand, the propositions of the *Politikverflechtungstheorie* about the structural weaknesses of joint decision systems when it comes to making painful decisions, are confirmed. On the other hand, we will see what makes the outcome of these systems better than their reputation. The rigidities of joint decisions systems – which stem from the fact that the federal government, in principle, depends on the consent of each of the *Länder* to get its political projects through – can be dissolved in two ways. First, an active way out of the joint decision trap is for federal actors to reduce the costs of an appropriate solution for themselves. They can do that by externalizing part of the cost to third parties not directly represented in their intergovernmental 'cartel'. Second, a passive way out of the joint decision trap opens up when the federal actors are pressed from outside to relinquish the self-supporting routines of their quasi-diplomatic negotiations, for the sake of common interest. Who are these third parties which in the first case are made to share burdens, and in the second case impose their priorities on the federal decision system?

The last category of third parties has already been named. They represent the other players in the German 'network state' (Lehmbruch 1996). In the words of Tsebelis (1995), they are institutional veto players like the Bundesbank or the Federal Constitutional Court, and, as the political system has been opened to the European integration, the European Central Bank and the European Court of Justice, as well as the European Commission. Veto players with more informal power are the political parties, interest groups, and public opinion, with the media having an important part. Solutions to political problems may be promoted by these actors. What counts in addition to the interplay of various elements of the political system with federalism, is the 'political will and skill' of the leading actors (Shonfield 1965), as well as other general determinants of state activity that have been analysed by comparative research.[25]

In the case of German unification, the key to a solution lay in it being perceived as a national project, which allowed for the political parties to build an informal grand coalition. The external and internal support for unification was also secured by a skilful and determined political leadership. Finally, the path to unification was evened by constitutional mandates.

An example of problem-solving in 'double interlocking politics' is regional policy. Until 1990, Germany's system of regional assistance for underdeveloped and declining regions was a sophisticated policy mix. It aimed at attracting capital to poor regions through incentives for investment and infrastructure. In the federal ministry of economics, regional structural policy was subordinated to the principles of ordo-liberalism, a special brand of liberalism that recognizes the need for state intervention in order to keep the market place competitive. This general market-oriented policy notwithstanding, the federal ministry of economics was partner to the (constitutionally fixed) 'joint task' of boosting the economy in underdeveloped and declining regions. As the *Länder* are authorized by the Basic Law to promote economic development autonomously, the economics ministries of the richer *Länder*, at least, were able to pursue strategies of endogenous development, which they did rather successfully, mustering even the support of business and trade unions in their *Land*. While this policy mix was quite successful until the late 1980s, it had two weaknesses. First, the joint decision system was slow and inefficient in responding to new economic problems. It protected the interests of the agrarian underdeveloped *Länder* of the south and did not equally attend to the needs of the northern *Länder* who suffered from structural change and high unemployment rates. Redistribution in this system was possible only with additional funding. The second problem of the jointly practised regional assistance was that its efficiency was diminished by the lack of competition control, because the federal government had no competence to enforce it. When regional policy became a genuine multilevel system in Germany after the accession of the German Democratic Republic, due to a more energetic handling of competition control by the European Commission and to eastern Germany's classification as an objective 1 area for European structural funds, both the redistribution problem and the competition problem were resolved.[26]

The intervention of third parties, however, does not always result in good political solutions. There are cases where third parties help keeping the joint decision trap closed. In 1997 and 1998 the Kohl government tried in vain to get a tax reform law over the Bundesrat hurdle. The law aimed at reducing the net tax burden by DM 30 billion and provided some measures to counterfinance the tax rebate. The failure of passing the law provoked harsh criticism, particularly by business representatives, who put the blame for blockade on federalism. The political parties, though, which previously had often acted as mediators in financial disputes between the federal and the *Länder* governments (Renzsch 1991), also deserve part of the blame, because neither the Social Democrats nor the Christian Democrats were inclined towards much compromise this time. Both parties expected to draw more advantage in the incoming elections to the federal parliament by accusing the other side of obstruction (Zohlnhöfer 1999).

The second way for collaborative federalism to improve its capacity for problem solving is burden shifting, thereby making appropriate solutions more palatable to all participants of the joint decision system. This observation contradicts the hypothesis of joint decision systems being less flexible politically than pluralist decision systems, due to the fact that the latter can make underrepresented interests pay for political decisions or non-decisions, while the former consist of governments whose interests can barely be neglected or treated differently (Scharpf 1988: 38). My theory test has demonstrated that joint decision systems often use cost externalization to third parties in order to avoid gridlock or suboptimal solutions. The classic example is the financing of unification (see above). In the first stage, the transfer sums were largely raised by extending the public debt and subjecting the social security systems to additional payments. The burden was thereby shifted to future generations and to self-administered organizations, both of which do not form part of the interlocking politics cartel. Other self-governed organizations who are often made to bear the cost of decisions in the federal system are the local governments. For example, a federal mandate to offer a kindergarten place to every child aged between three and six – which in turn was prompted by a ruling of the Federal Constitutional Court on abortion – was imposed on local governments without any extra funding. When the federal government curtails unemployment benefits, the cities and municipalities must step in with social assistance. Local governments thus pay for the consequences of restrictive labour market and social policy on the part of the federal government. The same is true for federal immigration policy, because the municipalities had to pay social assistance to ethnic Germans from the former Soviet Union (*Aussiedler*) and to asylum-seekers. It is interesting to see that in the case of asylum-seekers, a law curtailed the assistance rate, in an attempt to reduce the welfare magnet effects of social assistance. This law was passed very quickly when the city-states of Bremen, Hamburg and Berlin, who pay extraordinarily high rates of social assistance per inhabitant,[27] signalled to the other *Länder* that they were being overburdened financially.

Like external pressure on the intergovernmental decision-making system, cost-shifting does not always generate appropriate solutions either. That can be seen in the case of another self-governing institution, the universities. Education policy in Germany has undergone two major changes. From 1960 to 1973, the education system was expanded and modernized, making higher education accessible to a large proportion of the young, and founding universities in less developed regions, too. Federalism was no obstacle to educational reform, because the big political parties and the public supported it. When this consensus broke down in the aftermath of the students' rebellion, the oil crisis and academic unemployment, education stopped attracting ambitious politicians who wanted to reform society, and became a target of the federal and *Länder* finance ministers in search of possibilities to cut expenditure. University outlays decreased relatively, from 1.32 per cent of GDP in 1992 to 0.92 per cent of GDP in 1995. While the number of students has tripled from 1970 to 1990, the universities increased their academic staff by a mere 10 per cent. The universities which have to cope with overload and expenditure cuts at the same time, are being abandoned by politicians. Education politicians opened the universities, and the *Bundesverfassungsgericht* ruled out rejecting applicants for a university place, but the finance ministers did not assume the financial consequences. The result is a loss of public confidence and of international attraction to the educational system. The reforms that have been discussed so far result in a contradictory mix of market-oriented incentives for teachers and students alike, and bureaucratic devices meant to strengthen the performance of university professors in teaching and research, without giving the universities the financial and legal means to do a better job. Federalism has to bear great part of the blame for this situation, which can only have subsisted for such a long time because no one seems to be really responsible. Blame avoidance has come to the extreme that striking students found the chancellor and the education ministers of the *Länder* on their side – each laying the blame on the other jurisdictions.

A last type of burden-shifting should be noted. It has the rare consequence that federal actors are paying the costs for a decision they have not made. The failure to redefine *Länder* territories is of this type, a non-decision firmly supported by the public who identify with their states and do not wish them to disappear or change. This can be called burden-shifting only insofar as the *Länder* governments pay a price that preferences of the public have also caused: the renunciation of welfare gains believed to come out of bigger and more balanced political units.

The price of federalism in Germany

It has been argued that collaborative federalism is more flexible and innovative than predicted by the theory of interlocking politics, due to its interplay with other components of the political system. The federal and the *Länder* governments must take other formal veto players (Tsebelis 1995) into account, in the parliaments and political parties, in the Federal Constitutional Court, in the European Central Bank, the European Commission and the European Court of Justice. Moreover, the cartel of territorial actors must consider the informal domestic veto groups, like business associations, trade unions, and the public (which make themselves heard through the media and continual state elections). Finally, no cartel can ignore fundamental economic and social problems in the long run, at least not in a democracy. It has been shown that the interplay of federalism with all these factors is contingent. Two patterns have been identified – pressure by third parties and burden-shifting to third parties – which mostly, though not always, oil the interlocking decision machinery to produce political solutions better than predicted.

The theory of joint decision systems must therefore be widened to explain political outcomes not only from intergovernmental relations but also from the pluralist process of society and the intervention of 'quasi-governments', such as the Bundesbank. What the theory has won in explanatory power, though, has been lost in elegance and simplicity. Beyond the contingent interplay of all these factors, is there any particular logic of decision-making in collaborative federalism?

I contend there is. In his 'theory of incentives for political organizations', Mancur Olson (1995) suggested that big political parties in certain political systems resemble encompassing organizations. Such organizations have an incentive to enhance the general welfare of the society they work in, to redistribute income to their members with a minimum of social costs, and to stop doing this if the sum redistributed is small compared to the social costs involved in redistribution (Olson 1991: 68). Following this logic, Olson (1995: 29) suggests that in a two-party system, and in most advanced democracies, competition provides a strong incentive for a political party to boost economic growth and proceed with caution implementing redistributive programmes for their own clientele, designed to preserve the political majority.[28] What Olson claims for political parties can also be said of the 'cartel' of federal and Länder governments.

The Bundesrat and the Bundestag, as the places of federal accommodation and party competition, therefore, are interested in bringing about appropriate political solutions for the common good, combining them with their regional or party-political special interests. This helps to explain why in most of the cases federal laws pass the Bundesrat. Only when the logic of action diverges between the two big encompassing organizations – the federal and the party-political one – does a blockade become probable. This happens when a bill substantially affects the clientele of the opposition party (for example the abolition of wage payments in case of sickness), or is deemed an issue suited for partisan competition (tax reform), or a matter of *Weltanschauung*, e.g. the policy towards foreign nationals; then the logics of action of federalism and party competition fall apart and no agreement is to be expected. When the 'pie' available for distribution cannot be enlarged by the political decisions pending (federal financial reform), consent is also more difficult to achieve.

A debate about the strengths and weaknesses of collaborative federalism should therefore not focus on *Reformstau* (reform blockage) or suboptimal outcomes of political decisions. It should rather concentrate on the price to be paid when political problems are processed in a highly institutionalized collaborative federalism.

Problem-solving in joint decision systems entails high costs, which are often not apparent to citizens. Federalism works as a big atomizer of problems,[29] responding flexibly to new challenges, but producing new problems in the long run. Among the long-term problems caused by Germany's federalism are the following:

1   In contrast to other federal systems, it promotes big government, not a small state. Germany has a relatively high rate of public expenditure as a percentage of GDP, and it even outdoes unitary systems in the regional equalization of infrastructure and services. The disciplining function of interjurisdictional competition, which according to fiscal theory of federalism tames the state, is lacking.

2   The way federalism produces political decisions features a particular selectivity. It has been argued that federalism does not lend itself to Keynesian economic policies or to combating unemployment (Scharpf 1987), whereas supply-side economics and tight monetary policy pass the federal machinery easily. One consequence is the immense difficulty in combating unemployment in a tripartite effort, because the trade unions, having no real counterpart on the side of the state, prefer to fight on the wage front, excluding the unemployed. Social protection is high, which dampens the conflict over unemployment, but the insurance systems have severe structural and financial problems. The high costs of the welfare state narrow the possibilities of financing other important tasks adequately, such as education. While the expansion of the welfare state has been mainly financed through social insurance contributions, taxes as a percentage of GDP have remained stable over decades. But part of the welfare state expansion has also been financed with taxes, so that education has to compete with spending on internal security and structural policy for an ever shrinking tax base (Wachendorfer-Schmidt 1999).

3   As a consequence, collaborative federalism favours the satisfaction of demands made in the present, and tends to neglect those of the future. Of the present demands, federalism provides for those groups of the population whose interests are processed in the interlocking decision system, leaving marginal groups aside. It is true that the latter are much more disregarded in the competitive federalism of the United States of America (Peterson 1995). But the bias against the needs of future generations and of the society as a whole in the future seems to be particularly characteristic of Germany's federal state.

Notes

1   For the following, see Oeter (1998: 17–28).
2   The term was coined in the *Frankfurter Allgemeine Zeitung* (No. 277, 28 November 1998: 13), varying the older term '*Landesfürsten*', which pointed to the 'princely' status of the *Länder* heads in their respective parties and in the federation.
3   For an overview and comment, see Laufer and Münch (1998: 323–44). For pronounced statement in favour of competitive federalism, see for example Lambsdorff (1999).

4 For an overview of the debate on managing unification in Germany's social sciences, see Bulmahn (1997).

5 Kohl himself (1996: 213) gave a clue to his key experience with respect to unification. When he visited the GDR minister president Hans Modrow in Dresden on 19 December 1989, thousands of people waited for him, waving red-black-golden flags. Kohl took this enthusiastic reception for a sign that the East German regime was finished and German unity under way.

6 Only two days before, federal chancellor Kohl had reached an agreement with the state premiers of the Länder about how to finance the deficits of the GDR government which were to be expected as a consequence of the economic, monetary and social union. Kohl and the Länder heads of state decided to establish the German Unity Fund (Küsters 1998: 152).

7 The *Länder* had presented to the federal minister of the interior, Wolfgang Schäuble, a letter giving their views on the future federal order. *Eckpunkte der Länder für die bundesstaatliche Ordnung im vereinten Deutschland*, 5 July 1990. See document no. 342A, in Küsters and Hofmann (1998: 1305).

8 See note 7.

9 The Treaty of Unification (article 5) recommended that the legislative bodies in unified Germany (Bundestag and Bundesrat) form a joint commission that would have to deal with constitutional questions raised by unification. Particularly, the unification treaty pointed to the need of enhancing the discretionary power of the *Länder* and strengthening them with respect to the federal government. Furthermore, the Joint Commission on Constitutional Reform was to consider an amendment to Article 29 Basic Law. This article had last been amended in 1976, to the effect that the mandate of the Basic Law of 1949 to restructure the *Länder* in the Federal Republic was changed into an option. Thereby the government of federal chancellor Willy Brandt recognized that its efforts to comply with the mandate for restructuring the territorial boundaries within the Republic had failed. Brandt had established an expert commission that presented proposals for redrawing the map in 1973. The proposed solutions met with fierce resistance, not only in the Christian-Democrat-led big southern states but also in the small city-states under Social Democratic government that were to fuse with their neighbouring states (von Beyme 1999: 388). The amendment of Article 29 in 1994 inserted a new paragraph 8 that allowed for fusions of *Länder* on the basis of an interstate compact that was to be confirmed by popular referendum and by the Bundestag. The consent of the Bundestag was not necessary for a fusion of Brandenburg and Berlin (Article 29 Basic Law; Dittmann 1997: 241). Questions of the federal financial order were not tackled by the Joint Commission on Federal Reform. The Commission declared that issues of the financial constitution could not be treated because of the short period of time provided for the dealings of the Commission (Bundestags-Drucksache 12/6000: 114ff.). The Commission's restraint in the case of federal financial reform is further explained by the fact that the finance ministers of the federal government and of the *Länder* had already started bargaining on the financial reform scheduled for 1995. All in all, the proceedings of the Joint Commission on Constitutional Reform did not result in significant changes of the federal order. Hopes that unification would trigger major reform did not come true.

10 Article 4 cipher 3 Einigungs-Vertrag.

11 Staatsvertragsgesetz of 25 June 1990, Article 31, Section 2, 5f., Article 32.

12 Sachverständigenrat (1997: 324 and 1999: 218, 263), author's calculation.

13 They are paid with equal contributions by employers and workers, for old age insurance, health insurance, unemployment insurance, and (since 1995) long-term care insurance.

14 Gesetz zur Umsetzung des Föderalen Konsolidierungsprogramms (FKPG), 23 June 1993, BGBl I: 944.
15 See above.
16 By the mid-1990s, the welfare state in Germany had come to a critical threshold. High contributions to social insurance, high social expenditures as percentage of GDP, and the expectation that demographic changes (a growing proportion of persons over 65 years of age) and high unemployment would require further increases in social insurance contributions all added up to the assessment shared by most of the experts that social expenditure had reached a limit (Schmidt 1998: 145).
17 Comment of the Federal Council on the Single European Act, 16 May 1986, Bundesrats-Drucksache 150/86 Beschluss: 2.
18 Zustimmungsgesetz zur Einheitlichen Europäischen Akte, BGBl, 1986, II: 1102.
19 In the case of European policy, the *Länder* governments would first have to co-ordinate with their parliaments; second, the states would have to find a common position which they could then negotiate with the federal government; this in turn would have to co-ordinate the positions of its ministerial departments. Finally, talks with the European partner states in the European Community and with the European Commission could begin (Scharpf 1994a: 94–5).
20 See, for example, Reutter 1998 and Wachendorfer-Schmidt 2000.
21 The theory on interlocking politics is not a theory on federalism in general, nor does it pretend to predict the political performance of a federation, because it focuses on the 'politico-administrative system', attributing to it a high degree of autonomy with respect to its societal environment. Scharpf et al. (1976: 18) state that in a system with interlocking decision-making between the territorial actors, federal government and *Länder* suffer a loss of sovereignty and pay the price of a degree of immobility. In exchange, they obtain relief from political overload by claims of pluralist groups in modern society. Joint decision systems therefore can provide political stability. This stability is endangered when certain issues (like mass unemployment) become the centre of public and media attention, and are considered to have assumed critical proportions. Under these circumstances of politicization, the autonomy of inter-locking politics is undermined and its rules are no longer sacrosanct. The interlocking system, confronted with pressure from the pluralist-political process, is now forced to put the institutional self-interest of its participants behind, in order to build consensus for an appropriate solution. This hypothesis can be called the extended version of the *Politikverflechtungstheorie* (Wachendorfer-Schmidt 1999).
22 In the comparative analysis of parliamentary systems, Germany is often wrongly classified a 'bicameral' system. According to Article 77 paragraph 1 of the Basic Law, the federal parliament alone is the legislator. This agenda-setting function is not affected even when the consent of the Bundesrat is required. When the second chamber disagrees with the legislative proposal, the intermediation committee between the two chambers can make suggestions in order to facilitate the federal council's consent. Even then, the primacy of the Bundestag is not affected (von Beyme 1997: 292).
23 A political solution is considered appropriate if it meets the following three criteria: (1) efficiency (how much time is needed for a policy to be formulated and implemented, and how much time passes for a problem to be solved, supposing that it can and should be resolved by political decisions?); (2) effectivity (does the policy resolve fundamental problems of political steering and coordination?); (3) procedural changes (political decisions and their imple-mentation may require adaptations in the decision-making process and in the implementation process, or they may require major institutional reform). The

third criterion is therefore the capacity for institutional reform (Wachendorfer-Schmidt 1999).

24 This test is part of a research project on 'Interlocking politics in unified Germany' (see Wachendorfer-Schmidt 1999). The policy fields and political decisions under examination are: German unification, European integration, the constitutional reform of 1994, the reform of the federal railway and mail services, the introduction of compulsory insurance for the risk of long-term care, the constitutional amendment that restricted the right to political asylum, regional structural policy, the failure to redraw the *Länder* territorial boundaries, the incremental adaptation of the financial constitution, the failure to pass a tax reform law, and education policy.

25 For an overview, see Schmidt (1993).

26 The Europeanization of regional policy has produced a positive outcome in Germany, but some reservations must be made. Intervention by Brussels was accompanied by a change in the mode of political regulation, which passed in Germany's case from negotiated agreement in a highly institutionalized setting (the joint decision system) to hierarchical direction. This does not only mean that the preferences of lower-level actors are often overruled by central decision, and the information they have available may be ignored. It also poses serious problems of political accountability (see also Wachendorfer-Schmidt 2000).

27 In 1996, the city-states of Bremen, Hamburg and Berlin spent DM 1493, DM 1085 and DM 891 per inhabitant on social assistance. In contrast, in the big southern state of Baden-Württemberg outlay on social assistance was only DM 360 per inhabitant (*Süddeutsche Zeitung*, 3 December 1997: 27).

28 Olson claims this only for obligatory transfers of income from the political losers. He excludes transfers for the socially weak based on a general consensus, which benefit the whole of society and increase the general welfare (Olson 1995: 28).

29 See also Czada (1995), for the case of financing unification.

References

Abromeit, H. (1992) *Der verkappte Einheitsstaat*, Opladen: Westdeutscher Verlag.

Bach, M. (1999) *Die Bürokratisierung Europas. Verwaltungseliten, Experten und politische Legitimation in Europa*, Frankfurt and New York: Campus.

von Beyme, K. (1997) *Der Gesetzgeber. Der Bundestag als Entscheidungszentrum*, Opladen: Westdeutscher Verlag.

—— (1999) *Das politische System der Bundesrepublik Deutschland*, 9th edn, Opladen Westdeutscher Verlag.

Braun, D. (ed.) (2000) *Public Policy and Federalism*, Aldershot: Ashgate.

Bulmahn, T. (1997) 'Vereinigungsbilanzen', *Aus Politik und Zeitgeschichte* B40–41/97, September: 29–37.

Bundesministerium für Arbeit und Sozialordnung (1998) *Sozialbericht 1997*, Bonn.

Czada, R. (1995) 'Der Kampf um die Finanzierung der deutschen Einheit', Max-Planck-Institut für Gesellschaftsforschung, Köln, discussion paper 95/1.

—— (1996) 'Interessenvermittlung und Anpassungslernen in der Vereinigungspolitik. Grundmuster und intersektorale Varianten der Politikentwicklung' in A. Eisen and H. Wollmann (eds) *Institutionenbildung in Ostdeutschland. Zwischen externer Steuerung und Eigendynamik*, Opladen: Leske & Budrich, 337–58.

Dästner, C. (1998) 'Die Mitwirkung der Länder an der Wiederherstellung der Einheit Deutschlands', in E. Klein (ed.) *Die Rolle des Bundesrates und der Länder im Prozess der deutschen Einheit*, Berlin: Duncker & Humblot, 33–59.

Dittmann, A. (1997) 'Föderalismus in Gesamtdeutschland', in J. Isensee and P. Kirchhof (eds), *Handbuch des Staatsrechts der Bundesrepublik Deutschland*, vol. IX, Heidelberg: C.F. Müller Verlag, 229–58.

Eschenburg, T. and Benz, W. (1983) 'Der Weg zum Grundgesetz', in T. Eschenburg (ed.) *Geschichte der Bundesrepublik Deutschland. Vol. I. Jahre der Besatzung 1945–1949*, Stuttgart-Wiesbaden: Deutsche Verlagsanstalt und Brockhaus, 459–514.

Grimm, D. (1997) 'Blockade kann nötig sein', *Die Zeit* 42, 10 October: 14.

Gunlicks, A. (1989) 'Introduction', in A. Gunlicks (ed.), *Federalism and Intergovernmental Relations in West Germany: A Fortieth Year Appraisal*, special issue of *Publius* 19, 4: 1.

Häde, U. (1996) *Finanzausgleich*, Tübingen: Mohr Siebeck.

Hamilton, A., Madison, J. and Jay, J. (1993) *Die Federalist Papers*, Darmstadt: Wissenschaftliche Buchgesellschaft (American edition 1787/88).

Hesse, J.J. and Renzsch, W. (1990) 'Zehn Thesen zur Entwicklung und Lage des deutschen Föderalismus', *Staatswissenschaften und Staatspraxis* 4: 562–78.

Hrbek, R. (1986) 'Doppelte Politikverflechtung: Deutscher Föderalismus und Europäische Integration. Die deutschen Länder im EG-Entscheidungsprozess', in R. Hrbek and U. Thaysen (eds), *Die deutschen Länder und die europäischen Gemeinschaften*, Baden-Baden: Nomos, 17–36.

—— (1999) 'The Effects of EU Integration on German Federalism', in C. Jeffery (ed.), *Recasting German Federalism: The Legacies of Unification*, London and New York: Pinter, 217–33.

Jeffery, C. (ed.) (1999) *Recasting German Federalism: The Legacies of Unification*, London and New York: Pinter.

Katzenstein, Peter (1987) *Policy and Politics in West Germany: The Growth of Semisovereign State*, Philadelphia: Temple University Press.

Kohl, H. (1996) *Ich wollte Deutschlands Einheit*, Berlin: Propyläen.

Kohler-Koch, B. (1998) 'Effizienz und Demokratie: Probleme des Regierens in entgrenzten Räumen', in B. Kohler-Koch (ed.) *Regieren in entgrenzten Räumen*, special issue of *Politische Vierteljahresschrift* 29: 11–25.

König, T. and Bräuninger T. (1997) 'Wie wichtig sind die Länder für die Politik der Bundesregierung bei der Einspruchs- und Zustimmungsgesetzgebung?', *Zeitschrift für Parlamentsfragen* 4: 605–28.

Küsters, H.J. (1998) 'Entscheidung für die deutsche Einheit. Einführung in die Edition', in H.J. Küsters and D. Hofmann: *Dokumente zur Deutschlandpolitik. Deutsche Einheit. Sonderedition aus den Akten des Bundeskanzleramtes 1989/90*, bearbeitet von Küsters und Hofmann, München: R. Oldenbourg Verlag, 21–236.

Küsters, H.J. and D. Hofmann: *Dokumente zur Deutschlandpolitik. Deutsche Einheit. Sonderedition aus den Akten des Bundeskanzleramtes 1989/90*, bearbeitet von Küsters und Hofmann, München: R. Oldenbourg Verlag.

Lambsdorff, O. Graf (1999) 'Eine Kur gegen den verkappten Zentralismus. Zum Föderalismus gehört die Trennung der Aufgaben, der Ausgaben und der Steuerkompetenz', *Frankfurter Allgemeine Zeitung* 203, 2 September: 19.

Laufer, H. and Münch, U. (1998) *Das föderative System der Bundesrepublik Deutschland*, Opladen: Leske & Budrich.

Lehmbruch, G. (1996) 'From State Authority to Network State: The German State in Developmental Perspective', in M. Muramatsu und F. Naschold (eds), *State and Administration in Japan and Germany*, Berlin: De Gruyter.

—— (1998) *Parteienwettbewerb im Bundesstaat*, 2nd edition, Opladen: Westdeutscher Verlag.

Oeter, S. (1998) *Integration und Subsidiarität im deutschen Bundesstaatsrecht*, Tübingen: Mohr Siebeck.

Olson, M. (1991) *Aufstieg und Niedergang von Nationen*, 2nd edition), Tübingen: Mohr.

—— (1995) 'Eine Theorie der Anreize für politische Organisationen', in K. Bentele, B. Reissert and R. Schettkat (eds), *Die Reformfähigkeit von Industriegesellschaften. Fritz Scharpf Festschrift zu seinem 60. Geburtstag*, Frankfurt and New York: Campus, 23–46.

Owen Smith, E. (1994) *The German Economy*, London and New York: Routledge.

Peterson, P.E. (1995) *The Price of Federalism*, Washington, D.C.: The Brookings Institution.

Renzsch, W. (1991) *Finanzverfassung und Finanzausgleich*, Bonn: Dietz.

—— (1994) 'Föderative Problembewältigung: Zur Einbeziehung der neuen Länder in den föderativen Finanzausgleich ab 1995', *Zeitschrift für Parlamentsfragen* 25, 1: 116–38.

Reutter, W. (1998) 'Deutsche Asylpolitik', *Staatswissenschaften und Staatspraxis* 9, 1: 85–101.

Sachverständigenrat zur Begutachtung der gesamtwirtschaftlichen Entwicklung (1997) *Jahresgutachten 1997/1998*, Bundestags-Drucksache 13/9090, 18 November.

—— (1999) *Jahresgutachten 1999/2000*, Bundestags-Drucksache 14/2223, 26 November.

Scharpf, F.W. (1987) *Sozialdemokratische Krisenpolitik in Europa*, Frankfurt and New York: Campus.

—— (1988) 'The Joint Decision Trap: Lessons from German Federalism and European Integration', *Public Administration* 66: 239–78.

—— (1994a) 'Der Bundesrat und die Kooperation auf der "dritten Ebene"', in F.W. Scharpf *Optionen des Föderalismus in Deutschland und Europa*, Frankfurt and New York: Campus, 59–91.

—— (1994b) 'Regionalisierung des europäischen Raums. Die Zukunft der Bundesländer im Spannungsfeld zwischen EG, Bund und Kommunen', in F.W. Scharpf, *Optionen des Föderalismus in Deutschland und Europa*, Frankfurt and New York: Campus, 92–116.

—— (1994c) 'Kann es in Europa eine stabile föderale Balance geben?', in F.W. Scharpf, *Optionen des Föderalismus in Deutschland und Europa*, Frankfurt and New York: Campus, 117–30.

—— (1997) *Games Real Actors Play*, Boulder, CO: Westview Press.

—— (1999) *Regieren in Europa. Effektiv und demokratisch?* Frankfurt-New York: Campus.

Scharpf, F.W., Reissert, B. and Schnabel, B. (1976) *Politikverflechtung. Theorie und Empirie des kooperativen Föderalismus in der Bundesrepublik*, Kronberg: Scriptor.

Schäuble, W. (1991) *Der Vertrag. Wie ich über die deutsche Einheit verhandelte*, Stuttgart: Deutsche Verlags-Anstalt.

Schindler, P. (1994) *Datenbuch zur Geschichte des Deutschen Bundestages. IV 1983 bis 1991*, Baden-Baden: Nomos.

Schmidt, M.G. (1993) 'Theorien der international vergleichenden Staatstätigkeitsforschung', in A. Héritier (ed.), *Policy-Analyse. Kritik und Neuorientierung*, special issue of *Politische Vierteljahresschrift* 24: 371–93.

—— (1996) 'The Grand Coalition State', in J. Colomer (ed.), *Political Institutions in Europe*, London and New York: Routledge, 62–98.

—— (1998) *Sozialpolitik in Deutschland. Historische Entwicklung und internationaler Vergleich*, 2nd edition, Opladen: Leske & Budrich.

—— (1999) 'Immer noch auf dem "mittleren Weg"? Deutschlands Politische Ökonomie am Ende des 20. Jahrhunderts', in R. Czada and H. Wollmann (eds), *Auf dem Weg zur Berliner Republik?*, special issue of *Leviathan* 19: 491–513.

Seibel, W. (1996) 'Innovation, Imitation, Persistenz: Muster staatlicher Institutionen-bildung in Ostdeutschland seit 1990', in A. Eisen and H. Wollmann (eds) *Institutionenbildung in Ostdeutschland. Zwischen externer Steuerung und Eigendynamik*, Opladen: Leske+Budrich: 359–416.

Shonfield, A. (1965) *Modern Capitalism: The Changing Balance of Public and Private Power*, Oxford: Oxford University Press.

Tsebelis, George (1995) 'Decision Making in Political Systems: Veto Players in Presidentialism, Parliamentarism, Multicameralism and Multipartyism', *British Journal of Political Science* 25, 3: 289–325.

Wachendorfer-Schmidt, U. (1999) 'Der Preis des Föderalismus in Deutschland', *Politische Vierteljahresschrift* 40, 1: 3–39.

—— (1999) 'Gewinner oder Verlierer? Der Föderalismus im vereinten Deutschland', in R. Czada and H. Wollmann (eds), *Auf dem Weg zur Berliner Republik?*, special issue of *Leviathan* 19: 113–140.

—— (2000) 'Regional Policy in Germany – the European Union as the "Great Healer"?', in D. Braun (ed.), *Public Policy and Federalism*, Aldershot: Ashgate.

Wolfrum, R. (1995) 'The Constituent Power and the Birth of the New Länder', in C. Starck (ed.), *Studies in German Constitutionalism*, Baden-Baden: Nomos, 126–39.

Wollmann, H. (1996) 'Institutionenbildung in Ostdeutschland: Rezeption, Eigenentwicklung oder Innovation?', in A. Eisen and H. Wollmann (eds), *Institutionenbildung in Ostdeutschland. Zwischen externer Steuerung und Eigendynamik*, Opladen: Leske+Budrich: 79–112.

Zohlnhöfer, R. (1999) 'Die große Steuerreform 1998/99: Ein Lehrstück für Politikentwicklung bei Parteienwettbewerb im Bundesstaat', *Zeitschrift für Parlamentsfragen* 30, 2: 326–45.

5 Swiss federalism in comparative perspective

Klaus Armingeon

Introduction

The Swiss federation has no sovereignty. Federal institutions can only assume tasks which are explicitly enumerated in the constitution. Constitutional change must be approved by popular vote. A majority of the population and a majority of cantons have to approve the change. Sovereignty resides with the 26 states (*Kantone*) (Article 3 Constitution), to the extent that it is not restricted by the constitution.[1] The cantons have major competencies in various policy fields, including tax policy.[2] With regard to their discretionary powers, Swiss cantons are comparable to the states of the USA. However, Swiss cantons are strongly interlocked with federal agencies. Federal agencies depend on cantonal administrations for policy implementation and the cantons are dependent upon transfers from the federal state. In this regard, Swiss federalism shares important traits with the German model of federalism. Judged by the major findings of research on federalism, Switzerland is in the worst of all possible worlds:

1 The large discretionary power of the American states implies complexity, duplication, confusion and inefficiency. This is a prominent critique easily found in textbooks on American federalism (Ripley and Slotnick 1993: 72–8).
2 Centralization and the 'attraction of the larger budget of central government' are inherent features of modern democratic welfare states (Castles 1999: 28). This centralization tends to deprive a given state's citizens of political autonomy which they formerly enjoyed. It is detrimental to the idea of federalism. In the worst case, federalism is eroded. In the best case, there is a costly and burdensome process of moving back and forth between centralization and devolution (Lösche 1989: 64–81; Kern 1997).
3 Interlocking politics between states and the federation are prone to policy blockade due to distributive conflicts between regional and central units (Scharpf 1994).

4   Interlocking politics between states and the federation are prone to policy blockade due to the different logics of political actors. A logic of co-operation and compromise is based on the need for large majorities in nearly all important policy areas, created by rules such as the frequent mandatory inclusion of the German second chamber into the process of policy-making. A logic of competition is based on the needs of competitive democracy where majorities have to be won in elections (Lehmbruch 1976; 1998).

5   In avoiding policy blockade, co-operative federalism tends to externalize costs to those not represented in the federal–state arena. Examples include future generations, asylum-seekers or sectors with weak power resources like universities (Wachendorfer-Schmidt 1999).

Sharing some major traits of both German and American federalism, Swiss federalism is prone to the deficiencies of both models. Does Swiss federalism work? Why does it work, instead of succumbing to these potential problems? These are the guiding questions of this chapter. In the following sections, the deficits and achievements of Swiss federalism will be discussed in comparative perspective. The major thesis states that, judged by its goals, Swiss federalism performs well. The major explanations for the positive performance will then be discussed. Here I will present the hypothesis of three favourable sets of factors: (1) the loose coupling of the states and the federation minimizes distributive conflicts in a system of interlocking politics (Benz 1998); (2) a congruence between the logics of political action on all levels of the political system prevents blockade due to the confrontation of conflictual and co-operative strategies; (3) there is an enhancement of efficient co-operative and solidaristic federalism due to the absence of exit-options, the threat of direct democracy at the state and federal level and the connected bargaining rounds of consociational democracy and corporatism (Armingeon 2000a; Armingeon 2000b).

For a discussion of achievements and deficits, the criteria of successful federalism must be identified. However, a tried-and-true checklist for the comparative evaluation of federalism does not exist. Hence I will start from the goals frequently assigned to federalism (Nüssli 1985; Kriesi 1995: 65–7; Kilper and Lhotta 1996). The following list of goals is hardly contested and it generates the criteria for evaluation used in the remainder of this chapter:

1   constraint on central government due to powers vested in the states;
2   integration of heterogeneous societies into stable democracies;
3   compatibility with distributive fairness, i.e. federalism should do no harm to the weak by externalizing costs onto those who cannot efficiently oppose;
4   compatibility with democratic legitimization, i.e. federalism does not hinder democratic control;

5   Ease of policy innovation due to limited and competing regions where policies are tested;
6   Preservation of regional socio-cultural and political/regional distinctiveness;
7   Proximity of state agencies to citizens, which favours political participation;
8   High transparency and efficiency of policy-making due to the minimization of distance between citizens and central agencies;
9   Compatibility with national government, i.e. in the fields where national government has competencies, it must be able to govern.

Deficits

Research finds that Swiss federalism falls short in several respects when judged by this list of goals. This applies to participation, transparency, efficiency, democratic legitimization and inefficient central government.

Participation

Although the 26 states and the approximately 3,000 local communities offer a wide range of possibilities of political participation, this institutional supply has not produced a large demand for participation. Rather, turnout at national elections and popular votes is low. In 1999, 43 per cent of the enfranchised population voted in the national election. This is the lowest rate found among the established democratic OECD nations. With few exceptions, participation in popular votes has varied between 30 and 40 per cent in the period 1970–99. Interest in politics is medium-to-low compared to other European countries. Party membership and party attachment are as strong as in Europe, on average (Gabriel and Brettschneider 1994; Armingeon and Freitag 1997). Two qualifications are appropriate, though. First, in general, participation in local elections is higher than in cantonal elections. In the latter, turnout is higher than in national elections. This pattern is particularly pronounced in villages and small towns; it is not found in large cities (>50,000 inhabitants). However, these are only the nine largest cities where 17 per cent of all Swiss residents live (Ladner 1991: 201). Second, the amount of participation is hard to compare, since direct democracy creates more challenges for citizens, in particular with regard to the information required for a decision. In addition, it reduces the importance of elections and hence lowers the incentives for electoral participation. Finally, it structures the field of political mobilization. Old and new social movements do not focus on lobbying and extra-parliamentary actions. Rather, they concentrate on popular votes: organizing, preparing initiatives and referenda and mobilizing citizens for them (Kriesi 1999a).

Transparency, efficiency, democratic legitimization

There are two dimensions to the interlocking politics between cantons and federations: vertical and horizontal. In the vertical dimension, the federal state co-operates with cantons. The federal state has no administration of its own to implement decisions. Implementation of federal law is carried out by the cantons. The constitution stipulates that cantonal agencies must have considerable discretionary power and that they are entitled to fiscal compensation. About 29 per cent of all federal expenditures are allocated to cantons.[3] The federation in turn receives a small contribution for federal social security from the cantons, amounting to an eighth of the sum (1990) which they receive from the federation. Hence there is a massive transfer to the cantons. About 70 per cent of these transfers are linked to clearly specified tasks (like road construction, universities). The remaining 30 per cent of transfers are intended to equalize the resources between cantons ('*Finanzausgleich*', '*péréquation financière*').[4] Most of the transfers, tied to a particular task, are given as a subsidy, depending on the canton's own contributions and its fiscal power. Hence, the more a canton spends in a certain field of policy, the greater its entitlement to federal subsidies, and the lower the canton's fiscal capacity, the more it gets from the federal government. This system has been criticized for its lack of transparency and efficiency. The lack of transparency is due to a large number of different schemes in the system. The lack of efficiency is due to the failure to equalize the fiscal capacity of the cantons, although massive payments have been made. In addition, poor cantons have often failed to mobilize the resources necessary to trigger federal subsidies. In other cantons, considerable sums of money were spent on policies, which while not very necessary, were very cheap to finance, since federal subsides were available (Eidgenössisches Finanzdepartement and Konferenz der Kantonsregierungen 1999). On these grounds, political elites at the federal and cantonal level are attempting to overhaul this system of fiscal equalization in the years to come.

On the horizontal dimension, limited payments are made between cantons, compensating for services provided by only a few cantons (e.g. universities). These payments are minor, amounting to 19 million francs per annum in 1997 (less than 2 Euro per capita).[5] More important are treaties and institutions for the accommodation of cantonal policies. In 1980, 311 intercantonal treaties were in force. Less than a dozen were signed by all the cantons and 90 per cent were of purely regional importance. The most important institutions of intercantonal harmonization are the conferences of cantonal ministries. They are a means of voluntary co-ordination without any legislative competencies. However, major agreements of these conferences become *de facto* cantonal law. For example, the conference of cantonal ministries of education (Erziehungsdirektorenkonferenz), founded in 1897, issues recommendations which are considered to be binding, although cantons are not forced to accept these decisions (*Neue Zürcher Zeitung*, 24

January 1997 13). In 1993, a conference of cantonal governments was created in order to influence federal foreign policy. The efficiency of these conferences is open to question. The major problem is their democratic legitimization. They settle major questions – e.g. harmonization of school degrees or public order – without having a formal democratic mandate (Vatter 1999: 99; Wälti 1996: 126–7).

Another major problem of legitimization is the veto position of a small group of cantons. These veto rights are based on previous societal conflicts which have largely withered away in the course of modernization. The major example of a potential 'tyranny of the minority' (Schmidt 1997: 236) is the power of cantons in amending the constitution. In a referendum, a majority of the Swiss population and a majority of cantons must vote in favour of the amendment. Hence each vote counts twice: as part of the vote of the population of the whole country and as part of the vote of the cantonal population. If the majority of a cantonal population votes in the affirmative, the cantonal vote is 'yes'. Guaranteeing minority rights by means of this 'double majority' made sense in times of conflict between the Protestant-liberal majority and a strong Catholic-conservative minority concentrated in a few cantons. In the meantime, denominational conflicts have largely ceased to be of major importance. At the end of the twentieth century, no state, except the canton of Bern, can be clearly labelled Protestant, since the share of Catholics is more than 20 per cent of cantonal population. Hence Catholics do not have to fear domination by Protestant cantons – if they care about denominational control at all. In addition, the double majority made sense when the population of the cantons did not differ very much, as was the case at the founding of the federal state in 1848. However, since then the disparity in cantonal population size has grown, due to a relative decline of the number of people living in the small (mostly mountainous and agricultural) cantons. This implies that the weight of an individual vote in the small cantons has increased considerably. In 1848, the vote of a citizen in Appenzell Innerrhoden on a constitutional amendment was equal to the votes of eleven citizens of the canton of Zürich (1:11). In the 1990s, this ratio has increased to 1:38 (Kriesi 1995: 67–9; Vatter and Sager 1996; Linder 1999: 179–85). Raimund Germann (1991) has calculated an illustrative example. If 51 per cent of citizens in the smaller 11.5 cantons[6] oppose a popular initiative, while all the remaining citizens are in favour, nine per cent of the citizenry would dominate the remaining 91 per cent! These are extreme theoretical cases. In reality, when referenda and initiatives have failed due to an insufficient number of cantonal votes, it was about a quarter of the citizens, living in the smaller cantons, which were decisive in these popular initiatives (Linder 1999: 181).

One source of inefficiency has been the variation of cantonal laws regulating entry to certain professions and limitations on economic competition between firms in different cantons. These barriers were abolished by reforms in the mid-1990s (Armingeon 1999b: 740).

Inefficient central government

The federal government has limited resources and limited legal means to force cantonal administrations to comply with federal law and its aims. For example, implementation of the law on asylum-seekers reflects, to a large extent, political power distributions in the respective cantons (Spörndli et al. 1998). Another example is the implementation of a law which limits the acquisition of land and real estate by persons and firms residing abroad. Some cantons implemented the law according to its intentions, others changed it substantially and one turned the intention of the law on its head, by supporting the sale of real estate to foreigners (Linder 1994: 68–9; 1999: 177–8). The inefficiency of central government is due to variation in the efficiency of cantonal administrations. In particular, smaller cantons lack the administrative and technical resources for an adequate implementation of complex federal law (Kriesi 1995: 75; Wälti 1996: 133). Various proposals haven been put forward to strengthen central government. However, this is very difficult to achieve since there are no majorities for the reduction of cantonal autonomy (Wälti 1996: 114).

Achievements

These deficiencies of Swiss federalism have to be weighed against its achievements, all concerning the core goals of federalism. Swiss federalism has been successful as a constraint on central government. The people are highly satisfied with Swiss democracy, of which federalism is a central element. In addition Swiss federalism is sustainable, encourages policy innovation, preserves regional socio-cultural and political differences and is a major means of integration in a highly heterogeneous society.

Constraints on central government

Judged by the share of local and regional government expenditure of general government expenditure, Switzerland is one of the most decentralized states in the OECD. There are no signs of centralization (Table 5.1).[7] Similar results were found in an in-depth study of several indicators of centralization (Nüssli 1985). There are at least two reasons for Switzerland's decentralized structure. First, right from its beginnings in the nineteenth century, the Swiss political system has been conceived of as a confederation of cantons with the central state reserved for the fulfilment of certain clearly defined tasks. The federal government can only deal with matters explicitly enumerated in the constitution as tasks of the federation (Constitution Article 42.1). Cantons, in contrast, can decide which tasks they will tackle and they are entitled to exercise all powers which are not transferred to the federation (Constitution Articles 3, 43). Arguments between the federal and cantonal states should be resolved by negotiation and intermediation (Constitution Article 44.3). The federation has to safeguard cantonal autonomy (*Eigenständigkeit*), the cantonal constitutional polity and the cantons' existence and territory (Constitution Articles 47, 52, 53). Cantons organize their polities according to their wishes, decide on their constitutions (Constitution Article 51) and choose their political institutions and leaders (Vatter 1999: 82–4; Kriesi 1995: 50–3; Germann 1999: 388–94). A second major barrier to centralization is the system of direct democracy. The people have been very reluctant to extend competencies to the federal state. For example, the attempt to establish central Keynesian economic management failed, as did the plan to grant the federation permanent powers of direct taxation. At present, the federal state gets about a quarter of its revenues from direct taxes which – after 150 years of a federal state – are still based on temporary legislation.

Satisfaction and trust

The people strongly support the federal system. When asked in 1998, 28 per cent of Swiss citizens stated that federalism is of particular importance and should not be changed at all, 52 per cent were of the opinion that it is good and only minor adaptations should be done, while a small minority of 14 per cent considered federalism totally outmoded, ready for major change or abandonment (Univox Survey, January 1998). Swiss citizens are highly satisfied with the way their democracy works (Table 5.2). Part of this high proportion might be explained by the workings of Swiss federalism, since this is a core element of Swiss democracy.[8]

Table 5.1 Local and regional government final consumption (% general government final consumption) in federal and selected unitary political systems

Country	1960	1992	Change
Federal countries			
Australia	55	68	+13
Austria	51	65	+14
Canada	54	79	+25
Belgium	22	34	+12
Germany	70	86	+16
Spain	32*	63	+31
Switzerland	73	80	+ 7
USA	42	57	+15
Unitary countries			
France	23	45	+22
Netherlands	53	55	+ 2
Norway	49	62	+13
United Kingdom	33	39	+ 6

*1980
Source: Lane et al. 1997: 74, 80; Lane and Ersson 1999: 188.
Note: Government final consumption consists of goods and services for public administration, defence, health and education. It excludes all transfer payments.

Table 5.2 Satisfaction with the way democracy works (% responding 'works well')
1996/98

Norway	88	Great Britain	71
Switzerland	84	USA	71
Australia	84	New Zealand	67
Germany (West)	83	France	67
Ireland	81	Spain	63
Canada	75	Germany (East)	61
Japan	74	Sweden	60
		Italy	29

Source: Klaus Armingeon/Andreas Diekmann: *Role of Government*, Switzerland 1998; ISSP 96 (Role of Government).

Indicators of trust in political institutions, and particularly in federalism, support the finding that the Swiss people are satisfied with the federal system (Table 5.3). Trust in democratic institutions in Switzerland in 1998 corresponds to the European average in 1990 (Listhaug and Wiberg 1995).

Sustainability

The Swiss public debt and deficit are low in international comparison. In 1997, the public debt amounted to 52 per cent of GDP, and the public deficit was 2.3 per cent of GDP (*Die Volkswirtschaft*, December 1999). Judged by the Maastricht criteria for the European Monetary Union or by the average debt and deficit of democratic OECD countries, this is an outstanding success. In 1997 only Australia and Norway had a lower public debt. In 1997, the Swiss public deficit was high in longitudinal comparison. However, it was modest compared to the average deficit EU-nations officially reported in that particular year before the evaluation of their capability to enter the Monetary Union (OECD: Economic Outlook, June 1999). Hence

Table 5.3 Confidence (% responding 'a great deal/quite a lot') in political institutions 1998

Federal Government	63
Parliament	49
Civil service	48
Army	47
Trade unions	41
Police	72
Legal system	62
Cantonal institutions	57
Local institutions	62
Cantonal education system	82*
Political parties	19

Source: Klaus Armingeon/Andreas Diekmann: *Role of Government*, Switzerland 1998, Brunner and Sgier 1997.
Note: *1989.

there are few signs that Swiss federalism has externalized its costs to future generations. In addition, no indication can be found that it has external-ized costs to those outside of the 'federalist power cartel' (Wachendorfer-Schmidt 1999: 16).

Innovation

As federalist theory claims, Swiss federalism allows for policy experiments and hence supports policy innovation. Policies against drug abuse are a case in point. Several cantons have experience with quite different strate-gies, singling out several policies which proved to be quite successful. Subsequently, these policies have been adopted on the federal level. With regard to active labour market policies, cantons are trying a variety of measures.

Preservation of regional socio-cultural and political differences

After 150 years of a federal state, the Swiss cantons are still very different. Electoral behaviour and party systems vary nearly as much between cantons as do national party systems and voting patterns across Western Europe (Armingeon 1998). Cantonal rules for cantonal elections and referenda and the use of direct democracy (i.e. number of referenda and initiatives) are very different (Lutz and Strohmann 1998; Vatter 1997; 1998b). There are still French-, Italian- and German-speaking cantons without any indication of convergence. In some cantons (such as Wallis, Obwalden, Uri, Appenzell Innerrhoden) the share of Catholics is larger than 90 per cent; in other cantons (Bern, Schaffhausen, Appenzell Ausserrhoden) this share is less than 30 per cent (Kriesi 1995: 68). Tax burdens vary enormously. If the Swiss average is 100, the index of tax burden on income and property in the canton of Zug is 56, while the same index for the canton of Jura is 133. This means that taxes paid by an ordinary wage-earner increase by a factor of 2.4 if he or she moves from the canton of Zug 70 km westwards to the canton of Jura (Bundesamt für Statistik 1998: 445). Societal organization, habits, the distribution of 'social capital' and the distribution of the risk of unemployment vary strongly between the Swiss states (Freitag 1999).

Integration

Swiss federalism was intended to integrate society with regard to its differ-ent linguistic and denominational groups. At the founding of the federal state in 1848, the denominational question was of utmost importance, but it is of minor relevance at the end of the 1990s. The linguistic divide, however, still exists and is of great relevance. Federalism grants rights of representation of these linguistic groups in all domains of the federal political system. Hence there are few doubts that federalism has reached its goal of integrating socio-cultural groups.

Explanations

Swiss federalism has a number of deficits. On the other hand, its achievements are obvious as well. It is a success story if evaluated against the criteria of constraints on central government, sustainability, integration of territorially concentrated socio-cultural groups, preservation of socio-cultural and political regions, and people's satisfaction with the way democracy works. It is also a success story if Swiss federalism is compared to US and German federalism. The Swiss people are much more satisfied with their democracy than US citizens are with theirs. Swiss federalism has seen neither policy blockade nor the externalization of costs, as some analyses have found in the German case.

How might one explain this favourable result? I offer three groups of arguments. First, the Swiss federal system is a system of loose coupling (Benz 1998: 563–5). In systems of tight coupling, (a) negotiations are mandatory; (b) actors have an imperative mandate, making any major move in negotiations dependent on agreement or legitimization by the delegating constituency; (c) the interlocking is highly formal and institutionalized and (d) it is a system of co-decision where actors can be pitted against one another with a high likelihood of stalemate and with clearly discernible winners and losers in the case of a decision. In contrast, a system of loose coupling is much less prone to deadlock. In such a system (a) negotiations are not mandatory and actors have an exit option; (b) actors do not have to legitimize each decision *vis à vis* their constituency, but can include the public welfare in their set of goals; (c) the interlocking is largely informal; and (d) decisions are not made in a formal procedure with all relevant actors, but instead a decision is made by a few actors after hearing and evaluating arguments and information from other actors. There is no co-decision (Linder 1999: 135–89). This loosely coupled system does not tend to deadlock and does not need to solve the problems of inflexibility by externalizing costs.

Second, the various actors in the Swiss federal systems operate according to the same logic of negotiation and compromise. Deadlock is avoided since there are no clashing logics like the ones of party competition and of federalist co-operation as it has been found in Germany.

Third, the loosely coupled system of negotiation is enhanced by several institutional and structural characteristics which increase the incentives for co-operative, solidaristic behaviour and which motivate actors not to exit negotiations.

Loose coupling

Loose coupling is brought about by at least seven political and institutional characteristics of Switzerland.

1   The Swiss national parliament is a symmetrical bicameral institution (Huber-Hotz 1991). The council of states (Ständerat) is composed of

two representatives from each canton with the six half-cantons having only one councillor. The councillors are not appointed by the cantonal parliaments or government but instead are elected directly by the citizens of the cantons. Hence they do not have to defend the interests of the regional government. Their function is to search for political solutions compatible with the stance of their political party, the interests of the cantons and the public good.

2   Whenever legislation is proposed on a certain matter, the groups and institutions to be affected by this legislation have to be consulted in advance ('*Vernehmlassungsverfahren*'). This gives the cantonal government and parliament an opportunity to express their arguments, wishes and fears in case of legislation relevant to them. On the other hand, those making the decision are not bound by the position of the cantons, although it is expected that the cantonal arguments are seriously evaluated and taken into account.

3   The same logic underlies the representation of cantons on expert commissions. Legislation is frequently prepared there. Cantonal experts are incorporated into these commissions if they deal with matters of concern to the cantons. These expert commissions have no right to make decisions on laws. Rather they prepare a draft and often the proposal of the commission is later turned into law with only minor amendments.

4   A major means of federal governance are the subsidies offered to cantons if they undertake a particular measure and finance parts of it. Hence the federation tries to stimulate cantonal activity via subsidies. This leaves much discretionary power to the cantons, which can decide not to take a particular subsidy and hence not to implement the goals of the federation.

5   Due to its lack of resources, the federal government can hardly control the implementation of its measures by the cantons. In addition, the cantons have considerable leeway in implementation due to their constitutional prerogatives. Article 46.2 of the constitution stipulates that, in the implementation of federal law, the federal government has to give substantial manoeuvring room to the cantons and has to take account of cantonal differences.

6   The loose coupling of federal and cantonal politics presupposes that there is not – as in Germany – uniformity of living standards (*Einheitlichkeit der Lebensverhältnisse*) across all states. As in the USA, in Switzerland it is an accepted norm that taxes, public services, social assistance, educational and health systems differ from one canton (and often from one local community) to the other.

7   One could argue that competition between states leads to strong pressure for convergence between the cantonal living standards, thereby reducing the chances of smooth loose coupling. Once people migrate, e.g. from states with high taxes to low taxes, state governments are forced to

accommodate policies. However, federalism in Switzerland is not – unlike in the USA – primarily competitive. Rather it is solidaristic by redistributing resources to poorer (mostly mountainous) cantons thereby allowing for minimum standards of public services and inhibiting migration to rich (and densely populated) regions. In addition, in contrast to the USA, regional mobility is low in Switzerland. In a representative survey in 1998, 39 per cent stated that they had lived less than 10 years at the present place, while 36 per cent had been there for 20 years or more (Armingeon/Diekmann: Schweizer Arbeitsmarktsurvey). In the United States in 1992, 63 per cent had lived for less than 10 years at the present address and 18 per cent for 20 and more years (Cross National Election Project: 1992 American National Study). Hence although living conditions are very heterogeneous across states, in Switzerland there is little danger that cantonal governments are forced to converge due to migration.

Strategic logic

The congruent strategic logic of negotiation and accommodation in the federalist arena is supported by the structure of the party systems, the composition of cantonal governments and the composition of local governments. The Swiss party system is weakly centralized. Party organizations, party manifestos and major coalitions and cleavages between parties vary between cantons or between groups of cantons (Ladner 1999: 218; Kriesi 1998; Linder 1999: 88–92; Klöti 1998). The focal point of party organizations is the cantonal level and the issues and cleavages of state politics. National political parties are federations of state party organizations. Some authors (Kriesi 1995: 144) even argue that national party organizations are precarious units. A major implication is that the odds are low that centralized political parties will pursue the politics of party competition incompatible with the style of negotiations seen in the federalist arena. Whenever a national party decides on an important issue, this has to be accommodated between the state party organizations often holding quite different views.

With one exception,[9] cantonal governments are broad coalitions where the major means of decision making is negotiation and mutual accommodation. In 1998, three cantons were governed by a five-party coalition. In nine states there was a government made up of four parties, and in 13 cantons three parties shared power (Vatter 1998a; Germann 1999: 406–8). Hence party competition cannot enter the federal arena, since – in contrast to Germany – states are not under the leadership of either a left or a centre-right party.

Local communities have considerable discretionary power. For example, they levy income taxes, which vary considerably across communities. These local income taxes are in the range of 30–45 per cent of the total income taxes paid by an average employee. Local communities are strongly inter-locked with the cantons. The composition of the local governments follows a pattern of coalitions similar to the cantonal level (Geser et al. 1994; Geser 1999). Hence once a cantonal government decides to pursue a conflictual policy in the federal arena, this would bring it into conflict with the closely allied local governments following a logic of negotiation.

Incentives for co-operation

The co-operative behaviour of cantonal representatives is enhanced by at least three structural traits of the political system of Switzerland. First, due to size, some cantons are dependent on co-operation; they do not have an exit option. Second, negotiation, not majority rule, is the dominant tech-nique of reaching decision in the other two major political arenas apart from federalism: corporatism and consociational democracy at the federal level. Finally, direct democracy at all major levels of the political system (local, cantonal and federal level) penalizes political elites which con-sistently pursue conflictual policies.

Federalism is mainly a political organization of large nations (Lijphart 1999: 215). Switzerland – the size of the German state of Baden-Württemberg – is small, composed of 26 autonomous states. In international comparisons, even large cantons like the one of Zürich have small popul-ations (1.2 million). In intercantonal comparison, cantons are very different in size. More than a quarter of the total population live in the two largest cantons – Zürich and Bern – amounting to about 2 Million inhabitants. The total population of the five smallest cantons (Uri, Obwalden, Nidwalden, Glarus, Appenzell Innerrhoden) amounts to 160,000 inhabitants. Fourteen thousand people live in the smallest state, Appenzell Innerrhoden. This implies that resources vary between cantons, as does the size of the public sector (Kriesi 1995: 71–2). Some cantons are too small to provide basic public services and, some economists argue, they are too small to create an environment for competitive firms (Frey 1995). For these small cantons, there is no choice but to co-operate with other cantons.

Negotiation is the dominant means for reaching decision in federal politics as well as in collective labour relations. These consociational and corporatist arenas have various overlaps with the federal arena. Function-ally, there is some accommodation between these three fora, as seen for example in recent austerity policies in 1998. Representatives of the cantons, the social partners and the large national parties met at a round table to agree on austerity measures. On the personal level, in this small country with its small political elites, leaders in these different arenas know each other. Sometimes a person may even act in two arenas. Hence co-operative behaviour is stabilized by the surrounding fora of decision-making. Conflictual strategies in the federalist arena would be in sharp contrast to the style of policy-making in the remaining arenas.

Probably the strongest incentives for co-operative behaviour stem from direct democracy. Referenda and initiatives are used at the local, cantonal and national levels. In order to avoid a referendum and a possible defeat, political leaders seek to build broad coalitions when a policy is designed (Neidhart 1970). If a cantonal government tried to bring about a solution with the smallest possible majority, the defeated groups and regions would probably call a referendum with the possible result that the reform is repealed. Hence there are strong incentives to be co-operative right from the beginning.

Conclusion: why Switzerland? why not Germany? why not the USA?

The guiding questions of this chapter concerned the performance of Swiss federalism. It was argued that, judged by the major goals of federalism, the balance is favourable. Deficits are discernible, though. Some of them – like the smallness and heterogeneity of cantons – can be seen as conducive to the smooth working of the federal system. They can be conceived of as the operating cost of a functioning federalist order. Compared to the USA, the complexity, duplication, confusion and inefficiency caused by federalism seem to be less marked. In addition, the Swiss people are far more satisfied with their democracy – a central part being federalism – than are the people of the USA Compared to Germany, Swiss federalism externalizes fewer costs to future generations or groups outside the federalist power cartel and is less prone to policy blockade[10]. These differences can be explained by some findings of this chapter. In contrast to the USA, a major difference is the solidaristic character of Swiss federalism (Linder 1999). This allows for fiscal equalization and harmonization without flattening the socio-cultural and political differences between the cantons. Mitigated competitiveness results from a bundle of factors, including low population mobility, and negotiation and accommodation as the dominant patterns of settling societal conflicts. This pattern is based on institutional character-istics as well as the historical development of policy-making in Switzerland (Lehmbruch 1993; 1996). In contrast to Germany, loose coupling – including the acceptance of heterogeneity in living conditions and the absence of formalized structures of co-decision — creates flexibility. The lack of it has led to policy blockade or externalization of costs in Germany. In addition, in all relevant sectors of Swiss politics, the same political logic of negotiation and compromise is applied, avoiding clashes of different logics of political actors.

Notes

1 Six of these cantons are 'half-cantons'; these are represented in the second chamber by one (not two) representatives and they count as 0.5 canton when the votes of cantons are tabulated in referenda and initiatives.

2 The tasks and competencies of the federation lie predominantly in foreign relations, national defence, tariff law, the currency and monetary system, postal services, telecommunications, mass media, railways, aviation, nuclear energy, international treaties, federal universities, civil and criminal law, right to asylum and scientific research. The tasks and competencies of cantons are primarily the police, churches, the health system, funerals, energy, regional construction and planning, grants to students and pupils, education and higher education, cantonal administration, imprisonment and regional economic policy. The federation and states share competencies in the fields of agriculture, environmental protection, labour law, road construction, pensions and health insurance. Cantons share competencies with local communities in the fields of cantonal roads, some aspects of the health system, environmental protection, regional planning and sports (Schenkel and Serdült 1999: 473; Armingeon and Freitag 1997: 29).

3 This implies that the weak Swiss central state is actually even weaker (i.e. about a third in terms of expenditures) than is suggested by the figures on the distribution of revenues and expenditures between general and central governments. In 1997, about 38 per cent of all public expenditures were made by the federal government (Eidgenössische Finanzverwaltung 1999: 8–9). After deducting the net transfers to cantons, the share of central government is reduced to about 28 per cent.

4 The scheme of equalizing cantonal resources was introduced in 1959. Federal transfers are distributed according to an index of the fiscal capacity ('*Finanzkraft*', '*capacité financière*') of cantons. Until 1995, the composition of this index has changed ten times, using 16 separate criteria. Since 1991, the index has been composed of an indicator of the cantonal revenue per capita, the share of the cantonal public sector, the yield of selected taxes of the respective canton and its local communities plus an indicator, measuring the size of the agricultural sector in the mountainous vs. non-mountainous regions and the density of population (Dafflon 1994: 5; Dafflon 1995: 64–5; Mäder and Schedler 1996).

5 The difference from Germany is obvious: in 1998 the horizontal equalization (*Länderfinanzausgleich*) has had a volume of DM 14 milliard; this amounts to about 82 Euro p.c. (Statistisches Bundesamt 1999: table 20.1.3).

6 Since there are 20 cantons and 6 half-cantons (i.e. 23 'full' cantons), 12 cantons constitutes a majority.

7 Adding social security transfers to individuals, most of which are paid out by the central government, would strengthen unitary traits of Switzerland. However, this applies to other federal countries as well. In contrast to these countries, Switzerland has experienced a massive increase in social security transfers in the 1990s. Expenditures for major welfare programmes have grown from 17 per cent of GDP in 1990 to 23 per cent of GDP in 1996 (Kriesi 1999b: 107). But even taking that into account, Switzerland is still a rather decentralized country (Armingeon 1999a: 731; Castles 1999: 34; Linder 1999: 150).

8 Considering Table 5.2 it is remarkable that of the seven federal political systems, five are in the upper half of the list. Of the group of long-established federal democracies, only the USA is in the lower half.

9 Appenzell Innerrhoden is governed by only one political party, the Christian Democrats. However, the party system in this canton is at an embryonic stage; there are hardly differentiated and organizationally consolidated party organizations. Hence the notion of one-party government is not appropriate (Steiner 1969).

10 I cannot discuss here the extent to which this diagnosis empirically applies to Germany. Arthur Benz has, in various analyses, argued convincingly that there might be deficits, but that in general German federalism is working.

References

Armingeon, K. (1998) 'Interregionale und internationale Unterschiede der Wahlentscheidung. Das Wahlverhalten in Schweizer Kantonen im westeuropäischen Vergleich', *Politische Vierteljahresschrift* 39, 2: 282–300.

—— (1999a) 'Politische Reaktionen auf steigende Arbeitslosigkeit', in A. Busch and T. Plümper (eds), *Nationaler Staat und internationale Wirtschaft. Anmerkungen zum Thema Globalisierung*, Baden-Baden: Nomos,: 169–96.

—— (1999b) 'Wirtschafts- und Finanzpolitik', in U. Klöti et al. (eds), *Handbuch der Schweizer Politik*, Zürich: Verlag Neue Zürcher Zeitung, 725–66.

—— (2000a) 'Consociationalism and Economic Performance in Switzerland 1968–1998', in T. Ertman (ed.), *The Fate of Consociationalism*, London: Oxford University Press.

—— (2000b) 'Renegotiating the Swiss Welfare State', in G. Lehmbruch and F. von Waarden (eds), *Renegotiating the Welfare State*, London: Routledge and Kegan Paul.

Armingeon, K. and Freitag, M. (1997) *Deutschland, Österreich und die Schweiz. Die politischen Systeme im Vergleich. Ein sozialwissenschaftliches Datenhandbuch*, Opladen: Leske & Budrich.

Benz, A. (1998) 'Politikverflechtung ohne Politikverflechtungsfalle. Koordination und Strukturdynamik im europäischen Mehrebenensystem', *Politische Vierteljahresschrift* 39, 3: 558–89.

Brunner, M. and Sgier, L. (1997) 'Crise de confiance dans les institutions politiques suisses? Quelques résultats d'une enquête d'opinion', *Revue Suisse de Science Politique* 3, 1: 105–13.

Bundesamt für Statistik (1998) *Statistisches Jahrbuch der Schweiz. 1999*, Zürich: Verlag Neue Zürcher Zeitung.

Castles, F.G. (1999) 'Decentralization and the Post-war Political Economy', *European Journal for Political Research* 36, 1: 27–53.

Dafflon, B. (1994) 'Expertise sur les aides financières et les indemnités de la Confédération aux cantons', in R.L. Frey et al. (eds), *Der Finanzausgleich zwischen Bund und Kantonen. Expertise zu den Finanzhilfen und Abgeltungen des Bundes an die Kantone im Auftrag der Eidg. Finanzverwaltung und der Konferenz der kantonalen Finanzdirektoren*, Basel, Fribourg, Neuchatel.

—— (1995) *Fédéralisme et Solidarité. Etude de la préréquation en Suisse*, Fribourg: Institut de Fédéralisme Fribourg Suisse.

Eidgenössisches Finanzdepartement; Konferenz der Kantonsregierungen (ed.) (1999) *Der neue Finanzausgleich zwischen Bund und Kantonen. Konkretisierung der Grundzüge vom 1. Februar 1996. Schlussbericht der vom Eidg. Finanzdepartement (EFD) und der Konferenz der Kantonsregierungen (KdK) gemeinsam getragenen Projektorganisation*, Bern: Solothurn.

Eidgenössische Finanzverwaltung (ed.) (1999) *Oeffentliche Finanzen der Schweiz 1997*, Neuchatel: Bundesamt für Statistik.

Freitag, M. (1999) 'Soziales Kapital und Arbeitslosigkeit. Eine empirische Analyse zu den Schweizer Kantonen', Basel, Bern: unpublished manuscript.

Frey, R.L. (1995) 'Europäische Integration, Regionalstruktur und Föderalismus', *Aussenwirtschaft* 50: 295–309.

Gabriel, O.W. and Brettschneider, F. (eds) (1994) *Die EU-Staaten im Vergleich. Strukturen, Prozesse, Politikinhalte*, Opladen: Westdeutscher Verlag.

Germann, R.E. (1991) 'Die Europatauglichkeit der direktdemokratischen Institutionen der Schweiz', *Schweizerisches Jahrbuch für politische Wissenschaft* 30: 257–69.

—— (1999) 'Die Kantone: Gleichheit und Disparität', in U. Klöti et al. (eds), *Handbuch der Schweizer Politik*, Zürich: Verlag Neue Zürcher Zeitung, 388–420.

Geser, H. (1999) 'Die Gemeinden in der Schweiz', in U. Klöti et al. (eds), *Handbuch der Schweizer Politik*, Zürich: Verlag Neue Zürcher Zeitung, 422–68.

Geser, H. et al. (1994) *Die Schweizer Lokalparteien*, Zürich: Seismo.

Huber-Hotz, A. (1991) 'Das Zweikammersystem. Anspruch und Wirklichkeit', in Parlamentsdienste (ed.), *Das Parlament - 'Oberste Gewalt des Bundes'?* Bern and Stuttgart: Haupt, 165–82.

Kern, K. (1997) 'Die Entwicklung des Föderalismus und den USA: Zentralisierung und Devolution in einem Mehrebenensystem', in S. Cattacin and I. Kissling-Näf (eds), *Subsidiäres Staatshandeln*, special issue of *Revue Suisse de Science Politique* 3: 171–96.

Kilper, H. and Lhotta, R. (1996) *Föderalismus in der Bundesrepublik Deutschland*, Opladen: Leske & Budrich.

Klöti, U. (1998) 'Kantonale Parteiensysteme. Die Bedeutung des kantonalen Kontexts für die Positionierung der Parteien', in H. Kriesi, W. Linder and U. Klöti (eds) *Schweizer Wahlen 1995*, Bern, Stuttgart, Wien: Haupt, 45–72.

Kriesi, H. (1995) *Le Système Politique Suisse*, Paris: Economica.

—— (1998) 'Die Ständeratswahlen 1995', in H. Kriesi, W. Linder and U. Klöti (eds), *Schweizer Wahlen 1995*, Bern, Stuttgart, Wien: Haupt, 193–218.

—— (1999a) 'Movements of the Left, Movements of the Right: Putting the Mobilization of Two New Types of Social Movements into Political Context', in H. Kitschelt et al. (eds), *Continuity and Change in Contemporary Capitalism*, Cambridge and New York: Cambridge University Press, 398–423.

—— (1999b) 'Note on the Size of the Public Sector in Switzerland', *Revue Suisse de Science Politique* 5, 2: 105–8.

Ladner, A. (1991) *Politische Gemeinden, kommunale Parteien und lokale Politik*, Zürich: Seismo.

—— (1999) 'Das Schweizer Parteiensystem und seine Parteien', in U. Klöti et al. (eds), *Handbuch der Schweizer Politik*, Zürich: Verlag Neue Zürcher Zeitung, 214–60.

Lane, J.-E. and Ersson, S.O. (1999) *Politics and Society in Western Europe*, 4th edn, London, Thousand Oaks, New Delhi: Sage.

Lane, J.-E. et al. (1997) *Political Data Handbook. OECD Countries*, 2nd edn, Oxford: Oxford University Press.

Lehmbruch, G. (1976) *Parteienwettbewerb im Bundesstaat*, Stuttgart, Berlin, Köln, Mainz: Kohlhammer.

—— (1993) 'Consociational Democracy and Corporatism in Switzerland', *Publius: The Journal of Federalism* 23, 2: 43–60.

—— (1996) 'Die korporative Verhandlungsdemokratie in Westmitteleuropa', in K. Armingeon and P. Sciarini (eds) *Deutschland, Österreich und die Schweiz im Vergleich*, special issue of *Revue Suisse de Science Politique*, Zürich: Seismo, 19–41.

—— (1998) *Parteienwettbewerb im Bundesstaat. Regelsysteme und Spannungslagen im Institutionengefüge der Bundesrepublik Deutschland*, 2nd edn, Opladen: Westdeutscher Verlag.

Lijphart, A. (1999) *Patterns of Democracy: Government Form and Performance in Thirty-Six Countries*, New Haven: Yale University Press.

Linder, W. (1994) *Swiss Democracy: Possible Solutions to Conflict in Multicultural Societies*, Basingstoke: Macmillan.

—— (1999) *Schweizerische Demokratie — Institutionen, Prozesse, Perspektiven*, Bern, Stuttgart, Wien: Haupt.

Listhaug, O. and Wiberg, M. (1995) 'Confidence in Political and Private Institutions', in H.-D. Klingemann and D. Fuchs (eds), *Citizens and the State. Beliefs in Government Vol. 1*, Oxford: Oxford University Press, 298–322.

Lösche, P. (1989) *Amerika in Perspektive. Politik und Gesellschaft der Vereinigten Staaten*, Darmstadt: Wissenschaftliche Buchgemeinschaft.

Lutz, G. and Strohmann, D. (1998) *Wahl- und Abstimmungsrecht in den Kantonen*, Bern, Stuttgart, Wien: Haupt.

Mäder, H. and Schedler, K. (eds) (1996) *Perspektiven des Finanzausgleichs in der Schweiz*, Bern, Stuttgart, Wien: Haupt.

Neidhart, L. (1970) *Plebiszit und pluralitäre Demokratie. Eine Analyse der Funktionen des schweizerischen Gesetzesreferendums*, Bern: Francke.

Nüssli, K. (1985) *Föderalismus in der Schweiz: Konzepte, Indikatoren, Daten*, Grüsch: Rüegger.

Ripley, E. and Slotnick, E.E. (eds) (1993) *Readings in American Government and Politics*, 2nd edn, Belmont: Wadsworth.

Scharpf, F.W. (1994) 'Die Politikverflechtungsfalle. Europäische Integration und deutscher Föderalismus im Vergleich', in F.W. Scharpf (ed.) *Optionen des Föderalismus in Deutschland und Europa*, Frankfurt am Main and New York: Campus, 11–44.

Schenkel, W. and Serdült, U. (1999) 'Bundesstaatliche Beziehungen', in U. Klöti et al. (eds), *Handbuch der Schweizer Politik*, Zürich: Verlag Neue Zürcher Zeitung, 470–507.

Schmidt, M.G. (1997) *Demokratietheorien*, 2nd edn, Opladen: Leske & Budrich.

Spörndli, M. et al. (1998) 'Diener dreier Herren? Kantonalbehörden und die Vollzugsvielfalt der arbeitsmarktlichen Bestimmungen im schweizerischen Asylrecht', *Revue Suisse de Science Politique* 4, 3: 53–77.

Statistisches Bundesamt (ed.) (1999) *Statistisches Jahrbuch für die Bundesrepublik Deutschland und für das Ausland 1999*, Stuttgart: Metzler-Poeschel.

Steiner, J. (1969) 'Typologisierung des schweizerischen Parteiensystems', *Schweizerisches Jahrbuch für Politische Wissenschaft* 9: 21–40.

Vatter, A. (1997) 'Die Wechselbeziehungen zwischen Konkordanz- und Direktdemokratie', *Politische Vierteljahresschrift* 38, 4: 743–70.

—— (1998a) 'Konstanz und Konkordanz. Die Stabilität kantonaler Regierungen im Vergleich', *Revue Suisse de Science Politique* 4, 1: 1–21.

—— (1998b) 'Politische Fragmentierung in den Schweizer Kantonen', *Kölner Zeitschrift für Soziologie und Sozialpsychologie* 50, 4: 666–84.

——(1999) *Föderalismus*, in U. Klöti et al. (eds), *Handbuch der Schweizer Politik*, Zürich: Verlag Neue Zürcher Zeitung, 77–108.

Vatter, A. and Sager, F. (1996) 'Föderalismusreform am Beispiel des Ständemehrs', in S. Hug and P. Sciarini (eds), *La réforme des institutions* special issue of *Revue Suisse de Science Politique*, Zürich: Seimo, 165–200.

Wachendorfer-Schmidt, U. (1999), 'Der Preis des Föderalismus in Deutschland', *Politische Vierteljahresschrift* 40: 3–39.

Wälti, S. (1996) 'Institutional Reform of Federalism: Changing the Players Rather Than the Rules of the Game', in S. Hug and P. Sciarini (eds), *La réforme des institutions*, special issue of *Revue Suisse de Science Politique*, Zürich: Seismo, 113–41.

6 When adversaries collaborate

Conditional co-operation in Australia's arm's length federal polity

Martin Painter

Under what conditions do the constituent units of a federal system co-operate to solve joint problems, when regional and national interests and agendas overlap? Can the potential for debilitating conflict and gridlock in intergovernmental relations be avoided by resorting to particular types of institutional arrangement, or adopting particular strategies of action? Answers to these questions will differ considerably depending on the underlying character of the federal arrangements.

We can identify two contrasting models of intergovernmental relations in federal systems, depending on the underlying constitutional rules (see Figure 6.1) (Painter 1991). The first is an image of competitive federalism, in which governments keep their distance and provide separate bundles of services as they compete for public support, and co-operate when it suits them individually. Such an image is most familiar in federal systems such as the United States of America, which can be characterized as decentralist, 'arm's length' federations (Kincaid 1991). The second is a contrasting image of collaborative federalism, in which governments are engaged in a variety of interlocking institutional arrangements that routinize joint action, or even under some conditions compel it. Federal systems that embody a variety of interlocking institutional arrangements, such as Germany, best merit this label. Many federal systems contain elements of both models in different degrees, and scholars may argue about which best applies. This is the case in Australia, where such is the extent of Commonwealth-dominated, routinized intergovernmental co-operation – albeit in sub-constitutional rather than constitutionalized forms – that the arm's length distinctiveness of state governments is often questioned (Painter 1998).

The images (Figure 6.1) embody both an empirical and an evaluative component. Advocates of collaborative federalism propose that competition leads to debilitating confrontation, often to the point of deadlock; to unilateralism and to unwarranted jurisdictional intrusions, particularly by the federal government; and to contradictory and uncoordinated policies. Collaboration produces better co-ordinated outcomes that achieve a more satisfactory balance of regional and federal perspectives. Critics of

	Negative	*Positive*
Competition	Duplication	Responsiveness
Collaboration	Gridlock	Co-ordination

Figure 6.1 Evaluations of intergovernmental relations: competition versus collaboration.

collaborative federalism point to the democratic deficit that exists when the executives of the two levels of government come together to strike their bargains, and to the debilitating effects of potential deadlock in complex multi-party negotiations. Some also warn against cartel-like collusion between collaborating, empire-building governments. Left to their own devices to go it alone and compete with each other, governments may offer a more diverse set of policies that are more responsive to public demands. Where public pressures on both governments demand a joint response, they will come together to co-operate in an unfettered manner if it is in the interests of their constituents; and so long as the competitive dynamic operates, governments will remain answerable to citizens rather than merely to each other in the deals that they strike.

Leaving aside the heat that these debates can engender, experience suggests that both competitive and collaborative models are capable of producing suboptimal outcomes where joint action is desirable. The purpose of this chapter is to help clarify the circumstances under which these outcomes might be avoided, first by outlining a vocabulary for the empirical analysis of joint action, and second by applying it to some empirical cases. Particular attention will be drawn to the experience of recent cooperative initiatives in the Australian federal system, and to the factors that were conducive to those that brought some success.

Institutional analysis

A general framework for analysing institutional arrangements, conceived as a set of rules that order the relationships among actors, has been suggested by Elinor Ostrom (1986). Ostrom proposes a seven-fold classification of the 'working rules' governing actors in a variety of 'action arenas':

1 *boundary rules* determine who is eligible to participate;
2 *scope rules* specify the range of matters over which actors can take action;
3 *position rules* specify what positions eligible participants hold;
4 *authority and procedural rules* prescribe what actions particular position holders can take;
5 *information rules* establish the information that actors may, or must, reveal to others;
6 *aggregation rules* prescribe the way collective decisions are taken (for example, majority vote or unanimity);

7   *payoff rules* specify how costs and benefits are to be distributed as the result of a decision.

Various forms of 'strategic action' can be encompassed in this framework – confrontation, bargaining, coalition-building, joint problem-solving and opting out, for instance. Ostrom's approach also demands specifying the nature of the subject matter in dispute – for instance, zero-sum problems (where gains for some are only possible at the expense of losses for others) produce different kinds of bargaining from positive-sum problems (where outcomes that provide gains for all are possible). In addition, it is important to specify the norms and other aspects of the social context within which the arena is located (Ostrom 1986: 471–3).

In the current context, we are concerned with strategic actions that produce or impede co-operation and co-ordination among governments. One way of thinking about co-ordination is to see it as a familiar problem of achieving joint action among actors with different interests, each facing uncertainty about the actions of other players. In many such cases, even where it can be shown that benefits would accrue to each and all from co-operation to avoid perverse outcomes, the incentives to co-operate are typically not sufficiently strong or clear to outweigh the perceived gains from uncoordinated action. Game theorists model such situations as a 'prisoners' dilemma' or a 'tragedy of the commons': the safest and most risk-averse course of action for each individual where behaviours are interdependent, in the absence of certainty about the future actions of others, turns out to be mutually self-destructive: what good does it do me to refrain from depleting the common resource to exhaustion – be it fish in the ocean or clean air – when I cannot be certain that everyone else will also refrain? No one wants to be 'the sucker'.

Co-ordination traps in collaborative, competitive and mixed systems

Fritz Scharpf's (1988) analysis of the 'joint decision trap' in former West Germany models such a case of 'individual rationality' accompanied by 'collective ruin'. It provides an example of a collaborative system of intergovernmental relations that produced suboptimal outcomes. Amendments to the West German Basic Law in 1969 rewrote the rules relating to certain kinds of joint programmes (scope rules). In framing these programs, formal agreement was required from all governments (authority and boundary rules). Unable to act alone, the federal government was effectively a captive of the lowest common denominator of agreement among the *Länder*. The *Länder* adopted a decision rule that required unanimity, giving participants a potential veto, because the 'default condition' was the status quo (aggregation rule). As a result, a 'bargaining style' evolved that was inimical to dealing with some of the collective problems that had been identified. No one would accept being worse off, and all the benefits had to be distributed equally (pay-off rule) (Reissert 1978: 33–4). Poorer *Länder* expressed dissatisfaction with the resulting allocations, and with provisions that demanded matching contributions which they were sometimes not able to afford (pay-off rule). In addition, because the financial costs of joint programmes were shared, but the political benefits accrued equally to both levels, the federal budget became vulnerable to a series of raids by an intergovernmental cartel of public officials concerned solely to see their programmes and empires expand. The result was a steady, uncontrolled growth in *Länder* budgets (Scharpf 1988: 255–6). The federal government continued to make *ad hoc* financial and jurisdictional concessions rather than risk a constitutional confrontation, on each occasion 'tightening . . . the ropes that reduced its own ability to act'. More than this, however, the trap ensnared all those interests and groups (including the poorer *Länder*) who saw potential benefits in substantial changes to the status quo, because the institutional arrangements that resulted in inertia were themselves 'frozen'. They effectively 'block(ed) their own further institutional evolution', despite considerable agreement on the presence of counter-productive outcomes (Scharpf 1988: 267).

Scharpf is describing one case of a collaborative intergovernmental arrangement, arising from a specific set of working rules for joint action in the West German federal system. Particular constitutional provisions, including the distribution of powers between the levels of government and the composition and powers of the Bundesrat, constrained and shaped the working rules. The West German constitution divides powers along both jurisdictional and functional lines, in the latter case allocating to the federal government law-making power and to the *Länder* the implementation and administration of these laws. *Länder* nomination of members of the Bundesrat, and the need to gain the second chamber's consent to legislative proposals, reflects this direct involvement of the *Länder* in spheres of federal jurisdiction. The *Länder*'s decisive power in joint program formulation also stemmed from their possession of paramount jurisdictional powers over some sectors of policy, such as education.

Chandler (1987) contrasts the collaborative style of intergovernmental relations in West Germany with the more adversarial style in Canada. The constitutional rules in Canada set a framework within which different kinds of working rules apply in particular arenas of joint action. The principles underlying the Canadian division of powers are based on jurisdictional distinctions between various subject matters. The result is a system of parallel or arm's length rather than interlocking governments, with each government asserting the right of unilateral action in its separate jurisdiction. For this reason alone, one would not expect the conditions of the joint decision trap to be replicated in Canadian intergovernmental relations, despite the fact that complete jurisdictional disentanglement is impossible to achieve due to subject matter overlaps (Leslie 1987).

These overlaps create a continuing agenda of co-ordination problems and provide powerful incentives to co-operate for specific purposes. The co-existence of competitive and collaborative forms of interaction extends across all spheres of Canadian intergovernmental relations. Alongside the aggressive thrust and riposte of competitive unilateralism, provincial and federal ministers and officials are constantly engaged in networks of accommodation. In the case of agricultural policy (a sphere of concurrent jurisdiction) Skogstad (1987) has described a situation where *de facto* federal paramountcy was accepted, and a series of joint programmes initiated and implemented co-operatively in response to producer demands. There was broad agreement on the need for assistance to agriculture, and a willingness, in the face of the difficulties of reaching interregional agreement among producer groups, to pass the buck to the federal government and to deal bilaterally. Rather than assert their jurisdiction, provinces were mostly content with continuing involvement at official and ministerial levels in various consultative arrangements.

This example illustrates an important aspect of strategic action within the framework of the constitutional rules: where it is to the mutual benefit of the actors concerned, operating rules may evolve that facilitate bureaucratic accommodation and consensus. Networks are built across jurisdictions on the basis of a common experience of problem-solving, discussions proceed in a climate of shared understandings and reciprocity, and policy community norms evolve that facilitate agreement (Scharpf 1997: 136–9). For instance, Simeon (1972) describes the officials' meetings supporting the Conference of Ministers of Finance and Provincial Treasurers as a 'tight-knit group with an esprit of its own' and a sense of community. Brown's (1988) description of the operation of the Continuing Committee on Trade Negotiations (which was largely a consultative mechanism to keep the provinces informed of negotiations with the United States on free trade) concludes that it was 'an effective mechanism for the exchange of views and information', characterized by frankness and, for the most part, reasonableness. In the case of the federal government's negotiations with Quebec over the pension plan, as described by Simeon, information rules prescribing frank exchange but strict secrecy, at ministerial as well as official levels, produced the kind of reciprocity often found in interstate diplomacy (Simeon 1972: 57–61).

The effectiveness of these co-operative arrangements, however, may be threatened by the possible exercise of the power of the hold-out. Many operate in sectoral policy communities, and are vulnerable to 'whole-of-government' political intervention for strategic political purposes. In order to try to transfer some of the problem-solving potential of sectoral communities into the deadlock-prone arenas of high politics, and to reflect and support the authority of cabinets and first ministers, there may be a temptation to institutionalize these often informal arrangements, for example by integrating them with the 'peak' political institutions of intergovernmental 'high politics', and establishing a set of protocols and regular forums for negotiation and clearance. Elsewhere (Painter 1991), I have argued against this, because the avoidance of gridlock and perverse outcomes in a 'mixed' system such as Canada (i.e. where competitive and collaborative elements coexist uneasily) depends on the freedom of political manoeuvre provided by the underlying conditions of arm's length federalism: the ability to opt out, the flexibility afforded by bilateralism and multilateralism, and the possibilities in such a system for relatively loose, informal and productive forms of sectoral co-operation within and among policy communities and networks. Such forms have their own life, and are not destroyed permanently by the collateral damage of the thrust and riposte of adversarial high politics. What of the case of Australia?

Collaborative federalism in Australia

Australia, like Canada, is a 'mixed' system where co-ordinate parliamentary governments share overlapping functions, and are forced to co-operate while seeking to preserve an arm's length existence. A feature of these two federations is that co-ordination proceeds exclusively between the executive branches (hence the term 'executive federalism') and through largely informal, sub-constitutional machinery (Smiley 1987; Sharman 1991; Painter 1996b). A major obstacle to close co-operation in such a system is the fear of loss of executive autonomy (or 'sovereignty') that might result from domination by another government with greater functional capacities – money, administrative resources, knowledge and so on. It is often safer to keep one's distance and deny the existence of a co-ordination problem at all. Hence, for example, it took over a hundred years of effort before a standard gauge railway system directly linked all mainland Australian state capitals (a feat finally achieved in 1995).

In the Australian federal system, the Commonwealth government is the dominant actor, largely due to its exclusive occupancy of major fields of taxation – in particular sales tax, corporations tax and income tax. State governments are highly dependent on Commonwealth general and specific purpose grants for their revenues. Their experience throughout most of the history of federation has been of continual expansion and encroachment by the Commonwealth. In many areas of policy, the Commonwealth can wield unilateral power despite the states' jurisdictional claims. Central command is thus a not uncommon form of co-ordination. Yet there are limits, set largely by the continuing jurisdictional powers and administrative capacities of the states. The Commonwealth may face High Court constitutional challenges, as well as political challenges from state premiers, if it proceeds with heavy-handed, unilateral national initiatives. It most often needs the states' co-operation to implement such schemes.

Some intergovernmental machinery reflects the brute power of the Commonwealth, for example the annual financial premiers' conferences, where the federal government each year presents a 'take it or leave it' fiscal package to the states. If the Commonwealth would prefer to proceed unilaterally in this way, the states' preferred method of co-ordination is what we might call 'unfettered co-operation'. They want to agree to co-operate on their own terms through decision-making processes that do not reduce their autonomy. Some intergovernmental machinery reflects the norms and style of this mode of co-operation. Most intergovernmental ministerial councils in Australia, for example, traditionally worked under the guise of being merely 'consultative' bodies where formal votes were almost unheard of. Conventions stressed their consensual style, and much was done behind the scenes in official committees, by 'gentleman's agreement'.

Given the limits of the Commonwealth's unilateral powers, and the limitations on the scope and intensity of joint action in a system of unfettered co-operation, a third, more collaborative mode of co-ordination has evolved. Figure 6.2 depicts this mode of co-operation as an ideal type, using the vocabulary of Ostrom's institutional analysis. For the sake of the current analysis, it is contrasted with an unfettered, arm's length model. Although the collaborative model evolved from a long period of institutional experimentation and adaptation, in recent years the machinery of collaborative federalism has proliferated rapidly (Painter 1998: 92–120).

The shift from unfettered to collaborative forms of co-ordination in Australia is a long-term trend, but during the 1980s and 1990s there was an increasing number of ventures in closer intergovernmental collaboration, each involving similar elements: a formal agreement; uniform or complementary legislation; an intergovernmental administrative agency; a supervising ministerial council which, for some purposes, made decisions by majority vote rather than unanimity; and an agreement to 'pool' funds and make expenditure of them subject to these joint decision-making arrangements (Painter 1996a). Among such arrangements were the National Crime Authority (1984), the Murray-Darling Agreement (1987), the Australian Securities Commission (1991), the National Vocational Education and Training Agreement (1992), and the National Competition Policy Agreement (1995). These schemes typically dealt with pressing issues over which the states enjoyed jurisdiction but where, in an increasingly complex world, it was recognized that a greater degree of uniformity in national coverage was needed. In every case, the Commonwealth was the prime mover, with state governments expressing varying degrees of enthusiasm and commitment. The resulting forms of joint legislative and executive action effectively pooled the powers of each government in an intergovernmental arrangement.

From unfettered to collaborative co-ordination

What might explain the emergence of more collaborative forms of co-ordination in the Australian federal system? Three types of explanation might be advanced. First, we could look to secular trends in the agenda of

	Unfettered co-operation	*Collaboration*
Scope rules	Each government's jurisdiction over all or any set of decisions relating to subject matter X is limited only by provisions of the constitution.	A specific range of decision about subject matter X is, by agreement, the shared responsibility of all governments party to the agreement.
Authority rules	Each government can choose whether or not to be bound by any agreement about X arising from any consultative process with other governments.	No policy about X is made in any jurisdiction other than with the approval of a joint ministerial council of all governments.
	Each parliament acts independently in making and amending laws about X.	No parliament can make or amend laws about X other than by a procedure that maintains conformity with the laws of all other jurisdictions.
	Administration of policy and enforcement of laws about X is undertaken by agencies responsible only to each separate government.	Administration of policy and enforcement of laws about X is undertaken and/or monitored by a National Commission, which reports to the ministerial council.
Information rules	Governments will consult with each other and exchange information before determining policy about X.	No decision about X can be taken without considering the advice of a National Commission.
Aggregation rules	No consultative forum can take decisions about X other than by unanimous agreement.	All decisions on policy about X are taken under voting method P (e.g. two-thirds majority).
Pay-off rules	The Commonwealth and states direct funds independently to X in a manner that mutually supports a unanimous agreement.	Funds for X are pooled by both state and Commonwealth governments, and allocations made by joint agreement under voting method Q (and on recommendations of the National Commission).

Figure 6.2 Contrasting models of intergovernmental co-ordination.

co-ordination problems. Exogenous pressures such as globalization and technological change have arguably created a larger agenda of pressing new co-ordination problems, and unfettered coordination has thereby been rendered obsolete. But how do we explain the emergence of a collaborative response to replace unfettered co-ordination? An institutional explanation might suggest the importance of path dependency, with piecemeal collaborative innovations and experiments in institutional arrangements being diffused throughout the system by adaptation and imitation, such that collaborative forms become a dominant feature (Painter 1998: 103–20).

But a third type of explanation is needed to understand the change process, that is a focus on the motives and the strategic choices of actors responsible for critical events and outcomes. A closer look at the recent spate of new collaborative machinery provides a rich source of data for exploring this type of explanation. In the early 1990s the Commonwealth launched an initiative in 'co-operative federalism', dubbed by Prime Minister Hawke a 'new partnership'. A series of Special Premiers' Conferences (SPC) was held in 1990 and 1991, and in 1992 a new institution, the Council of Australian Governments (COAG), was established, meeting twice yearly until 1996, and more infrequently since then (Fletcher and Walsh 1992; Painter 1996a; 1998). Regular meetings of officials facilitated the work of this peak institution. The main agenda items during this period concerned economic restructuring – the removal of interstate barriers in national markets, regulatory reform and other 'pro-competitive' measures, and the modernization of infrastructure (Carroll and Painter 1995). All these areas lay at the heart of state government jurisdictions, involving many state-owned services and enterprises. Despite deep-seated traditions and strong interests surrounding the preservation of the status quo within state governments themselves, considerable progress on an agenda of co-ordinated reform was achieved, largely through the crafting of collaborative arrangements for joint decision-making. How did this come about?

The focus by the prime minister and state premiers on a new process – the 'new partnership' – led to the creation of new consultative and decision-making machinery through which resources could be mobilized to seek agreement. The political leaders, through regular interaction in 1990 and 1991, developed a new level of commitment to joint problem-solving. Premiers' chief officials and advisers were personally involved as emissaries and crisis managers in many of the jointly mandated working parties. These central agency officials – appropriately dubbed the 'central agencies club' – were familiar to each other, had similar perspectives on 'whole of government' issues, and were in continual contact (Weller 1996). Instead of leaving matters of disagreement languishing in working parties of minor officials, log-jams could be cleared rapidly through the exercise of personal authority from the top. In SPC and COAG, the central agency officials set up and managed a complex set of steering committees and working parties, setting agenda, fixing timetables and monitoring progress. The institutionalization of this 'peak level' machinery around regular meetings of SPC and COAG was an important new ingredient in intergovernmental relations.

But energy, commitment and organization are only some of the necessary ingredients. COAG decisions required unanimity, and the pressures to reach agreement often led to intense conflict of the kind familiar in Australia's arm's length, adversarial federal politics. But the internal logic of the 'co-ordination game' under conditions of unanimity contributed to the collaborative outcomes. The careful management of the agenda by the central agency club coupled with the intense pressures to agree – due to the 'urgency' of the problem, the successful mobilization of external interests, or the extent to which political leaders had made public commitments – took governments operating under a unanimity rule down decision paths that led to the setting up of collaborative institutions, rather than to some other solution. Under the pressure to take the final steps to sign an agreement and in order to avoid deadlock, governments chose to search for compromises in the institutional arrangements for future joint decision-making, often in order to disguise or sweep under the table substantive points of disputation. These compromises took the form of decision rules, information rules and other safeguards to allow the hold-outs to 'fight another day' over the more intractable substantive issues. Important roles in clarifying ambiguities in the these issues were surrendered to collaborative institutions, such as a ministerial council or a national commission of experts. Here, the existence of a growing repertoire of such 'ready made' solutions was often important – for example, the adoption of a complex ministerial council aggregation rule that would satisfy at one and the same time the Commonwealth's wish to take initiatives, and a small state's fear of being swamped by a large state majority. Of such institutional niceties and complexities are collaborative forms of co-ordination made.

We can see other strategic reasons why the parties to these agreements would want to formalize them in such a way that they broke with the more informal, arm's length traditions of intergovernmental co-ordination. Formal intergovernmental agreements – rather like treaties between foreign powers – were an increasing feature of intergovernmental co-ordination. Such agreements are 'extra-constitutional', and the High Court has ruled they are not enforceable between the parties as if they were a private contract (Howard et al. 1982: 8–9). They are political instruments, compromises between the general wish to retain political flexibility and a specific interest in limited co-operation. Often, what provided the 'glue' to make the parties stick to an agreement was money (specifically, of course, Commonwealth grants to the states, often pooled in a 'national' fund under the auspices of a ministerial council).

In this context, a formal agreement seeks not only to bind executives to each other but also to help bind the respective parliaments. Some of the most intractable problems of commitment arise in the case of schemes where a surrender of legislative as well as executive autonomy is envisaged. The political reality is of legislatures that are not always compliant to a government's bidding (Moon 1995). But the symbolic weight of a formal agreement, when taken back to a legislature, is a powerful weapon in the hands of the executive. Faced with proposed legislation implementing such agreements, legislators often complain at being presented with *faits accomplis*. Technically speaking, they need not consider them as such, but the political pressure brought to bear by the fanfare surrounding a national agreement is often strong.

Thus formal agreements assisted political executives to buttress each other's power in their relations with parliament. But there could be further parliamentary obstacles: if the current legislature can be coerced or persuaded to agree, future ones may not feel bound. Over time, joint legislative schemes may lose their uniform character if legislatures do not amend them in concert to adapt them to changing conditions. A formal agreement can seek to prevent this by proposing 'template' legislation which is passed in one jurisdiction and then 'adopted' in others. Future amendments agreed to by unanimous decision of a ministerial council, once passed by the 'host' legislature, automatically become law everywhere, without the need for separate amending acts. This legislative device is the ultimate tool of collaborative federalism, involving the surrender of un-fettered parliamentary sovereignty to an executive cabal, and for that reason, while naturally finding favour with political executives, it aroused considerable hostility in state parliaments, with some governments on occasion bowing to pressures not to adopt this method of harmonization of laws.

Indeed, all these collaborative institutions existed in a wider institutional setting that still expressed the norms and traditions of arm's length federalism, where Commonwealth unilateralism coexisted with the states' struggles to maintain the conditions of unfettered co-operation. In that context, they were no more (and no less) than the product of statements of political intent and mutual understanding among a particular group of political leaders. Successor governments were under strong pressures to honour them, and the collectivity had a general interest in maintaining their integrity, because the majority of governments in some measure benefited from most of them, while all benefited from some. However, the understanding was clear that these were conditional commitments, more or less voluntarily entered into and, in principle, capable of being dissolved in the same manner.

The spirit with which they were interpreted and implemented reflected this. As circumstances changed and events unfolded, governments, national commissions and ministerial councils developed their own stratagems for achieving their ends, in the process sometimes side-stepping the finer detail of the formal agreement where this inhibited freedom of manoeuvre. A case in point was the National Road Transport Commission (NRTC), which found that it was impossible to get all states to follow a common timetable for adoption of a series of major legislative changes using template legislation, and reverted to agreeing to piecemeal, jurisdiction-by-jurisdiction initiatives according to the timetables and priorities of individual governments. As well, the complex voting rules established for the NRTC Ministerial Council were for the most part never activated, and a two-zone system for differential charges (one for the less-populated states, where road costs were lower, and another for the more densely populated states) was not implemented by the NRTC.[1] In spite of these departures from the strict letter of the collaborative procedures, the NRTC made considerable progress on achieving harmonization and uniformity in inter-state road use charging and regulation. It would appear that the 'fine print' in the agreements concerning voting and other rules was included primarily to cement an initial unanimous agreement (see above). On the ground, things were different. The issues that had prompted the various conces-sions and inclusions disappeared from the agenda, and some of the rationale for the precise nature of the institutional arrangements was for-gotten. Then, the manner in which joint decision-making actually occurred depended more on the strategies of the key players – particularly the members and officials of new national inter-jurisdictional executive and advisory bodies – and on more traditional, unfettered and *ad hoc* forms of intergovernmental decision-making.

In sum, the agreements themselves were entered into in a spirit such that nothing was so permanent or immutable as to be incapable of re-negotiation at a later date, and many things 'agreed to' left many important matters at the discretion of the actual decision-maker. Even where there were apparent external enforcement mechanisms, edges were blurred and guarantees softened. The National Competition Policy (NCP), adopted by formal intergovernmental agreement in 1995, required state governments to pass certain 'milestones' in implementing regulatory reform, restruc-turing government enterprises and so on. At three-yearly intervals, a check would be made to see that each state had complied, at which point funds in a long-term financial agreement, signed at the same time as the NCP agreement, would flow from the Commonwealth to each state.[2] However, what comprised 'compliance' was left to the interpretation by and advice of a body of experts, the National Competition Council, whose members were appointed jointly by all governments. As well, the actions needing to be taken to 'comply' were loosely defined, and left open to a good deal of discretion and interpretation by each government, in the name of 'local conditions' and 'special needs' (Harman and Harman 1996). As the decade of the 1990s drew to a close, several state governments began to have second thoughts about aspects of their earlier agreement to some of the principles of NCP, and the degree of compliance and uniformity weakened.

Meanwhile, the Commonwealth retained and continued to expand its scope for unilateral policy initiatives, and co-ordination by command and control. It chose its strategy according to a variety of considerations, and only in some circumstances did collaborative forms of co-ordination appeal. In the second half of the 1990s, the Commonwealth's fiscal powers continued to expand, in part as a result of new interpretations of the High Court removing entirely the states' access to excise, sales and like taxes, and in part as a consequence of the Commonwealth's decision in 1999 to introduce a new goods and services tax and to transfer the proceeds to the states. In return the states agreed to abolish some taxes and levies, and to the ending of the current system of general revenue grants. This change reasserted and reinforced the Commonwealth's fiscal dominance. The states made themselves dependent on a tax which only the Commonwealth could levy, while agreeing also to vacate additional fields of taxation clearly within their powers. At the same time the Commonwealth steered away from elaborate collaborative arrangements, with COAG becoming much less significant as a forum. In a number of specific service provision agreements with the states, the Commonwealth tended to prefer bilateral deals within a common framework set by the federal government, rather than jointly agreed collaborative outcomes.

Conclusion

Where intergovernmental relations are pursued in a collaborative mode, a new dimension is added to the meaning of the term 'executive federalism'. Not only are the intergovernmental agreements made by and between executives, with parliaments mostly rubber-stamping the results, but also an enlargement of the scope and power of executive government is achieved. So long as the new agencies established by agreement retain the support and confidence of governments, they enlarge their powers. This is a 'positive sum' outcome for the collectivity of executives. Even if in the process a particular government has lost exclusive possession of a slice of turf, the result is that the field on which they all play is enlarged.

The evidence suggests that in the Australian case, the emergence of more collaborative forms of co-ordination to solve collective problems represented a set of shifting compromises between, on the one hand, the need for concerted, harmonious and (in some cases) uniform action and, on the other, the continuing interests of each jurisdiction in remaining in control of important levers of power so as to retain a capacity to express diversity. The collaborative mechanisms were part symbolic and part instrumental in character. They were not so much fixed or rigid formulae as devices for initiating the terms and conditions of joint action, which emerged from subsequent events.

In most cases, the key initiative was to introduce a new 'national' player in the form of an expert commission, where none existed before, with varying combinations of regulatory, advisory and executive powers. Information rules – such as a requirement that no decision is taken until a report from such a body is received – were as important as the more specific decision rules, such as who sits where and who can vote on what. These new national bodies were not Commonwealth agencies, but were jointly mandated (although in most cases their statutory existence was owed to a Commonwealth act, the terms of which were set out in the intergovernmental agreement). Governments, in fact, remained mostly at arm's length, but new players were set down in the gaps between them. The collaborative forms allowed for the moderation of some of the potentially debilitating effects of unfettered co-operation (in particular, the inertial power of the hold-out and of the fear of uncertainty present in each actor's mind). At the same time, the underlying arm's length character of federal arrangements, in which these collaborative arrangements were uneasily nested, ensured sufficient flexibility to escape the potential gridlock effects of excessively rigid formulae and unnecessary uniformity. Different patterns of co-operation and co-ordination will continue to evolve in a variety of forms in the Australian federation, as different strategic opportunities and constraints face political executives from time to time.

Notes

1 The aggregation rules varied according to the nature of the decision taken by the Ministerial Council: recommended new legislation was subject to disapproval within two months by a *simple majority*; changes to the decision rules, along with agreement on funding of the Commission, required *unanimity*; the mass-distance heavy vehicle charges to apply in the separate zones could be disapproved by *simple majorities* in those zones; the level of the road use charge, comprising a portion of the Commonwealth excise tax on fuel, was subject to approval by a *simple majority* of the full Council; charging principles could only be changed by a *two-thirds majority* of the full Council; appointment and dismissal of the three members of the National Commission were also subject to a *two-thirds majority*; and changes to the boundaries of the zones required a three-quarters majority. Any other resolution of the Council could be carried by a *simple majority*.
2 The Agreement on financial matters was the key to the final deal. The real per capita value of financial assistance grants from the Commonwealth to the states would be maintained on a three-year rolling basis, and from 1997 special payments would be made to the states and territories so long as they met certain conditions. For the first tranche of $200 million in 1997/8, states and territories had to meet deadlines for review of regulatory legislation and implementation of competitive neutrality policy in the terms set out in the Competition Principles Agreement, and to achieve 'effective implementation of all COAG agreements' on electricity reform and the national framework for free and fair trade in gas and 'effective observance' of road transport reforms (i.e. those agreed to in the NRTC Agreement). In 1999–2000 a second tranche of $400 million would be paid, subject to continuing progress on the implementation of the same set of reforms, plus water industry reforms agreed to by COAG; and the third tranche, by 2001–2 of $600 million, would depend on 'having fully implemented, and continu[ing] to observe fully, all COAG agreements with regard to electricity, gas, water and road transport'.

References

Brown, D.M. (1988) 'The Federal-Provincial Consultation Process', in P.M. Leslie and R.L. Watts (eds), *Canada: The State of the Federation 1987–88*, Kingston: Institute of Intergovernmental Relations.

Carroll, P. and Painter, M. (eds) (1995) *Microeconomic Reform and Federalism*, Canberra: Federalism Research Centre, Australian National University.

Chandler, W.N. (1987) 'Federalism and Political Parties', in H. Bakvis and W.N. Chandler (eds), *Federalism and the Role of the State*, Toronto: Toronto University Press.

Fletcher, C. and Walsh, C. (1992) 'Reform of Intergovernmental Relations in Australia: The Politics of Federalism and the Non-politics of Managerialism', *Public Administration* 70, Winter:, 591–616.

Harman E. and Harman, F. (1996) 'The Potential for Local Diversity in Implementation of the National Competition Policy', *Australian Journal of Public Administration* 55, 2: 12–25.

Howard, C., Saunders, C.A. and Crommelin, B.M.L. (eds) (1982) 'The Co-operative Companies and Securities Scheme', Information Paper No. 4, Intergovernmental Relations in Victoria Program, Melbourne: Law School, University of Melbourne.

Kincaid, J. (1991) 'The Competitive Challenge to Cooperative Federalism: A Theory of Federal Democracy', in D.A. Kenyon and J. Kincaid (eds), *Competition Among States and Local Governments: Efficiency and Equity in American Federalism*, Washington, DC: The Urban Institute.

Leslie, P. (1987) *Federal State, National Economy*, Toronto: University of Toronto Press.

Moon, J. (1995) 'Minority Government in the Australian States: From Ersatz Majoritarianism to Minoritarianism?', *Australian Journal of Political Science*, 30, Special Issue: 142–63.

Ostrom, E. (1986) 'A Method of Institutional Analysis', in F.X. Kaufmann et al. (eds), *Guidance Control and Evaluation in the Public Sector*, New York: Walter de Gruyter.

Painter, Martin (1991) 'Intergovernmental Relations in Canada: An Institutional Analysis', *Canadian Journal of Political Science*, 24, 2: 269–88.

—— (1996a) 'The Council of Australian Governments and Intergovernmental Relations: A Case of Cooperative Federalism', *Publius: The Journal of Federalism*, 26, 2: 101–20.

—— (1996b) 'Federal Theory and Modern Australian Executive Federalism', in J. Halligan and I. Thynne (eds), *Public Administration Under Scrutiny: Essays in Honour of Roger Wettenhall*, Canberra: University of Canberra Press and Royal Institute of Public Administration Australia.

—— (1998) *Collaborative Federalism: Economic Reform in Australia in the 1990s*, Cambridge: Cambridge University Press.

Reissert, B. (1978) 'Responsibility Sharing and Joint Tasks in West German Federalism', in P.B. Spahn (ed.), *Principles of Federal Policy Co-ordination in the Federal Republic of Germany*, Canberra: Centre for Federal Financial Relations, Australian National University.

Scharpf, F.W. (1988) 'The Joint-Decision Trap: Lessons from West German Federalism and European Integration', *Public Administration* 66: 239–78.

—— (1997) *Games Real Actors Play: Actor-Centered Institutionalism in Policy Research*, Boulder, CO: Westview Press.

Sharman, C. (1991) 'Executive Federalism', in B. Galligan, O. Hughes and C. Walsh (eds), *Intergovernmental Relations and Public Policy*, Sydney: Allen & Unwin.

Simeon, R. (1972) *Federal-Provincial Diplomacy*, Toronto: Toronto University Press.

Skogstad, G. (1987) 'Federalism and Agricultural Policy', in H. Bakvis and W.N. Chandler (eds), *Federalism and the Role of the State*, Toronto: Toronto University Press.

Smiley, D.V. (1987) *The Federal Condition in Canada*, Toronto: McGraw-Hill Ryerson.

Weller, P. (1996) 'Commonwealth-State Reform Processes: A Policy Management Review', *Australian Journal of Public Administration* 55, 1: 95–110.

7 Federal constraints and regional integration in Canada

Stephen G. Tomblin

At the beginning of the twenty-first century, federal redistributive policies and traditional models of territorial management are under attack in Canada and there is new interest in building region states in richer provinces like Ontario and encouraging the integration of smaller 'have-not' provinces that cannot make it on their own in a new economic era. It is a time when the moral foundations and relevance of Canadian federalism and her institutional and cultural traditions are being questioned by critics who believe there is no alternative but to accept continental integration and strengthening the role of subnational regions in North America.[1] In an effort to transform the intellectual environment and the terms of the federal bargain, neo-liberal politicians and academics alike have raised questions about the merits of subsidizing Canada's east–west ties, whether in the form of equalization to poor provinces or federal transfers to individuals. These supporters of change present a view of the world in which economic factors loom very large. However, in Canada, forging a consensus on the regional integration question has always proved difficult even when economic conditions have changed. Much of this is the product of a highly competitive and decentralized federal system that makes it possible for even small provinces to operate independently and resist economic changes. Even in an era of integration, Canadian federalism is known for its uncoordinated power and policies.

The regional integration debate has emerged repeatedly without significant progress and any attempt to understand this issue should consider the role played by intergovernmental traditions and structures. Changing economic circumstances alone cannot explain the history of struggle over the integration question. The Canadian intergovernmental system has made it difficult to achieve a consensus on a new approach.

The objective of this chapter is provocative: to question the policy prescriptions of regional integrationists and to discuss the values of cultural and political sovereignty that are important to Canadian federal traditions but have received little attention in the regional discourse. Rather than focusing on economic arguments only, this analysis will assess various political challenges, constraints and problems associated with changing embedded social and political practices and replacing them with new ones. The intent here will be to provide a better understanding of both sides of the regional integration issue and the contemporary challenges of bringing about fundamental economic and political change and building consent for regionalization in a federal system like Canada.

Regional integration is a timely and significant issue in Canadian federal politics in the 2000s. It is also important to bear in mind that the regional idea has been a major source of political conflict in Canada for generations. In this respect, the regional integration issue has much in common with the Quebec question in that the debate emerges repeatedly but the federal system is designed in a way that makes it difficult to achieve a consensus or impose a solution. By design, Canadian federalism is about balancing opposite forces and defending and promoting cultural and economic diversity. As a result, any movement seeking to restructure societies and existing organizational structures and processes based on some new economic theory or logic must deal with the power and resilience of established interests and stakeholders who benefit from the old system of ideas, processes and institutions. The fact that there has never been a regional or national centre strong enough to act as an agent of change has added to the challenge of achieving effective regional integration.

We need also to recognize that the system of fiscal federalism in Canada is designed in a way that has always made it difficult to adopt new approaches. Indeed, a central issue in the regional integration debate has always been whether the poor provinces should be forced to adjust to market conditions and whether it makes sense for rich provinces to be subsidizing old cultures, unsound development policies and political boundaries in Atlantic Canada. The history of struggle over regional integration is inexorably connected to federal spending powers, previous national policies that discriminated against rich provinces and an institutional structure that encourages territorial competition. In this vein, the use of the federal government's spending power to interfere in provincial areas of jurisdiction has always been contentious, especially for the richer provinces and Quebec. As one would expect, the poor provinces of Atlantic Canada have had a more positive view of Ottawa's spending power that made it possible to create a national system of equalization and income transfers. In the past, rich provinces have opposed the principle of equalization and the idea that equal opportunities should be promoted across the country. In the 2000s, much of the push for regionalization is the result of Ottawa's unilateral decision to cap or reduce federal transfers for social welfare, post-secondary education and health services in 'have' provinces (Courchene and Telmer 1998: 224–33). This has resulted in a new attitude that every province should be more self-reliant and prepared to do whatever is necessary to compete in a new era when boundaries are more porous, and continental and regional forces are gaining strength. There is new pressure for abandoning provincialism in Atlantic Canada and for strengthening ties with New England.

In the past, Alan Cairns has noted that one of the great mysteries debated by Canadian scholars has been why all the provinces have always survived despite changing economic conditions and predictions by economists that the status quo was not an option (1988: 144). The following analysis will rely on Cairns's ideas about federalism in an attempt to explain why the regional idea continues to be a non-starter, despite globalization, continentalism, and new economic forecasts in the 2000s.

The major divisions in the regional integration debate are the result of scholars holding different ideas about state and society autonomy. The role of the state and whether the state shapes society or vice versa remains a central question in the study of federalism and politics generally. There are marked differences in the way we can approach the regional integration question. For those who assume that state choices and policies can or should reflect societal pressures or economic trends at the global level (the society-centred perspective), there is a strong belief that we should be witnessing the dawning of a new era of continental regimes, region states, and regional co-operation. According to this view, external forces determine future choices and policies. On the other hand, state-centred theorists like Cairns assume that federal institutions and inherited overlapping state–society linkages have and will continue to play a vital role in determining how premiers and governors respond to changing societal and international forces. From this perspective, federalism still matters in the struggle over regional integration in Atlantic Canada and New England because it ensures that the perceptions, attitudes and behaviours of the political leaders involved are shaped by past societal traditions and institutional frameworks. Informed by Cairns's ideas on federalism, the following analysis argues that these different traditions have made it difficult to achieve effective integration and that economic conditions alone do not determine policy responses. It is suggested that economic factors by themselves do not determine whether new ideas acquire influence. We must also consider the cultural and institutional structures of each of the societies involved and their previous experiences with related policies.

The embedded state

Cairns holds that even when 'homogenizing tendencies' or changing economic circumstances pose a challenge to provincial diversities, Canadian federalism provides a shield against outside forces because within this uncoordinated system of power-sharing and public policies, there is not a centre with the political will or power to bring about fundamental political change. According to this logic, even when external conditions change, federalism makes it possible for old identities and boundaries (whether national or sub-national) to survive.

A central issue in the regional integration debate centres on the influence of state autonomy and capacity. Cairns's embedded state theory of federal state–society relations explains how state and societal institutions interact to produce a unique set of cultural and policy traditions that affect the way problems are defined or perceived in the future. Cairns rejects the assumption that political change comes easily when environmental conditions change and he came up with the concept of 'embeddedness' to explain why. Whether we are dealing with the forces of modernization in the 1950s or globalization in the 1990s, Cairns's model offers critical insights for understanding the significance of inherited federal state–society traditions and how these complicate any drive for integration. According to Cairns:

> the tighter fusion of state and society engendered in recent decades by activist national and provincial governments simultaneously fragments the state and contributes to the multiplication and increased political salience of socio-economic cleavages. The overall Canadian federal state has become a sprawling diffuse assemblage of uncoordinated power and policies, while the society with which it interacts is increasingly plural, fragmented, and multiple in its allegiances and identities. The more we relate to one another through the state, the more divided we seem to become. Somewhat paradoxically, however, the web of state–society interdependencies is in one way stabilizing, for it locks state and society in countless discrete overlapping linkages; this makes it necessary for us to rethink the meaning of societal integration and of community.
>
> We must learn to think in terms of politicized societies caught in webs of interdependencies with the state, and we must think of the latter as an embedded state tied down by multiple linkages with society, which restrains manoeuverability.
>
> (1995: 33)

Defining regions

In reality, each of the provinces and states in Atlantic Canada and New England have different economic needs and historical experiences that are unique and complicate the search for common approaches. Newfoundland is a province that did not join Canada until 1949 and the provincial society has always been split between those who support integration with other industrial societies and those who do not. New Brunswick is a province with a French population of nearly 40 per cent and it experienced a modern revolution in the 1960s. Nova Scotia is known for its conservative culture and wealth, but its lack of bureaucratic traditions and internal territorial divisions have worked against the integration cause. Prince Edward Island is a small island with a population of only 120,000 and strong rural roots. The Atlantic provinces do not have the industrial, urban traditions found in New England and each of these provinces have relied upon a different mix of resource industries and interregional transfers for sustenance.

Maine also has strong rural traditions and when examining the regional integration question we need to consider that in its past it broke away from the more urban and industrial Massachusetts. Massachusetts is an economic powerhouse. This state is known for its manufacturing, research and new technologies. Connecticut is closely linked with New York City and much of this is due to the prominene of financial services in its economy. Vermont is known for its independent spirit, progressive environmental policies and the fact that it is the most rural state in America. New Hampshire is a state that has no income tax or sales tax and a reputation for self-reliance. Rhode Island is urban and industrial. These different economic traditions are reinforced by the institutional structures and cultures of each province and state.

There are various ways of defining regions and approaching economic problems and challenges. Janine Brodie has reviewed some of them. The formal approach is informed by the assumption that underdevelopment is caused by 'internal factors', such as geography or lack of entrepreneurial culture. On the other hand, the 'relational perspective' assumes that underdevelopment comes about when local people lose control over the development process to outsiders. It merges well with the idea of the embedded state. As illustrated by Brodie, 'It is an explicitly political approach to the study of regionalism' (1990: 18), and it highlights the interplay between various historical forces and the need to view one region in relation to others. According to Brodie, 'regions are the products of historical experience, human organization, and social organization. From a historical perspective, regions are, in a very real sense, political creations – the products of social alliances and conflicts' (1990: 17). According to this viewpoint, opening up boundaries to more powerful outside forces and relying upon their ideas and techniques in order to solve 'internal problems' may not be the best strategy. At a very basic level, region implies a sense of community, and a willingness to co-operate and work together on common projects – rather than at cross-purposes. Bringing this about is never easy, especially when there are different and competing cultural and institutional traditions involved and different perspectives on the benefits of integration and who the winners and losers are likely to be. It is only logical that embedded national and federal traditions would complicate the search for regional solutions in a continental era and we need to consider these differences.

The evidence from the past struggles over integration is consistent with Brodie's relational perspective. Premiers in Atlantic Canada have naturally tended to be suspicious of outsiders who have no understanding or appreciation of previous bad experiences with integrative policies or local culture. Even though these political actors have always been dependent on federal transfers, these monies have been used to defend provincial interests rather than to promote change and integration in the region. The biggest obstacle facing pro-integrationists has always been the fact that the policy process has always been dominated by political leaders with different agendas who play for different audiences and receive their information from public servants who are motivated by their own institutional self-interests. In a competitive federal system where political decision-making takes place between governments, such an approach is not well suited for co-ordinating policies across provincial boundaries. Even though the federal government would prefer the Atlantic provinces to co-operate more, it has been unwilling to impose a solution. Separate provincial state institutions, party systems, different inherited cultures and policy traditions have all worked against movements seeking fundamental changes. Another complicating factor is the fact that provinces own and control natural resources and any call to undermine the old resource-based economy and replace it with a knowledge-based one represents an attack not only on local cultures, but on the power and authority of the government. Finally, the insularity of intergovernmental arenas and the considerable political resources made available to the premiers as a result of federal redistributive traditions, have ensured that these political leaders have been well positioned to defend their territorial and jurisdictional interests. This will probably continue as long as federal transfers continue to support independent state-building traditions.

Central to this discourse and contestation over the need for change is the question of whether political actors in federal systems have any choice but to accept the new economic logic of the times as determined by new economic forces. Or, does federalism provide political actors with the capacity to set their own priorities and defend their territorial and jurisdictional interests? Regionalists have focused much of their energy on discussing the economic logic of reorienting Canadian politics toward a regional framework but we also need to recognize that federalism matters because it creates its own logic. It would be a good time to consider the various cultural and institutional constraints that have always worked against the regional idea in Atlantic Canada. In New England, existing federal state structures and traditions pose other problems for regionalists. This chapter assumes that the extent to which external pressures will result in fundamental change will depend, in part, on the strength or weakness of current federal institutions and practices. With this in mind, emphasis will be placed on understanding how different embedded federal ideas, interests and institutional practices have always complicated the parallel building of regions in New England and Atlantic Canada, and the even more ambitious idea of erecting a continental mega-region.

Whether in debates over modernization or globalization, neo-classical economists have tended to downplay the value of protecting cultural and federal traditions in underdeveloped regions and subsidizing unproductive economic activities. On the other side of this debate, critics of integration have tended to be more sceptical about the merits of abandoning redistributive national policies that deal with equity issues and make it possible to defend local community control over the economic development process, while preserving unique cultural, economic and institutional traditions. In Canada, these opponents of integration have tended to come from the left or from poor provinces. Since provincial governments in poor provinces rely more upon federal transfers and old resource-based economies for their economic survival, there is a natural reluctance to abandon traditional cultures and old models of territorial management. For the most part, pro-integrationists have tended to focus on understanding the environmental context as opposed to understanding the challenges associated with changing patterns of state–society relations and embedded social and political practices. As a result, their forecasts about the inevitability of political change have never proven to be very accurate.

In Canada, the rules of the political game and the closed nature of policy-making institutions have always made it possible for provincial politicians and bureaucratic actors to resist change. From the start, federalism was designed to be self-perpetuating and there have been few opportunities for outsiders to alter the terms of the discourse and mobilize new coalitions in support of the regional cause. Whether the stalemate over regional integration continues or not in the future will depend to a great extent on the political resources made available to those who feel threatened by market solutions and prefer the idea of provincialism and the need to preserve provincial identities, rooted in historical experience and cultural traditions. It is clear then that as long as federal traditions survive in Canada and premiers have the incentive and resources required to defend the status quo, there will be challenges for those involved in the political struggle for regionalization.

New versus old forces

Critics of the current system of national and subnational institutions in Canada believe that with the realities of continentalism and economic restructuring, old ideas and institutions will become less relevant and will need to be replaced. Thomas Courchene, a well-known mainstream economist, Preston Manning, leader of the official opposition in the House of Commons, and Doug Young, a former right-wing federal transport minister, among others, have criticized old federal redistributive practices in Canada in favour of building transborder regions that better reflect the economic realities of the times, but threaten the capacity of the smaller provinces to defend their cultures and economies against outside forces. Regionalists suggest that change is both necessary and inevitable if we are to come to grips with new economic problems and challenges.[2] Their preference for decentralization and a new neo-liberal policy paradigm is naturally more popular in the United States and richer provinces that are more self-reliant and do not rely very much on federal largesse for sustenance or protection. Those inspired by the idea of 'glocalization'

(Courchene and Telmer 1997: 271) hold that we are in the midst of a paradigm shift when the nation-state is losing power and subnational political activity and regional confederations consisting of provinces and states across national borders are on the rise (Duchacek 1986; Duchacek et al. 1988; Michelmann and Soldatus 1990; Brown and Fry 1993; Hooghe and Marks 1996; Gress 1996; Deeg 1996).

The idea of devolving power to the regions, reducing the power of Ottawa and the Atlantic provinces is also popular in Quebec, British Columbia, and Alberta, albeit for different reasons. British Columbia and Alberta have never been strong supporters of redistributing wealth along the east–west axis or relying upon national policies to deal with pressing economic development problems in poor provinces. These wealthy provinces do not benefit much from east–west oriented policies and have much to gain from trade liberalization. Quebec is a have-not province but it sees economic restructuring and reducing national powers as an opportunity to gain more autonomy. This willingness to sacrifice national redistributive policies for policy independence has made it more difficult for supporters of Canadian sovereignty and the east–west axis. In Ontario, the rise of the Harris government in the 1990s and the building of a new neo-liberal political movement has added further to the regional integrationist cause. Indeed, to appreciate fully the contemporary push for political restructuring, it is important to recognize that prior to 1957, Ontario governments opposed equalization and regional development subsidies for poor provinces. It is also important to note that equalization and regional programmes first emerged in 1957. In the 1990s, the debate over regional integration provided a new context for the rise of old ideological debates between territorial competitors.

Despite the efforts of these powerful forces of change who are committed to political and economic restructuring, we also need to recognize and take into account the arguments and capacities of those who oppose such changes. For the most part the regional integration debate in Canada has been an intergovernmental affair. Aside from the powerful business interests who are committed to reducing the force of state regulation, subsidies and political boundaries, discussions and debates over the pros and cons of the regional idea have been dominated by political actors and a select group of economists with limited political resources. As one would expect, such a context has ensured that territorial politics has remained a central focus.

Since both the American and Canadian federal systems have created problems for regional movements in the past, it would be useful to explore the internal factors that have worked against integration and to speculate on whether the current drive for regional integration is likely to be any more successful. Even though the focus of regionalists today is globalization rather than modernization, in various respects this is an old debate, and we should not lose sight of the fact that federalism, whether in Canada or the

United States, was designed to defend territorial communities against external forces. Since we can learn a great deal from past struggles over regional integration, this chapter will briefly review the historical struggle over regional integration to make the case that there are a number of built-in cultural and institutional constraints working against the regional idea in both New England and Atlantic Canada.

Given the fact that this debate has tended to be pushed by supporters of neo-liberalism and the idea that powerful external forces outside our control do and should determine policy choices, greater emphasis will be placed in this article on understanding the Atlantic Canadian perspective and the extent to which federalism and state capacity still matter and make it possible to defend local cultures and institutions against external threats. Clearly, external factors and changes in the international political economy are important for understanding new discourses, problems and political practices. On the other hand, we also need to recognize that inherited federal society–state traditions influence the way governments respond to external economic pressures. Indeed, homogenization is often seen as a threat to distinct societies, whether at the national or subnational level. Because it is a system designed to balance opposite forces, federalism ensures that change does not come easily and that territorial identities and boundaries are well defended against external forces.

Differences between American and Canadian federalism

A major obstacle to Atlantic/New England integration involves the very different cultural, institutional, historical and policy traditions of Canadian and US federalism. Federalism comes in different varieties and shapes and as Davis points out, 'there is often more in common between some federal and non-federal constitutions than between two or more federal constitutions: for example, in the choice between presidential and parliamentary executives, or between elected and appointed upper chambers' (1978: 141–2).

The Canadian federal system is an example of 'interstate federalism', and because of the traditions and practices of a cabinet-parliamentary system, power is heavily concentrated in the hands of the political executive and decisions tend to be reached 'between governments' as opposed to 'within' national institutions. Premiers dominate their legislatures in a way that allows them an opportunity to speak for their communities with the confidence and knowledge that they are in control of the public agenda. Comparable to international systems of decision-making, major decisions tend to be resolved at competitive intergovernmental bargaining sessions that normally take place outside of the public view. In such an environment, getting a political consensus among territorial competitors is never easy, and because of equalization even poor provinces have the political resources required to defend their interests and cultures against outside attacks. When we take into account that the regional idea represents an attack on province-building traditions that have been subsidized by Ottawa, it is little wonder that the combination of federalism and cabinet-parliamentary traditions have impeded progress. In sum, different provinces are shaped by different historical forces and structures, and a lack of common objectives, cultures and institutions has made it difficult to achieve a consensus on the merits of integration, whether at the national, regional or continental level.

Cairns states that 'New governments inherit massive program commitments put in place by predecessors. These programs are enmeshed in bureaucracies; they are supported by clientele expectations: they are protected by incremental processes of policy-making' (1986: 57). Such inherited patterns of state–society relations restrict the manoeuvrability of the governments involved, even when external circumstances change. Complicating matters further, as shown by Hartz (1964) and Horowitz (1966), Canadians are more collectivist in their orientations than Americans, and these inherited traditions and structures naturally influence the way the Atlantic premiers react to calls to change Canada's redistributive policy traditions. The main impetus for change in Canada at either level of government has been the state, not society.

In the United States, institutional and societal frameworks are very different. America is a country that has always placed greater value on market-oriented solutions and self-reliance. The market ethos is well embedded and the traditions of state intervention are weak. As stated by Robertson and Judd, 'Governments in the United States do less to reduce the risks and to rectify the inequalities that result from market capitalism because they raise less revenues, spend less money, and impose fewer restrictions on the uses of property than do comparable nations' (1989: 1). Americans have never used the state to deal with equity issues in the way that Canadians have.

There are other important differences between Canada and the United States. In the United States, an 'intrastate' system of federalism has emerged (Gibbins 1982). The American political system features a powerful legislative branch that is not dominated or fused with the executive branch, an integrated national-state party system, and nationally based policy communities. In the 'nation-centred' (Walker 1985: 2) US federal system, centripetal forces are more salient and state governments have less power than their provincial counterparts. Moreover, because governors do not control their legislatures and cannot represent their communities in the way premiers do, the executive-dominated form of federalism found in Canada has not emerged in the United States to the same extent.

There are other important differences as well. In the United States a system that separates power among the three branches of government and features an undisciplined party system ensures that local and regional issues are resolved 'within' Congress, rather than in closed intergovernmental bargaining sessions. State governments operating in such a context have had little choice but to use the same tactics employed by other pressure groups in Washington D.C. In the past decade or so, this 'intergovernmental lobby' has been housed in the 'Hall of States'.[3] The state and national governments are not co-equal political competitors and regional concerns tend to be dealt with 'within' national institutions. As a result, mobilizing regional interests at the subnational level has never been easy.

The regional idea

From the 1950s until the 1970s, the regional idea was associated with strengthening regional economies, reducing intergovernmental competition in disadvantaged areas, and solving the problem of regional disparity through the building of regional communities. It was a time when the nation-state was less constrained and Keynesianism remained popular. It was also a time when modernization theorists felt that given changing economic conditions the attrition of central power was inevitable (Simeon and Robinson 1990). The original intent of the regional idea was to enhance intergovernmental co-operation and policy harmonization. Yet, despite various attempts to promote effective integration in Atlantic Canada, little changed over the years. Province-building remained a powerful force and the effort to reinvent Atlantic Canada based on modernization theory never worked in practice, in part because the premiers were in a position to defend their territorial communities against outside attacks. Despite new economic forces, Canada remained a highly decentralized federal system.

The United States federal experience was different. Yet, even though modernization contributed to the power of Congress, regionalism remained a marginal force. During this time, integration at the regional level never went very far in either New England or Atlantic Canada, albeit for different reasons. History clearly shows that cross-border, transnational experiments between the Eastern provinces and New England states have not accomplished very much either.

Despite these failures, there seems to be growing interest these days (especially among Canadian neo-liberal thinkers in rich provinces) for strengthening regional province–state interactions, building borderlands (McKinsey and Konrad 1990),[4] or region states in North America. Guided by the premise that external socio-economic forces determine issues and how governments respond, various critics have argued that new socio-economic realities will eventually reinforce and nurture region-building in North America – just as regionalism and cross-border co-operation is increasing in Europe (Hooghe and Marks 1996; Gress 1996; Loughlin 1996).

In the past, such predictions about the inevitability of change in one direction have not proven to be very accurate, in part because, as Cairns observed, federalism is designed to ensure that opposite state–societal forces are constantly balanced and preserved. If we have learned anything in Canadian politics, it is that we should never underestimate the capacity of state actors to defend their territorial and jurisdictional interests against outside forces and trends. Federalism has always mattered because it provides a way for provincial state actors who disagreed with new policy innovations to defend their interests and cultures against outside influences or ideas. If we think about the regional issue from the perspective of state-centred theory at least (Nordlinger 1981), it is perhaps too early to assume that new socio-economic forces will necessarily result in the building of stronger links among provinces and states. This can be demonstrated by examining previous struggles over the regional integration question in New England (Vermont, New Hampshire, Maine, Massachusetts, Rhode Island, Connecticut) and Atlantic Canada (Newfoundland, New Brunswick, Nova Scotia and Prince Edward Island).[5] Despite the strong views of those who believe in the cause of regionalism, the basic design of federalism has created a number of institutional and cultural challenges that have complicated the task of strengthening cross-border regional processes in both Atlantic Canada and New England.

Prospects for the regional option?

The push for cross-border co-operation, viewed from one perspective, threatens existing national and subnational structures and cultures; or viewed from another, it provides a more logical way to deal with the new realities of economic interdependence and market competition in a modern, global age. The movement poses a threat to the traditions of federalism because it challenges the idea that existing communities should be preserved. If critics are right about continental and regional forces replacing redistributive, national ones, at some point, small poor provinces will have little choice but to accept the inevitable. Under these circumstances, regional integration may become a reality – and the moral and political traditions of Canadian federalism will be gone. The moral foundations of Canadian federalism and the goal of making it possible for provincial communities to rely upon their own cultural and institutional traditions to define and resolve problems could be lost in an era of homogenization and market-inspired public policies. In the future, much will depend on the power and influence of redistributive policies and the political resources made available for maintaining a balance between the forces of continentalism, nationalism and provincialism.

Yet, despite the Cascadia initiative in the Far West, Courchene's call for making Ontario a 'North American Region State', Preston Manning's push for Atlantic/New England integration, and the popularity of the regional discourse elsewhere, there are still a number of institutional and cultural obstacles standing in the way of transborder regionalism. And these obstacles will remain as long as current Canadian federal practices survive intact.

Clearly, in the past, Canada did not experience the trend toward centralization predicted by various academics, and this was influenced, in part, by the actions of the premiers themselves. As long as Canada remains united, it would appear that the Atlantic premiers will have the incentive and resources necessary to defend themselves against attacks from outside territorial and ideological competitors. Indeed, given recent attempts on the part of the federal government to allocate fiscal transfers for social programmes on a per capita basis while at the same time increasing equalization payments to poor provinces, Ottawa has effectively strengthened province-building in Atlantic Canada while undermining the region idea in both Ontario and the Far West (*The Globe and Mail*, February 17, 18, 19, 20, 22, 1999; *St John's Evening Telegram*, February 18, 19, 1999). It is no coincidence that despite globalization, a number of disagreements over lotteries, off-shore development, toll roads, and other issues are now threatening the future of the regional partnership. The Maritime/Atlantic Premiers have not met in a year (despite a 25-year tradition of meeting four times a year) and there are signs that a number of regional projects are being abandoned at the same time as outsiders are pushing the regional idea onto the public agenda (*St John's Evening Telegram*, March 10, 16, May 29, 1999). History seems to be repeating itself.

Since federalism is about maintaining a balance between opposite forces, it is perhaps too early to write off the federal government and province-building just yet. With billions of dollars in surplus to redistribute, Ottawa is well positioned to ensure that new forces are balanced and the country survives. Clearly, with increases in unconditional equalization payments in recent federal budgets, the poor provinces are well positioned to defend their territorial and jurisdictional interests (*St John's Evening Telegram*, March, 1999). In light of the success of the Liberals' popularity, even the Reform Party has decided it is time to soften its hard-edged, market approach (*The Globe and Mail*, February 17, 18, 19, 20, 22, 1999).

We need to recognize that integration is influenced by such things as compatibility of values, institutions, and the self-interests of the political actors involved – and not just by external economic considerations or trends. Different federal practices and institutions make it difficult to establish new partnerships involving provinces and states. Another complication is that it is too early to assume that Canada has fully embraced the neo-liberal model often pushed by regionalists and continentalists. Finally, it would be a mistake to underestimate the future of the nation-state and the extent to which Ottawa does benefit from having small, have-not provinces around.

New England regionalism

To understand the challenge of building new regions in this part of North America, we must look to the past to understand the long-standing institutional and cultural constraints that have always worked against regional co-operation. Regionalism and the idea of establishing new regional mechanisms 'between the state and nation' (Derthick 1974) has enjoyed a long history in the United States, but this model has never been strong enough to reverse the competitive tendencies among the New England states, nor each state's tradition of independence and individualism. These early policy debates influenced public policy discussions in Atlantic Canada later on (Sharkansky 1970; Derthick 1974; Pierce 1976; Price 1982; Branch 1988; Spectrum 1994). In 1925 the New England Council was launched by the New England business community and the governors (Wheeler 1952). The principal objective of the new organization was to sustain economic growth and to reverse the movement of manufacturing industries south. This lobby organization, which promotes and defends large and small businesses in the nation's capital, became a powerful defender of New England interests in Congress. In 1937 the New England Governors' Conference was first established and its objective was to coordinate regional development policies among the New England states. Until the 1960s, the New England Council provided staff support for this organization. From the start, the regional idea was associated with business and other supporters of the market model.

Despite 'considerable similarities in government structures – similarities not shared in general with the rest of the forty-nine states' (Lockard 1959: 4), there have always been various political, social, economic and ideological differences that have posed a challenge for those committed to the regional cause. Internal urban–rural splits between states like Massachusetts and Rhode Island and Vermont and Maine have made it difficult to agree on priorities. Ideological differences between the states have created other problems. For instance, the fact that New Hampshire has no income tax or sales tax is a problem for anyone seeking a common rate of regional taxation or seeking support for a new regional public policy. The power of Boston and the desire of the other states not to be marginalized has posed yet another challenge for regionalists. No region is a homogenous governmental, social or economic entity; and within New England there are different physical geographical, cultural, economic and political forces that complicate the search for common solutions (Pierce 1976; Daniels 1988; Bradshaw 1988; Palmer et al. 1992). This rather limited partnership was not designed to mobilize other kinds of interests, besides business, and this hurt the movement. On the other hand, New England regionalism is less controversial than Atlantic regionalism and this has much to do with history coupled with the market values that transcend state borders.

In the past, every campaign seeking greater co-operation among the New England states through policy harmonization and planning occurred because of the threat posed by the problem of 'sweeping employment and population growth away from the older metropolitan centers of the Northeast and North Central to the newer growth poles of the South and West' (Sternlieb and Hughes 1978: 7–8). But while the regional approach has offered a logical way to fight national policies and other forces that threatened the region, the governors operate in a context where there is little incentive or opportunity to reinforce common community linkages and values. US politics is designed to deal with national and local issues, not regional ones.

It has never been easy for governors to achieve very much on a regional basis when they have little influence over budgetary matters or the legislative process. Since regional and local issues are usually addressed in Washington, governors have never felt the need to put much time or effort into regional planning. Simply put, the American federal system was not designed to reinforce regional approaches to problem-solving. Regionalism in Canada is normally associated with executive federalism where equals square off for battle; in the United States regionalism involves lobbying in Congress. Within such a context, there has been little incentive or opportunity to construct a coalition behind a new regional vision.

Despite this, the regional idea became popular in the 1960s and 1970s, not only within New England, but throughout the United States. The idea attracted more attention in the early 1960s when President Kennedy put in place a new federal--state partnership called the Appalachian Commission to deal with the disparity problems of the Appalachian states (Derthick 1974; Bradshaw 1992; *JARC* 1995).

The new experiment provided an incentive to pressure for regional projects in other jurisdictions. As a consequence of this lobbying activity, the New England Regional Commission was established in 1965 along with other 'Title V' Commissions (Derthick 1974: ch 5). These new regional structures never had access to the resources made available to Appalachia, but they did help promote the regional cause. In New England for example, these funds provided staff support for the New England Governors' Conference.

The results of this new intergovernmental experiment have been mixed. Given the lack of political incentives and the institutional context, the governors have never spent much time worrying about regional issues. Nor did the fact that a federal co-chairman had veto power help the regional cause very much. Finally, the focus on research and planning rather than 'action plans' also provided a target for critics and another reason for the governors not to work together (*Boston Globe*, October 8, 10, 1972).[6] Yet, despite structural difficulties and a variety of other problems, there have been benefits associated with governors meeting to discuss common problems.

With the rise of the New England Congressional Caucus in 1972, regional lobbying efforts in the Congress were further strengthened. These new resources made it possible to hire new people and there is little question that these changes made it much easier to promote and defend New England's interests in Congress. On the other hand, this initiative further reinforced the pattern of dealing with regional issues in Congress as opposed to governors' meetings.

By the early 1980s, it was the era of Reagan's 'new federalism'. The Regional Commission, River Basins Commission, Congressional Caucus, and other regional organizations were eliminated. Only the Appalachian Commission survived. Regionalism had suffered yet another setback. Even though interstate co-operation was regarded as a good idea, there were even fewer political resources and incentives to mobilize regional interests and issues. Local and national priorities came first and states were encouraged to compete, not co-operate during the Reagan years.

Since Reagan's 'new federalism', the New England governors have carried on their activities – despite declining resources and incentives for promoting closer interstate ties. The New England Governors' Conference, in order to survive, was forced to reinvent itself. It became a non-profit, tax-exempt corporation in 1981. In the 1990s, even though the cause of regional cooperation is far from dead, it is not a significant movement either. The fact that the organization has continued, despite setbacks, indicates that the governors recognize that there are benefits associated with meeting and discussing common problems. The New England regional movement suffered another setback in 1991 when support staff for the Governors' Conference was significantly downsized. This was the result of the combination of a severe economic downturn and a growing debt problem. To complicate matters, globalization, the devolution revolution, competition over welfare downsizing, and other trends have increased competitive tendencies among the states. The cutting of the Advisory Commission on Intergovernmental Relations in 1996 provided yet another setback for the regional cause, since this organization was designed, in part, to encourage regional co-operation and to analyse intergovernmental issues and trends (McDowell 1997). All of this has added to the challenge of regional co-operation in New England in the 1990s. On the other hand, the re-establishment of the New England Congressional Caucus in this decade strengthened regional lobbying efforts in Washington.

Atlantic regionalism

It has never been easy getting a consensus on the regional idea in Atlantic Canada. Because the call for regional integration is normally associated with American-based market-oriented values, the regional idea has always been perceived as a threat to the social, cultural and political traditions of small have-not provinces, and the redistributive, federal traditions of Canada.[7] As a result, Atlantic Canadians have naturally tended to be more cautious when it comes to this issue. When we consider the competitive nature of Canadian federalism coupled with the stronger traditions of state intervention at both levels of government, it is little wonder that progress has been slow. One consequence of having the institutional structure organized on a competitive provincial basis is there are built-in incentives to ensure that the territorial and jurisdictional concerns of the provinces are well defended against outside forces.

As discussed, premiers operate in different contexts and they tend to be most concerned with the maintenance of the territorially based community they have inherited and making sure that their citizens' needs are well defended against outside threats. Lack of common regional institutions and experiences have further complicated the search for the regional cause. And because past commitments to defend and promote provincial interests and cultures against outside interests have become deeply embedded within the political landscape, each premier's manoeuvrability is restricted by past decisions and media expectations that new leaders will battle with outside territorial and ideological competitors for advantage. Under these circumstances, it is obvious that premiers would not be inclined to use their political capital to forge co-operative strategies that threatened their territorial and jurisdictional interests.

Things change yet they remain the same. In the past, province-builders survived and even flourished when integration and centralization were gaining momentum in places like the United States and Europe. As illustrated by Cairns:

> We have long known that institutions represent mobilization of bias, that states are historical products whose evolution is subtly channeled by incentives and disincentives of their institutional arrangements, arrangements that are usually peculiarly resistant to change. Institutional congealment and the mobilization of bias to which it contributes are supplemented by the congealment of past policies, which, deeply entangled with society, require Herculean efforts for modification.
>
> (Cairns 1986: 89)

Provincialism has always survived because the premiers have had the incentive, resources, and capacity to resist outside pressures for change.

Another complicating factor is that the regional agenda has tended to be pushed by outsiders who see Atlantic Canada's underdevelopment problem as an 'internal problem' caused by lack of talent or initiative. The tendency to blame the victims of underdevelopment for their own problems has made it difficult for premiers to stand by and simply allow outsiders to impose their own definition of the underdevelopment problem. As one would expect, it has never been easy for premiers to know the best way to respond to these ideologically inspired attacks, and even if there are benefits to regional co-operation, few premiers want to be seen as incapable of defending the provincial community against outside attacks. The fact that there are different perspectives on whether the problems of under-development in Atlantic Canada are the result of 'internal factors' or a product of previous imposed national solutions has created a number of problems for the premiers involved.[8] These outside attacks have also strengthened provincial identities, especially in Newfoundland where there has been a long tradition of being exploited by outside interests. The recent collapse of the cod fishery, ongoing battles over hydro power with Quebec, and recent cuts in federal social spending have all helped reinforce the need to maintain provincial control over the economy.

The response of the premiers to the regional integration question has varied over the years. In the past, the provinces of Newfoundland and Prince Edward Island have been the most suspicious of outside calls for restructuring based on the integrated, industrial model (Tomblin 1995). Being islands and dependent on their rural economies, and possessing distinct cultures, it makes sense that they would be more suspicious of the regional idea. New Brunswick has tended to be more open to the regional idea and restructuring generally, while Nova Scotia, which is a richer province, but more conservative and internally divided, has also gone out of its way to undermine the regional project. As a result, little has been accomplished over the years.

The struggle over regional integration goes back decades, and while, in the past, the focus was modernization rather than globalization, there have been various campaigns to bring about fundamental change (Tomblin 1995). In the early 1950s, the premiers who were forced to deal with the entry of Newfoundland into the confederation (and feeling pressured by business leaders, Ottawa, richer provinces and the New England regional model) met to discuss ways to work together in solving common problems. In 1953 the premiers and business representatives met to consider the merits of regional planning and they launched the Atlantic Provinces Economic Council (APEC) which was based on the New England Council model. Ottawa used a carrot and stick to push for regional co-operation. It was a time when economists and outside political interests felt it was time to build new cross-border connections within Atlantic Canada, as well as new linkages with New England (Tomblin 1995: 80–1). Faced with these challenges to their territorial and jurisdictional interests, it is little wonder that the premiers employed the defensive strategy they did. In the early 1960s, Newfoundland premier Joey Smallwood was experiencing political problems in his efforts to resettle rural communities and restructure the Newfoundland economy based on the industrial model. This and his battle with Ottawa over future federal financing resulted in the decision to pull out of the regional meetings entirely. The idea of Atlantica was dead but Maritime integration was not.

In the early 1970s, the idea of Maritime union was pushed firmly onto the public agenda and there were outside calls for changing the culture and institutional processes, and for building a political coalition in support of a new region. Faced with calls for transfer payment reductions and the national unity problem, the premiers responded by establishing a study on Maritime union. Even though the premiers felt compelled to react, they also knew that as long as they had unilateral powers, the status quo could not be changed without their approval and there would be limited institutional opportunities for mobilizing support for a new super-province. As long as federalism survived, the embedded institutional biases of the system made it difficult for experts, outside governments and interest groups to bring about fundamental change.

The Maritime Study advocated full political union and the authors were inspired by the European integration experiment. Consequently, it was argued that political change would not be possible unless old provincial structures were replaced with a Commission, a Joint Assembly, and Council of Maritime Premiers.

Even though '84% of the English-speaking Maritimers up to 45 years of age were favourably disposed to a full Maritime Union' (Jenkins 1976), the provinces of Nova Scotia and Prince Edward Island resisted the calls for a Commission and regional parliament. The Council was accepted because the premiers had nothing to lose. Organized around the principle of unanimity, and with all discussions taking place behind closed doors, the premiers were always well positioned to defend provincialism from outside attacks. Ironically, the Council of Maritime Premiers was designed first of all to strengthen powers of the premiers, and only then to provide an opportunity for the premiers to meet and discuss common problems. Federalism mattered since it provided both the resources and incentive for the premiers to gain control over the regional project.

The history of the Council of Maritime Premiers has been one in which premiers have defended themselves against outside territorial and ideological attacks and they have done so by exploiting their unilateral powers to ensure any regional co-operative efforts 'reflect and represent the integrity of the respective provinces' (Council of Maritime Premiers Annual Report 1976). Along the way, a number of agencies have been established to deal with things like education, municipal training, harness racing, and land registration (Council of Maritime Premiers Annual Report 1995–6). While there have been benefits to working together, this regional organization has tended to avoid issues that are controversial or threaten the territorial and jurisdictional interests of the premiers. The tendency has been to work together on narrowly technical and non-controversial issues, or finding ways to ensure that province-building survives.

Since the 1970s, some things have changed, for example Newfoundland came back into the regional fold in the 1990s' with the creation of the Atlantic Premiers' conference, but province-building has remained stronger than ever. Every few years there are new calls from outsiders for new regional approaches and Atlantic integration. These are often in response to the threat of Quebec independence, the fiscal imperative, populism in the Far West, or discussions about the new realities of modernization or globalization. History shows that controversial issues that go to the heart of province-building (such as the ongoing jurisdictional dispute between Nova

Scotia and Newfoundland over offshore oil and gas development) have not been resolved in this weak regional system. Interprovincial co-operation works best when the premiers feel threatened by outside forces and there is a benefit to confronting them in a unified way. In the future, the premiers will probably continue to adopt a strategy of conservative defiance – at least as long as federal traditions continue and they have the resources necessary to defend their communities against outside threats.

Prospects for north–south partnerships?

Imagine the advantages of New England and Atlantic Canada working together to defend and promote their common interests. While New England lacks natural resources, the Atlantic region would benefit by having access to capital and a market for her hydro power, natural gas and other resources. Given the combination of the internationalization of the North American economic system and the fiscal crisis of the welfare state, as pointed out by critics, it seems reasonable that there would be some advantages in working together. And with the number of close social and historical connections in this international region, one would think this could be used for bringing the territorial communities together (Brookes 1976; Conrad 1989; Jamelle 1991; Squires 1991). As argued by Wiseman, New England has had a profound impact on the political cultures of the Atlantic provinces (1996: 40).

In the context of a changing North America, where Ottawa is said to be losing power and Quebec, Alberta, British Columbia and even Ontario seem to be more open to abandoning old traditions and building transborder regional co-operative regimes, it seems that the strong central vision of Canada is gradually being replaced with a more market-oriented, decentralized one. Atlantic Canada is not driving this new agenda but it will probably be the biggest loser if federal transfers continue to decline, especially since provincial services are heavily subsidized by these transfers. On the other hand, future efforts to harmonize policies are further complicated by the fact that cross-border regionalism is perceived as a threat, and the premiers have had some experience dealing with this issue. As long as Canadian federalism survives and premiers have access to generous equalization benefits there will be little incentive for the premiers to change their approach. Regional integration will remain a non-starter as long as the premiers have the capacity and autonomy required to defend their interests against external forces that are perceived as threatening.

The struggle over the regional question in this part of North America is further complicated by cultural and institutional differences between the American and Canadian forms of federalism. Nor has it helped that there has been little attention focused on bridging these cultural or institutional differences, despite the fact that regionalism as an ideology and force has been around for awhile. The sellers of integration need to understand that whenever a solution is perceived as a threat by some of the partners involved, getting a consensus is going to be very difficult. From this perspective, we can learn much from the European integration experiment where there have been attempts to strike a balance between equity and efficiency considerations and to deal with cultural issues and not just economic ones (Hooghe and Marks 1996; Gress 1996; Loughlin 1996). Smaller, less developed countries in Europe are more open to experimenting in new partnerships because they do not feel as threatened by the prospects of integration. Proponents of regional integration need to adopt a better marketing strategy if they want to have more impact on the North American continent and succeed in mobilizing support for a new approach to problem-solving.

Unfortunately, the history of the New England Governors and Eastern Premiers Conference provides little evidence of such activity. To date, little focus has ever been placed on bridging differences or dealing with the different federal principles and traditions that have complicated regional decision-making. Since 1973, the governors and premiers have met various times to discuss energy, transportation, environmental initiatives, and other issues. There have been benefits associated with having premiers and governors meet, but little has been achieved in public policy terms. Without common regional institutions, shared experiences or regional identities to build upon, the premiers and governors have not had much success in reinforcing common approaches to problem-solving.[9]

This multi-state regional confederation rarely attracts much public or media attention, but given the extent to which the organization deals with highly technical issues, this is not surprising (New England and Eastern Canadian Secretariats 1988). In Canada, the tradition of meeting behind closed doors has not helped the regional cause very much – but open meetings in the United States have not generated much attention either. Canadian–US relations tend to attract little interest south of the border at the best of times.

To be sure, from the beginning it has been a challenge advancing the interests of so many jurisdictions and promoting co-operation between such different public and private sector communities. Nor has it helped that while some of the Atlantic premiers have been reluctant to give up power, various governors have failed to put much effort into the project.[10] All of this has hurt the transborder cause in a significant way.

It is also clear that the various differences between the states and provinces in their political cultures, institutions, structures of public administration, and interest group politics have further hampered efforts at resolving common problems (Harrigan 1994; Council of State Governments 1995; Dyck 1996).

Lubin states that,

> States and provinces have distinctive structures, constitutional jurisdictions and political cultures that can substantially complicate the search

for areas of common transborder initiatives. The mere fact that states operate with bicameral legislatures combined with separation of legislative from executive powers, as distinguished from unicameral Westminister model of provinces, does circumscribe the range of possible 'hands-across-the-border'collaborative efforts as well as the depth of what can be accomplished. Further complicating the task of the NEG/ECP is the fact that each government within the two neighboring federations constitutes a combination of distinctive political interests in relation to all other sister states and provinces as well.

(1993: 146)

There are various obstacles standing in the way of transborder regionalism in this part of the continent, and key differences between the presidential and parliamentary forms of government (coupled with the incompatible values and self-interests of the actors involved) have made it difficult to reinforce transgovernmental policy co-ordination and coalition-building between state and provincial governments. In Canada, since executive power is concentrated the premiers have more control over the policy process than governors do. Premiers have more control over the public purse, and as a result they can commit to long-term projects knowing that they will be implemented. Governors cannot make such assurances since they do not dominate the legislature or the budgetary process in the same way. It also needs to be highlighted that 'Premiers have real political and legal power, which they regularly utilize in federal-provincial negotiations' (Lubin 1993: 146). They use this power to defend and promote their territorial and jurisdictional interests. Governors, on the other hand, do not enjoy this status and they have no choice but to compete with state representatives and other interests in a complex bicameral Congressional system. These activities take away time and resources that are not available for regional planning. Under these circumstances, there is little incentive for mobilizing or building international regional communities.

Dissimilarities among provinces and states in their respective executive councils or cabinets further complicate the regional process. Another problem involves the different backgrounds of the actors involved and the way they approach problems. In Canada, premiers tend to rely upon the bureaucracy for information and these officials have their own institutional traditions and self-interests to protect. Senior state officials are politically appointed south of the border and tend to come and go very quickly. Clearly, this complicates planning and community-building efforts. Finally, the US practice of appointing representatives of the corporate sector to serve on sectoral committees adds yet another dimension to the clash between public versus private cultures. As one would except, having such different people involved in the process adds to the challenge of integration.

In terms of process, the tradition has been for the New Governors and Eastern Premiers to meet in June and they normally move back and forth between the two countries every year. The meetings are co-chaired by a premier and governor, and since 1979 secretariats in Halifax and Boston have played an important role in organizing these meetings. Whenever common policies have been accepted, special intergovernmental structures called sectoral committees have been established to implement decisions. The practice has been for these committees to report back each year. In this way, they remain accountable to the regional partners. Transborder regional efforts have also benefited by having a co-ordinating committee made up of one representative from each of the governments involved in deciding what appears on the agenda and making sure decisions are implemented.

Even though the NEG/ECP represents an exciting experiment in transborder co-operation, it has always been a challenge getting unanimous agreement, especially with difficult policy questions. In a conference where decisions are reached on the basis of consensus, premiers and governors have tended to ignore tough policy issues. As one would expect, it is a very difficult task for such a forum to achieve very much because few politicians relish giving up power and there are few incentives to work together. Since there are few funds or resources available to support the activities of sectoral committees, what usually happens is that provincial and state officials usually take on these tasks. In practice, because these officials have other concerns and priorities to deal with, it is not unusual for passed resolutions to be simply ignored. For example, according to some environmentalists, a 1998 agreement by the New England Governors and Eastern Premiers to cut mercury emissions in half by 2003 has not received much attention in Atlantic Canada, where there is less pressure to get this on the public agenda (*St John's Evening Telegram*). Without strong regional institutions and processes in place, regional co-operation remains a challenge.

Conclusion

The regional integration question, whether in Atlantic Canada or New England, has tended to be approached from the economic perspective. The purpose of this chapter was to pay more attention to understanding how different federal institutions and cultures complicate the task of integration. Moreover, in the past, when the federal model has been discussed there has been a tendency to view it as a model for change and as a mechanism for facilitating economic and political integration. We also need to recognize that federalism is conservative and risk-averse. At a time when pro-integrationists are arguing about the economic merits and inevitability of building new province–state mechanisms or borderlands on the continent, the chapter raised questions about the future prospects of Atlantic and New England integration given the different federal traditions and systems of policy formulation and implementation at both the national and sub-national levels in Canada and the United States.

In Atlantic Canada, there has never been a consensus on the merits of regional integration, and the recent threat posed by outside territorial and ideological competitors to local economies and cultures have probably strengthened, not weakened, the forces of provincialism. If there is a need for new arrangements for managing economic interdependence in Atlantic Canada and if there are, in fact, benefits to be gained by reforming provincial institutions and building a continental region, the sellers of such an approach need to do a better job in selling the idea without threatening or insulting the governments involved and the societies they represent. For the most part, the public has not been well informed on this issue and what information it has received has either come from outsiders who do not appear to care much about cultural traditions or from provincial governments who have their own interests to defend. Because Atlantic Canadians have not had good experiences with economic integration and since many blame past national policies for their disparity problem, there is little guilt associated with accepting federal compensation. There is also a natural reluctance to provide outsiders with a chance to gain further control over the development process.

Despite common economic problems, Atlantic Canada is not a monolithic entity – each province has its own socio-economic and political traditions to rely upon when dealing with the regional integration question and changing this will not come easy, especially if change is viewed as a threat. Logic would suggest that as long as Canadian redistributive traditions remain, or until neo-liberal thinkers can do a better job of convincing sceptics that regional integration makes sense, there will be little incentive on the part of premiers or bureaucratic elites to abandon provincial political institutions or boundaries in favour of regional ones, despite new economic forces at play. Whether this can continue in the future will depend on the capacity of the Atlantic premiers to mobilize support for redistributive policies. In recent years, the record has been mixed. The Atlantic premiers have managed to build a powerful coalition behind certain redistributive policies such as health and equalization, but the record for social welfare has not been as good. On balance, however, there are signs that the Atlantic premiers have secured support for themselves and the moral and institutional traditions of Canadian federalism and this is reflected in Ottawa's new interest in equity issues.

In New England the debate over regional co-operation has been less controversial but there are few signs that regionalism is gaining strength. Rather, the idea of New England is more important to the tourist trade than as a model for political problem-solving and decision-making. Despite changing economic trends and arguments of economists that there are benefits to regional integration, there is little evidence that we are seeing new borderlands emerging. America is still a place where national and local politics matter most and this is the result of American federal structures and traditions.

As far as neo-liberal economic thinkers are concerned, the time is ripe for new regional forms of co-operation. Yet, experience shows that new regional forms and mechanisms have not and probably will not play much of a role in mobilizing support for the regional idea in either New England or Atlantic Canada. By providing a comparative study regionalism in New England and Atlantic Canada this chapter sheds light on the various political obstacles that will complicate the drive for building a mega-region in this part of North America.

Notes

1 According to Samuel V. LaSelva (1996), the moral foundations of Canadian federalism are based on the idea that there is an acceptance of different cultures at the provincial level and that equalization and the social welfare state were specifically designed to ensure that these moral traditions were put into practice.

2 For details on Courchene's assessment of how Ontario is becoming a region state and the implications for redistributive practices in Canada, see Courchene (1997) and Courchene and Telmer (1997). Preston Manning has also been calling for increased north–south trade links, and he argues that given the new economic realities and the political logic of the 1990s, it only makes sense that the 'Atlantic' vision which is the 'east coast equivalent to 'Cascadia' (the emerging trade zone in British Columbia, Alberta, and the US Pacific Northwest) should be expanded. He is a great supporter of Atlantic and New England integration and reducing the role of Ottawa in social and regional development matters. See 'Atlantica', excerpts from Address by Preston Manning, Leader of the Reform Party, to the Saint John Board of Trade, Saint John, New Brunswick, 11 May 1995. Doug Young, former federal transport minister, in 1991, argued that the Atlantic region had no real choice but to accept the fact that integration was the only viable option, in light of new forces shaping the continent and federation. See Young, 'Atlantic Canadian Political Union', presented at the Atlantic Provinces Political Studies Association Meetings Saint John, New Brunswick, 26 October 1991.

3 The Hall of States is behind the Congress and houses state government offices, regional organizations, and the National Governors' Association main office.

4 'The premise of the Borderlands Project is that North America runs more naturally north and south than east and west as specified by national boundaries, and that modern communications and efficient transportation help blur distinctions between regional neighbors. Such an approach naturally appeals more to those interests that benefit from north–south, as opposed to east–west approaches to problem-solving.

5 The part of Canada often refered to as the Maritimes is a made up of Nova Scotia, Prince Edward Island and New Brunswick.

6 For example, the attack on the Regional Commission by the *Boston Globe* in the 1970s hurt the regional movement in a significant way. Based on interviews.

7 Canada's welfare state and system of equalization that emerged in the Keynesian era has been very generous to Atlantic Canadians, who have no doubt benefited from Ottawa 's unlimited taxing powers. Executive federalism provides the forum for resolving issues related to federal finance, but Ottawa has always had

the final say. On the other hand, the system of fiscal federalism in Canada has been moving in the direction of decentralization over the decades as a result of globalization, the fiscal imperative and the Quebec question. This has made it possible for even poor provinces to set their own priorities and continue the traditions of province-building. Canadian fiscal federalism is a complex system where most tax bases have been co-occupied (with the exception of resource and property tax) and this has made it difficult to strike the right balance between equity and efficiency principles with the federation. It has also been a challenge co-ordinating tax systems through tax agreements that have taken on various forms in different provinces. In some cases, these have involved bilateral agreements, or as in the case of the 1996 goods and services tax (GST) tax harmonization agreement between Ottawa, Newfoundland, Nova Scotia and New Brunswick, multilateral agreements. Equalization and other federal transfers still provide around 40 per cent of the revenues for poor provinces like Newfoundland and this explains, in part, why there tends to be more support in Atlantic Canada for not restricting national spending power. The principle of equalization and the commitment to ensuring the equal treatment of the provinces was entrenched in the constitution in 1982. The formulae used to calculate equalization payments are negotiated every five years between Ottawa and the provinces.

8 As argued by Savoie, 'People from economically disadvantaged areas frequently argue that national economic policies are largely responsible for the economic underdevelopment of their respective regions and that more should be done in regional development. Meanwhile, those from more developed regions are likely to argue that far too much public money is committed to inefficient economic activity in slow-growth areas' (Savoie 1992).

9 The New England Governors and Eastern Premiers Conference involves the four Atlantic premiers, Quebec, and the six New England governors, and the Northeast International 'region' refers to New England and Eastern Canada. The conference began in 1973 and meetings have been held on an annual basis with the exception of 1991, 1992 (when the transborder mechanism nearly ended) and 1996, when Prince Edward Island Premier Catherine Callbeck at the last minute decided to cancel the meetings.

10 One of the former governors interviewed by the author suggested that he was often distressed that some of his peers seldom attended these meetings, and when they did, they often showed up without having read any of the conference materials. Such a lack of interest in regional matters has added to the problems of the conference.

Acknowledgement

This research is supported by the Institute of Social Economic Research at Memorial University. I wish to thank Lesley Tomblin, Chris Dunn, Ute Wachendorfer-Schmidt, David Dyment and Jim Feehan for reading early versions of this draft and providing comments.

References

Bradshaw, M. (1988) *Regions and Regionalism in the United States*, Basingstone: Macmillan.
—— (1992) *The Appalacian Regional Commission: Twenty-Five Years of Government Policy*, Lexington: University Press of Kentucky.

Branch, M. (1988) *Regional Planning: Introduction and Explanation*, New York: Praeger Publishers.

Brodie, J. (1990) *The Political Economy of Canadian Regionalism*, Toronto: Harcourt Brace Jovanovich.

Brookes, A. (1976) 'Out-migration from the Maritime Provinces, 1860–1900: Some Preliminary Considerations', *Acadiensis* 5, 2: 26–56.

Brown, D. and Fry, E. (eds) (1993) *States and Provinces in the International Economy*, Berkeley, CA: Regents of the University of California.

Cairns, A. (1986) 'The Embedded State: State-Society Relations in Canada', in K. Banting (ed.) *State and Society: Canada in Comparative Perspective*, Toronto: University of Toronto Press.

—— (1988) *Constitution, Government and Society*, Toronto: McClelland and Stewart.

—— (1995) *Reconfiguration*, Toronto: McClelland and Stewart.

Conrad, M. (1989) 'Chronicles of the Exodus: Myths and Realities of Maritime Canadians in the United States, 1870–1930', in S. Hornsby, V. Konrad and J. Herlan (eds), *The Northeastern Borderlands: Four Centuries of Interaction*, Fredericton, British Columbia: Canadian–American Center, University of Maine and Acadiensis Press.

Council of Maritime Premiers (1976) Press Release, Charlottetown, PEI, 25–26 May.

Council of Maritime Premiers Annual Report (1995–6).

Council of State Governments (1995) *The Book of States*, Lexington, Kentucky.

Courchene, T. (1998) 'Chaste and Chastened: Canada's New Social Contract', in R. Blake (ed.) *The Welfare State in Canada: Past, Present, Future*, Concord: Irwin Publishing.

Courchene, T. and Telmer, C. (1997) *From Heartland to North American Region State*, Toronto: University of Toronto, Faculty of Management.

Daniels, B.C. (1988) *The Fragmentation of New England*, New York: Greenwood Press.

Davis, R. (1978) *The Federal Principle*, Berkeley: University of California Press.

Deeg, R. (1996) 'Economic Globalization and the Shifting Boundaries of German Federalism', *Publius: The Journal of Federalism* 26, 1: 27–52.

Derthick, M. (1974) *Between State and Nation: Regional Organizations of the United States*, Washington, DC: Brookings Institute.

Duchacek, I. (1986) *The Territorial Dimension: Within, Among, and Across Nations*, Boulder, CO: Westview Press.

Duchacek, I., Latouche, D. and Stevenson, G. (eds) (1988) *Perforated Sovereignties and International Relations: Trans-Sovereign Contacts of Subnational Governments*, New York: Greenwood Press.

Dyck, R. (1996) *Provincial Politics in Canada*, Scarborough: Prentice Hall.

Gibbins, R. (1982) *Regionalism: Territorial Politics in Canada and the United States*, Toronto: Butterworths.

Gress, F. (1996) 'Interstate Cooperation and Territorial Representation in Intermestic Politics', *Publius: The Journal of Federalism* 26, 1: 53–71.

Harrigan, J. (1994) *Politics and Policy in States and Communities*, New York: Harper Collins.

Hartz, L. (ed.) (1964) *The Founding of New Societies*, New York: Harcourt Brace & World.

Hooghe, L. and Marks, G. (1996) 'Europe with the Regions', *Publius: The Journal of Federalism* 26, 1: 73–91.

Horowitz, G. (1966) 'Conservatism, Liberalism and Socialism in Canada: An Interpretation', *Journal of Economics and Political Science*, 32, 2: 143–71.

Jamelle, D.G. (1991) 'The Maine Connection: Quebec to New Brunswick', in R. Lecker (ed.) *Borderlands: Essays in Canadian-American Relations*, Toronto: ECW Press.

Jenkins, W.A. (1976) Comments on the Paper on the Council of Maritime Premiers by A.A. Lomas, 28th Annual Meeting of the Institute of Public Administration of Canada, Halifax.

JARC (1995) Appalachia, special issue of *Journal of the Appalachian Regional Commission* 28, 1&2.

LaSelva, S.V. (1996) *The Moral Foundations of Canadian Federalism: Paradoxes, Achievements, and Tragedies of Nationhood*, Montreal: McGill-Queen's University Press.

Lockard, D. (1959) *New England State Politics*, Princeton: Princeton University Press.

Loughlin, J. (1996) 'Europe of the Regions and the Federalization of Europe', *Publius: The Journal of Federalism* 26, 4: 141–62.

Lubin, M. (1993) 'The Routinization of Cross-Border Interactions', in D. Brown and E. Frye (eds), *States and Provinces in the International Economy*, Berkeley, CA: Regents of University of California.

McDowell, B.C. (1997) 'Advisory Commission on Intergovernmental Relations in 1996: The End of an Era', *Publius: The Journal of Federalism* 27, 2: 111–27.

McKinsey, L. and Konrad, V. (1990) *Borderland Reflections: The United States and Canada*, Orono, Borderlands Project.

Michelmann, H. and Soldatos, P. (eds) (1990) *Federalism and International Relations: The Role of Subnational Units*, Oxford: Clarendon Press.

New England and Eastern Canadian Secretariats (1988) *Review of the Conference of New England Governors and Eastern Premiers: Fifteen-Year Overview of Discussions, 1973–1987, Sixteenth Annual Conference*, New Port Rhode Island.

Nordlinger, E. (1981) *On the Autonomy of the State*, Cambridge: Harvard University Press.

Palmer, K., Thomas Taylor, G. and LiBrizzi, M.A. (1992) *Maine Politics and Government*, Lincoln: University of Nebraska Press.

Pierce, N. (1976) *The New England States*, New York: Norton and Company.

Price, K. (ed.) (1982) *Regional Conflict and National Policy*, Baltimore: Johns Hopkins University Press.

Robertson, D.B. and Judd, D.R. (1989) *The Development of American Public Policy: The Structure of Policy Restraint*, Boston: Little, Brown.

Savoie, D.J. (1992) *Regional Economic Development: Canada's Search for Solutions*, 2nd edn, Toronto: University of Toronto Press.

Sharkansky, I. (1970) *Regionalism in American Politics*, New York: Bobbs–Merrill Company.

Simeon, R. and Robinson, I. (1990) *State, Society, and the Development of Canadian Federalism*, Toronto: University of Toronto Press.

Spectrum (1994) *Exploring Regionalism*, special issue of *Journal of State Government* 67, 3.

Squires, S. (1991) 'Newfoundland to the Boston States: Season Cross-border Migration', in R. Lecker (ed.), *Borderlands: Essays in Canadian-American Relations*, Toronto: ECW Press.

Sternlieb, G. and Hughes, J.W. (1978) *Revitalizing the Northeast*, New Brunswick, NJ: Rutgers University, Center for Urban Policy Research.

Tomblin, S. (1995) *Ottawa and the Outer Provinces*, Toronto: Lorimer Press.

Walker, D. (1985) *The Contemporary Condition of American Pluralism: A Comparative and Chronological Assessment*, Washington: Advisory Commission on Intergovernmental Relations.

Wheeler, W. (1952) *New England Council: Its Beginnings, Its Work, and Its Future (1925–1952)*, printed and bound for the Newcomen Publications by Princeton University Press.

Wiseman, N. (1996) 'Provincial Political Cultures', in C. Dunn (ed.), *Provinces*, Toronto: Broadview Press.

Part III

The comparative political economy of federalism and decentralization

8 Federalism, fiscal decentralization and economic performance[1]

Francis G. Castles

Introduction

The strongest strand of comparative research with an interest in the policy consequences of federalism has concentrated not on the economy, but on the growth of the welfare state and public expenditure. In a series of empirical studies now going back more than two decades, this literature has identified the weak development of the public sector and the welfare state in federal nations (Wilensky 1975; Cameron 1978; Castles and McKinlay 1979) and in those with constitutional structures containing many veto-points to centrally initiated policy reform (Huber et al. 1993; Schmidt 1996; Castles 1998). By contrast, despite a real theoretical interest in the possible macro-economic policy consequences of constitutional and fiscal decentralization, the fact that the topic sits astride the demarcation line between political science and economics has not been conducive to the emergence of any substantial body of empirical research findings. Such a research effort is vastly beyond the scope of one short chapter, so the goal here is an exploratory one. In what follows, I seek to establish whether the evidence is such as to provide the basis of a prima facie case for a correspondence between a nation's degree of political and/or fiscal decentralization and its economic performance. Clearly, the stronger the case, the greater the need for further research.

Two lines of argument

It is possible to identify two lines of argument linking political and fiscal decentralization to the character of macro-economic objectives. One is a set of propositions emanating from public choice theory, which suggest that, in order to contain the supposedly revenue-maximizing proclivities of national governments, it is necessary that there be restraints on the capacity of the central state to take certain kinds of policy initiatives. The most familiar argument in this mode is that, because governments have an inherent tendency to put a higher priority on revenue maximization than on monetary stability, they cannot be trusted with the control of monetary policy, which is more appropriately located in the hands of independent central banks. In a somewhat similar vein, the 'dispersal of fiscal authority among differing levels of government' has been seen 'as a means of controlling Leviathan's overall fiscal appetites' (Brennan and Buchanan 1980: 181). The notion that decentralized government is more economically efficient – partly in virtue of its lesser imperial growth potential and partly because of its tendency to promote competition at the subnational level – has been the staple argument of those favouring a stronger degree of 'fiscal federalism' in existing federal nations, such as Australia and the United States. The clear implication of much theorizing in the public choice model is that federalism and decentralized control of the fisc are likely to be conducive to higher levels of economic growth, more efficient factor utilization and lower levels of inflation.

Public choice theory starts from a neo-classical and deductivist framework very different from the inductivist, comparative public policy approach which has characterized research focusing on the links between decentralization and the growth of the welfare state. More in the latter tradition is a second line of argument, which points to differing degrees of freedom for macro-economic policy manoeuvre in countries characterized by differential degrees of fiscal decentralization. Using a comparative case-study approach, Fritz Scharpf has argued that the capacity of national governments to utilize demand management techniques in a Keynesian manner to boost economic growth and unemployment is a function of the existing magnitude of public budgets and the extent to which they are controlled by the central government (Scharpf 1991: 212–13). Effectively, this turns the public choice argument on its head. If the key to economic growth and full employment is central control of a large centralized budget, then it will be federal states and nations with high levels of fiscal decentralization which are likely to perform least well.

While there are major differences between theorists concerning the general economic efficiency and employment generating implications of decentralized political and fiscal structures, there would seem to be greater unanimity on the question of inflation. Building on Scharpf's notion of the differential degrees of 'fiscal difficulty' experienced by large, centralized states and small, decentralized ones, Busch (1993: 65–9) argues that nations face a real economic performance trade-off, since increases in aggregate demand facilitated by large public budgets and a centralized fisc are likely to create substantial inflationary pressures. Using data for 17 OECD countries, Busch demonstrates that countries manifesting the preconditions for effective Keynesian control of the economy had significantly higher rates of inflation than other OECD countries in the period 1973–86.

Theoretical debate on linkages between decentralization and economic outcomes has only borne limited empirical fruit. Public choice theory is about the logic of economic institutions, and has been little concerned with the empirical testing of hypotheses. Almost the only major concern of that school of thought to be taken up seriously by empirical economic policy research has been the insight that central bank independence is linked to lower rates of inflation. Some of this work has involved sophisticated econometric modelling (see Alesina 1989; Grilli et al. 1991). In contrast, the work on 'fiscal difficulty' we have briefly reviewed here must be seen as having a rather more tentative character, since it does not use appropriate modelling techniques to take account of other obviously crucial factors conditioning macro-economic performance.

The research design

The research design employed here involves assessing the impact of a variety of measures of political and fiscal decentralization on robust models accounting for substantial degrees of cross-national variance in the long-term performance parameters of the post-war political economy.

Measures of decentralization

Five measures of decentralization are featured in Table 8.1. Sources and notes to that table provide precise details of the operationalization of each variable and our presentation here merely highlights some of the implications involved in the use of the various measures.

Federalism   This measure is largely unproblematical. Six countries – three Anglo-American and three German-speaking – have been federations throughout the post-war period. Belgium became a federal state in 1993, but this was too late to affect any of the performance measures used in this study.

Constitutional structure   Huber, Ragin and Stephens (1993) in their welfare state research argue that federalism is but one of a number of constitutional veto-points limiting centralized political intervention. Others include the existence of a presidential form of government, strong bicameral pro-cedures, territorial constituencies and referendum procedures. The constitu-tional structure variable used here is an additive index of the strength of such veto-points in Western nations (for details, see notes to Table 8.1).

Fiscal decentralization   This measure, which is simply the sum of state and local taxes as a percentage of total tax revenue, is the simplest and most unambiguous measure of the territorial decentralization of the fisc. Other taxes are levied on behalf of supranational bodies (the EU), by central governments or by agencies with national scope (social security funds). The revenues listed in the third column of Table 8.1 derive exclusively from taxes levied at a subnational level. Since we are attempting to capture the reality of fiscal centralization over the post-war period as a whole, our

Table 8.1   Measures of political and fiscal decentralization

Country	Federalism	Constitutional structure	Fiscal decentralization	Fiscal centralization	Fiscal difficulty
Australia	1	4	21.3	78.6	4.1
Canada	1	4	44.7	43.3	5.8
Ireland	0	0	4.4	82.2	3.1
New Zealand	0	0	6.4	93.3	–
UK	0	2	8.8	73.9	3.4
USA	1	7	28.8	41.0	7.9
Denmark	0	0	29.9	66.9	2.8
Finland	0	1	24.1	59.5	3.8
Norway	0	1	20.4	54.4	3.5
Sweden	0	0	32.0	49.2	3.6
Austria	1	2	21.6	51.8	4.2
Belgium	0	1	4.8	62.2	3.3
France	0	2	8.5	48.9	4.7
Germany	1	4	30.8	33.4	6.7
Italy	0	1	2.6	60.8	4.4
Netherlands	0	1	10.0	56.4	3.4
Greece	0	2	4.3	65.7	4.5
Portugal	0	0	4.4	70.1	4.3
Spain	0	1	8.6	50.2	6.2
Switzerland	1	6	39.9	27.0	11.3
Japan	0	2	25.0	46.6	7.3
OECD average		2.0	18.1	57.9	4.9

Sources and Notes: Federalism is coded: 0=no, 1=yes.

Constitutional structure from Huber, Ragin and Stephens (1993) as modified by Schmidt (1996). This variable is an additive index where: federalism 0=no, 1=weak, 2=strong; parliamentary/presidential government: 0=parliamentary, 1=president or collegial executive; proportional representation/single-member districts: 0=proportional representation, 1=modified proportional representation, 2=single-member, simple plurality system; bicameralism: 0=no second chamber or second chamber with very weak powers, 1=weak bicameralism, 2=strong bicameralism; Referendum: 0=none or infrequent, 1=frequent.

Fiscal decentralization is equivalent to the share of state and local taxes in total revenue, data averaged from 1973, 1983 and 1992, from OECD, *Revenue Statistics*, various dates.

Fiscal centralization is equivalent to central government revenue as a share of total revenue, data averaged from 1973, 1983 and 1992, from OECD, *Revenue Statistics*, various dates.

Fiscal difficulty is equivalent to the reduction in the central government's revenue share that would be required to secure a 1 per cent of GDP increase in demand. Data on the central government share of revenues from the previous column of the table; average receipts of government for 1973, 1983 and 1992 calculated from OECD, *Historical Statistics*, various dates.

measure is based on averaging OECD data for the years 1973, 1983 and 1992.

Fiscal centralization   It is important to distinguish fiscal decentralization as defined above from fiscal centralization or, as I have elsewhere called it, 'discretionary fiscal centralization' (see Barwise and Castles 1991). Fiscal centralization as defined here measures the share of the tax take going to the central government. Because it also excludes supranational and social security taxes, it is not simply the mirror-image of fiscal decentralization (see correlation matrix in Table 8.2 below). The reason for the label 'discretionary' preceding the centralization variable rests on an argument analogous to that underlying Scharpf's 'fiscal difficulty' hypothesis: namely, that the central government cannot manipulate social security and supranational taxes with the same ease as it does the main categories of tax under its direct control. So a demonstrated link between fiscal centralization and economic performance would imply that central control of the fisc has a direct effect on policy outcomes. As in the case of fiscal decentralization, the data here is averaged for the years 1973, 1983 and 1992.

Fiscal difficulty   There is no routinely available data on the central government's share of public expenditure, so, appropriately enough, we use the available OECD data on the share of revenues accruing to central government to measure fiscal difficulty on the revenue rather than the expenditure side of the budget. Thus, rather than following Scharpf's lead in assessing how difficult it is for national governments to deliver demand stimulus through central government public spending, we look at the implications of delivering a comparable stimulus to the economy via a central government tax cut. The figures in the final column of Table 8.1 show the percentage by which the share of central government taxes would have to fall in different countries in order to secure a 1 per cent of GDP increase in demand. As in the case of our other fiscal measures, the data presented here involves averaging over the years 1973, 1983 and 1992.

Only a single measure of each of the five decentralization variables is provided in Table 8.1, possibly conveying the erroneous impression that political and fiscal structures are unchanging. That is obviously untrue, but it is fair to point out that change of a kind that would influence the cross-national relativities we are concerned with here is most uncommon. Partly that is because constitutional structures are designed to resist change. In the period covered here, only one country (Belgium) in the OECD has become a federation and constitutional change influencing numbers of veto-points has been very minor. Partly, it is because national tax structures are also relatively unchanging, with the averaging procedure used to derive our tax decentralization and centralization measures leading to no major changes in the ordering of nations. Of the measures provided here, only

Table 8.2 Correlation matrix of political and fiscal decentralization variables

	Federalism	Constitu-tional	Decentral-ization	Central-ization	Difficulty
Federalism	1				
Constitutional	0.83	1			
Decentralization	0.64	0.54	1		
Centralization	−0.48	−0.57	−0.63	1	
Difficulty	0.56	0.77	−0.51	−0.77	1

'fiscal difficulty' is subject to substantial change over time of a kind affecting cross-national relativities, but that is because it is as much a measure of the growth of the public sector as of the decentralization of the state.

We conclude this discussion of our decentralization measures by seeking to establish the extent to which they capture the same dimension of the functioning of the modern state. Table 8.2 presents a simple correlation matrix for the five variables, which shows the strongest affinities to be between federalism and constitutional structure (0.83), fiscal centralization and fiscal difficulty (0.77), and fiscal difficulty and constitutional structure (−0.77).

The first two of these linkages are, in some part, definitional, since federalism is used in the elaboration of the constitutional structure index and fiscal centralization in the elaboration of the fiscal difficulty measure. There are no obvious definitional reasons why constitutional structure and fiscal difficulty should be so closely akin. A 0.70 correlation implies that two variables share half the same variance. Given that these are all supposedly measures of the decentralization of the state, it is appropriate to note that most of the other linkages identified in Table 8.2 are quite moderate. Indeed, the 0.64 correlation between federalism and fiscal decentralization is the strongest link between political and fiscal measures proper (i.e. excluding the hybrid fiscal difficulty term) and it could very well turn out that these two dimensions of decentralization have substantially different implications for policy outcomes.

Measures of outcomes

Table 8.3 provides data for three major parameters of post-war economic performance. They are measures of the fulfilment of the three main objectives of contemporary economic policy-making: high economic growth, low inflation and low unemployment. The definition of each of the variables is in accord with standard practice. Data sources and definitions are to be found in the notes to Table 8.3.

The precise operationalization of the three measures for this study involves certain choices. A narrow focus on specific years chosen because

Table 8.3 Performance parameters of the post-war political economy in 21 OECD nations

Country	Per capita economic growth, 1960–1992	Average rate of inflation, 1960–93	Increase in unemployment 1974/1979– 1990/1994
Australia	1.9	6.5	4.5
Canada	2.5	7.6	3.0
Ireland	3.3	8.1	7.4
New Zealand	1.1	8.2	–
UK	2.4	7.6	4.2
USA	1.9	4.9	−1.9
Denmark	2.3	6.7	2.9
Finland	2.6	7.2	7.6
Norway	3.3	6.4	3.8
Sweden	1.9	6.8	3.3
Austria	2.9	4.4	1.9
Belgium	2.8	4.7	3.5
France	2.7	6.3	6.0
Germany	2.5	3.5	3.5
Italy	3.2	8.5	4.5
Netherlands	2.4	4.4	1.9
Greece	3.7	12.0	6.6
Portugal	4.3	12.6	−0.9
Spain	3.6	9.7	14.0
Switzerland	1.6	3.9	–
Japan	5.1	5.2	0.5
OECD average	2.8	6.9	4.0

Sources: Per capita economic growth, 1960–1992 is the annual average increase in per capita GDP and is calculated from an update of Summers and Heston (1991).

Average rate of inflation, 1960–1993 is equivalent to the average annual rate of increase of the consumer price index over the period. Data is from OECD, *Historical Statistics, 1960–1993*, 1995.

Increase in unemployment, 1974/1979–1990/1994 is the increase in the average unemployment rate between the period 1974 to 1979 and 1990 to 1994. Data from OECD, *Historical Statistics, 1960–1994*, 1996.

they are likely to demonstrate the operation of hypothesized causal mechanisms might be one approach. Another – and that chosen here – is to examine variables over the long-term, allowing us to ascertain the extent to which decentralization variables have been associated with post-war performance as a whole. In so far as we locate strong associations in the data, that leaves for further research the question of whether such impacts have been constant over the whole period or focused at particular junctures. Because the thrust of comparative labour market research has been on the rise of unemployment since the mid-1970s, we adopt a comparable restriction of focus.

In the case of both economic growth and inflation, our operationalization is in terms of annual average rates of change: i.e. the annual average rate of per capita economic growth and the average annual rate of increase in the consumer price index. For both growth and inflation, the period under investigation is the entire post-war span from 1960 to the early 1990s. In the case of unemployment, we are concerned with the shaping role of decentralization on the trajectory of post-war change, so the dependent variable is operationalized as the increase (or decrease) in average levels of unemployment as between different periods. For unemployment, the period under investigation is that from the First Oil Shock recession of the 1970s to a period terminating with the recession of the early to mid-1990s.

Methodology

Although exploratory research in new areas and with novel variables is often justified in using case-study methods and in arguing for *a priori* conclusions on the basis of bivariate findings, such conclusions are necessarily preliminary. It is clear that, in a multi-causal universe, hypotheses are only fully grounded in so far as they are tested in the context of models which substantially account for the phenomena in question. Where the focus of research is on determining the causal impact of particular variables or categories of variables, this obviously involves a substantial task of data-gathering, since models must be elaborated across a wide range of subject areas.

Such modelling exercises are also methodologically problematic, because of the very considerable number of explanatory variables which must be examined in order to do justice to the relevant scholarly literature. The difficulty is that the low case numbers available for cross-national research permit us only to investigate a limited range of hypotheses using conventional cross-sectional designs, while the use of pooled time-series designs using multiple dependent variables makes an already major data-gathering exercise quite prohibitive in terms of cost and energy. To get around these difficulties, I have relied on the extensive database gathered in the context of my recent work on the determinants of post-war public expenditure development and labour market trends (Castles 1998). I have also utilized the same research strategy that was used in this work, combining a simple cross-sectional design with bivariate analysis as a means of exploring the full range of hypotheses suggested in the literature, and using a variant of stepwise regression to generate models maximizing levels of explained variance (adjusted R^2) on the basis of variables satisfying a minimum criterion of statistical significance ($t > 2.00$). The standard approach to cross-sectional investigation which excludes possible explanations by failing to test potentially relevant hypotheses rests on what I call 'disingenuousness by omission'. My own approach also clearly leads to some degree of model misspecification, but does allow discussion of a much wider range of potentially relevant hypotheses. It is transparent in a way the standard approach is not.

The precise application of this methodology in the present study involves the elaboration of stepwise regression models for each of the political economy variables itemized in Table 8.3. In addition to the criteria used for model specification in my earlier work, I further take account of the robustness of the findings by establishing whether the statistical significance of terms is a function of the inclusion of particular cases in the analysis. Having elaborated basic models with a capacity to account for much of the cross-national variance in each performance parameter, I include each of our measures of political and fiscal decentralization in turn, seeking to establish whether they are themselves statistically significant and robust. Basic models for each performance parameter, together with successive elaborations of the effects of the decentralization measures, are reported in Tables 8.4 to 8.6 respectively and are discussed below.

The models

Economic growth

Of a long listing of hypotheses concerning the factors influencing post-war economic growth, including catch-up (initial level of real GDP), investment levels and investment growth, employment growth, corporatism, party control and a wide variety of measures of change in different categories of public expenditure (see Castles and Dowrick 1990), the basic economic growth model as shown in Table 8.4 consists of a single, but enormously strong, term for catch-up. The notion that post-war economic growth has been characterized by a powerful tendency to convergence is now well established (Dowrick and Nguyen 1989) and is graphically demonstrated by the extremely high t-value for the relationship between the catch-up term, 1960 GDP per capita, and subsequent rates of economic growth. All other potential explanations pale beside this pattern of convergence, although the change in gross fixed capital formation, our measure of investment growth, does produce a further significant term for the full sample of 21 countries, which is shown in the notes to the basic model. It does not feature as part of the basic model as such, because the finding is not robust, depending exclusively on the coincidence of very high levels of investment and exceptionally good performance in Japan, the OECD's economic growth phenomenon.

Successively introducing our five decentralization measures into the single term basic model for economic growth reveals that no less than four of them are significantly related to economic growth, with federalism the

Table 8.4 Economic growth models

Basic model	Coefficient	Standard error	t-Value
Intercept	4.865		
1960 real GDP per capita	−0.0003662	0.00004483	8.168
Adj R^2=0.767			

Sources: Economic growth from Table 8.3. 1960 real GDP per capita from Summers and Heston (1991).
Notes: 21 cases in regression. Adding an investment growth term to the model produces the following equation: 1960–1992 economic growth=3.872 − 0.0003131 (0.00004240) 1960 real GDP per capital+0.204 (0.071) 1960–1992 change in gross fixed capital formation. Figures in parentheses are standard errors. Adj R^2=0.831. 1960–1992 change in gross fixed capital formation is the average annual percentage increase in gross fixed capital formation from OECD, *Historical Statistics, 1960–1992*, 1994.

Basic model+federalism	Coefficient	Standard error	t-Value
Federalism	0.364	0.254	1.432
Adj R^2=0.779			

Sources: Federalism is from Table 8.1.
Notes: 21 cases in regression.

Basic model+constitutional structure	Coefficient	Standard error	t-Value
Constitutional structure	0.143	0.053	2.688
Adj R^2=0.824			

Source: Constitutional structure is from Table 8.1.
Notes: 21 cases in regression. The t-value for constitutional structure is below 2.00 if New Zealand is excluded from the regression.

Basic model+fiscal decentralization	Coefficient	Standard error	t-Value
Fiscal decentralization	0.023	0.008	2.762
Adj R^2=0.827			

Source: Fiscal decentralization is from Table 8.1.
Notes: 21 cases in regression. The t-value for fiscal decentralization is below 2.00 if New Zealand or Japan are excluded from the regression.

Basic model+fiscal centralization	Coefficient	Standard error	t-Value
Fiscal centralization	−0.017	0.005	3.267
Adj R^2=0.845			

Source: Fiscal centralization is from Table 8.1.
Note: 21 cases in regression.

Basic model+fiscal difficulty	Coefficient	Standard error	t-Value
Fiscal difficulty	0.109	0.042	2.633
Adj R^2=0.832			

Source: Fiscal difficulty is from Table 8.1.
Notes: 20 cases in regression (no data for New Zealand). The t-value for fiscal difficulty is below 2.00 if Japan is excluded from the regression.

one exception. In all instances, the signs of these terms indicate that decentralized political and fiscal arrangements are associated with superior long-term economic growth rates. However, only in the case of fiscal centralization is the resulting model a robust one, with the other decentralization terms ceasing to be significant when either Japan and/or New Zealand are excluded from the analysis. Whereas Japan's influence on these models stems from its exceptionally strong growth performance, New Zealand's arises from the coincidence of the weakest growth trajectory in the OECD and a constitutional structure and fiscal arrangements as centralized as any in the advanced world.

At first glance, these findings conflict with our casual impressions of the post-war economic growth record of many OECD nations. Looking to one extreme, Switzerland and the USA have amongst the poorest growth records in the OECD, but they are federal, have more constitutional veto-points than any other OECD countries, have exceptionally high levels of state and local taxes, are almost at the bottom of the distribution in respect of the central tax take, and have the two highest readings for fiscal difficulty. At the other extreme, Ireland and Portugal exhibit opposite characteristics. Moreover, these are not impressions derived from just a few extreme cases. Four of our five measures produce bivariate correlations with growth which are signed as indicating that decentralization is inversely related to economic performance. The exception is fiscal decentralization, but even here the correlation is negligible (-0.04). If nothing else, this strongly underlines the methodological point that only full model specification provides us with the evidence required for well-grounded conclusions. Turning again to our examples at the extremes, it is impossible to know what is going on in respect of the economic growth performance of these countries until we have discounted the fact that Switzerland and the USA started out the post-war period very rich and that Ireland and Portugal started out very poor. If we don't know how much catch-up matters, we can't establish how much political and fiscal decentralization matter either.

Inflation

The basic model for inflation consists of three terms: corporatism, sectoral transformation and the growth of civilian public consumption expenditure. For the regression reported here, the latter term is not robust and is dependent on the inclusion of Japan in the analysis. The model is, however, reported in this form, since the term for public consumption becomes wholly robust in a number of the subsequent specifications including measures of decentralization. As in the case of economic growth, this model has strong resonances with the standard literature in the field. The role of corporatism as a factor containing inflationary growth has produced a huge literature (see, for example, Bruno and Sachs 1985; Crouch 1985; Crepaz 1992), while the role of public spending has been much demonized by the

Table 8.5 Inflation models

Basic model	Coefficient	Standard error	t-Value
Intercept	2.008		
Corporatism	−1.115	0.346	3.226
1960–1993 sectoral transformation	0.166	0.032	5.185
1960–1993 increase in civilian public consumption expenditure	0.307	0.111	2.757
Adj R²=0.648			

Sources: Inflation from Table 8.3. Corporatism scores from Crepaz (1992), with data for Greece, Portugal and Spain supplied by Professor Hans Keman of the Free University of Amsterdam. 1960–1993 sectoral transformation is equivalent to the percentage of the employed population leaving the agricultural sector, calculated from OECD, *Historical Statistics, 1960–1993*, 1995. Increase in civilian public consumption expenditure calculated from OECD, *Historical Statistics, 1960–1993*, 1995 and SIPRI, *Yearbook*, various years.

Notes: 21 cases in regression. The t-value for civilian public consumption expenditure is below 2.00 if Japan is excluded from the regression.

Basic model+federalism	Coefficient	Standard error	t-Value
Federalism	−1.375	0.714	1.914
Adj R²=0.697			

Source: Federalism is from Table 8.1.
Note: 21 cases in regression.

Basic model+constitutional structure	Coefficient	Standard error	t-Value
Constitutional structure	−0.411	0.165	2.499
Adj R²=0.731			

Source: Constitutional structure is from Table 8.1.

Notes: 21 cases in regression. The t-value for civilian public consumption expenditure is below 2.00 if Japan is excluded from the regression. The t-value for constitutional structure is below 2.00 if New Zealand is excluded from the regression.

Basic model+fiscal decentralization	Coefficient	Standard error	t-Value
Fiscal decentralization	−0.073	0.023	3.155
Adj R²=0.77			

Source: Fiscal decentralization is from Table 8.1.
Note: 21 cases in regression.

Basic model+fiscal centralization	Coefficient	Standard error	t-Value
Fiscal centralization	0.06	0.015	3.908
Adj R²=0.809			

Source: Fiscal centralization is from Table 8.1.
Note: 21 cases in regression.

Basic model+fiscal difficulty	Coefficient	Standard error	t-Value
Fiscal difficulty	−0.26	0.142	1.834
Adj R²=0.756			

Source: Fiscal difficulty is from Table 8.1.

Notes: 20 cases in regression (no data for New Zealand).

government overload and public choice schools of thought. Public consumption expenditure which is focused substantially on public service provision might be thought of as particularly conducive to inflation because of an inherent tendency to low productivity growth in the service sector (see Baumol 1967). Finally, the strong positive link between inflation and sectoral transformation, measured as the shift from agricultural employment into other sectors of the economy, confirms the standard view that rapid economic development is a source of an overheated economy.

It is also appropriate to mention two variables which do not feature in the analysis, both of them, according to the Busch's paper earlier cited (Busch 1993), important determinants of inflation. They are central bank independence and a measure of distributional conflict, the strike coefficient. In the former case, we do not have data for Ireland or the countries of Southern Europe and cannot replicate his findings for our full sample of cases. Busch's analysis suggests that there is a strong positive connection between central bank independence and decentralization, so that it is possible that any links we might establish between our measures and inflation are really to be attributed to the way in which central banks function. For the 17 countries for which we have a coding of the degree of bank independence (Busch 1993: 60), the correlation with federalism is a moderate 0.54 and there are comparable degrees of association with constitutional structure (0.51) and fiscal decentralization (0.49). The correlations with fiscal centralization (-0.78) and fiscal difficulty (0.67) are still stronger.

The omission of a distributional conflict variable, despite a bivariate relationship between the post-war strike coefficient (for a variable definition, see note 2 below) and inflation which is stronger (0.82) than any of the terms featuring in the basic model, is in order to reduce the risk of endogeneity. The problem is that, whilst distributional conflict is undoubtedly a trigger for inflationary wage rises, inflation itself is often part of a vicious circle fostering further union militancy and strike activity. We do not believe that the omission of an explicit distributional conflict term from our modelling leads to undue misspecification of the relationships involved, because we have reason to think that two of the variables figuring in our basic model – corporatism and sectoral transformation – are amongst the main factors conditioning whether distributional conflict emerges in the first instance.[2]

Turning now to our decentralization measures, we find that no less than three – constitutional structure, fiscal decentralization and fiscal centralization – are significantly associated with inflationary outcomes, with decentralization once again conducive to superior post-war economic performance. While the model specification including constitutional structure is lacking in robustness on at least two counts, the models including the fiscal variables are quite satisfactory on this score. Of the two robust models, the one including fiscal centralization has somewhat the greater explanatory power, leaving us with the finding that this variable features as the strongest of our measures in respect of both economic growth and inflation.

Given that this measure is the one most closely associated with central bank independence in Busch's 17-country data-set, it will be tempting for some to interpret this finding as supporting the view that bank independence provides the crucial institutional basis for sound macro-economic performance. Whilst that might possibly be the case, such an interpretation is not supported by the data at our disposal. Seventeen-nation regressions of economic growth and inflation replicate the findings of the models including fiscal decentralization in Tables 8.4 and 8.5. Moreover, in each case, these models perform better than do specifications in which central bank independence replaces fiscal centralization, with the bank term having no effect whatsoever in the growth model. This does not rule out central bank independence as being a factor contributing to superior macro-economic management in the post-war period, but it does suggest that it is far from being the whole story.

Unemployment

The basic model for change in the level of unemployment between 1974/79 and 1990/94 as reported in Table 8.6 consists of four terms: corporatism, sectoral transformation, right-wing cabinet incumbency and change in real earnings. The hypotheses tested to derive this model highlight the potential influence on labour market performance of a wide range of factors. They include productivity growth, exposure to international trade, changes in employment composition, part-time employment, inflation, real earnings growth, cultural factors (including religious belief), union density, the institutionalization of class conflict, partisan control of government, public expenditure development and unemployment benefit replacement rates (see Castles 1998).

We have already demonstrated an inverse relationship between post-war inflation levels and corporatism. The negative association between corporatism and unemployment in the basic model represents the other major plank of the fashionable argument of the 1980s that labour quiescence through labour discipline has brought major gains to working-class movements in certain countries (see, e.g., Cameron 1984; Crouch 1985). That the shift out of agriculture produces unemployment as well as inflation is unlikely to be a source of surprise, reflecting the difficulty of retraining an unskilled labour force for either manufacturing or service occupations. The finding of a negative relationship between unemployment growth and right-wing partisan control will be far more controversial, but is interpreted in Castles (1998: 239) as a proxy for a variety of policy initiatives promoted by the Right to underwrite the efforts of employers 'to create the basis for a more flexible or market-determined operation of labour markets'. That differences between nations in the trajectory of unemployment growth will

Table 8.6 Unemployment models

Basic model	Coefficient	Standard error	t-Value
Intercept	4.345		
Corporatism	−1.736	0.422	4.114
1974–1994 sectoral transformation	0.34	0.082	4.133
1979–1993 change in real earnings	1.808	0.434	4.167
1974–1994 right cabinet seats	−0.091	0.016	5.814
Adj R^2=0.844			

Source: Unemployment from Table 3. Corporatism scores from Crepaz (1993), with data for Greece, Portugal and Spain supplied by Professor Hans Keman of the Free University of Amsterdam. 1974–1994 sectoral transformation is equivalent to the percentage of the employed population leaving the agricultural sector, calculated from OECD, *Historical Statistics 1960–1994*, 1996. Average annual real change in hourly earnings in manufacturing from OECD, *Historical Statistics 1960–1993*, 1995. 1974–1994 right cabinet seats is equivalent to the average annual percentage of cabinet seats held by the major party of the right, with data from Schmidt (1996a) and the definition of the major party of the right according to criteria in Castles (1982).
Note: 18 cases in regression.

Basic model+federalism	Coefficient	Standard error	t-Value
Federalism	−0.274	0.859	0.318
Adj R^2=0.832			

Source: Federalism is from Table 8.1.
Note: 21 cases in regression.

Basic model+constitutional structure	Coefficient	Standard error	t-Value
Constitutional structure	−0.036	0.278	0.131
Adj R^2=0.831			

Source: Constitutional structure is from Table 8.1.
Note: 21 cases in regression.

Basic model+fiscal decentralization	Coefficient	Standard error	t-Value
Fiscal decentralization	−0.002	0.032	0.066
Adj R^2=0.831			

Source: Fiscal decentralization is from Table 8.1.
Note: 21 cases in regression.

Basic model+fiscal centralization	Coefficient	Standard error	t-Value
Fiscal centralization	0.003	0.027	0.096
Adj R^2=0.831			

Source: Fiscal centralization is from Table 8.1.
Note: 21 cases in regression.

Basic model+fiscal difficulty	Coefficient	Standard error	t-Value
Fiscal difficulty	0.133	0.263	0.506
Adj R^2=0.834			

Source: Fiscal difficulty is from Table 8.1.
Note: 20 cases in regression (no data for New Zealand).

be, in part, a response to the relationship between real wages and productivity is an argument which derives directly from the neo-classical model (Gregory 1993: 62).

When we turn to our five measures of decentralization, there is almost no story to be told, because there are no significant findings to report. Perhaps that should occasion little comment. The only obvious linkage in the literature is via the capacity of countries with low levels of fiscal difficulty to use Keynesian demand management techniques to boost employment. We have operationalized the fiscal difficulty measure on the tax side, whereas both Scharpf and Busch provide measures for the expenditure side of the budget. It is, therefore, possible that our lack of a significant finding for this variable is a result of discrepancies between the two measures, together with the obvious truth that Keynesian strategies were built more around increasing public expenditure than reducing taxation. However, comparing the few cases in which the variable has been operationalized in expenditure terms with those same countries as shown in the final column of Table 8.1, reveals no discrepancies of any magnitude. Were this correspondence to be demonstrated widely across the full distribution of OECD nations,[3] it would seem to suggest that decentralization was unlikely to be prominent in the list of the reasons why Keynesian policy intervention has failed to rein in the growth of unemployment since the mid-1970s.

Conclusions

There are only four points I wish to make here. The first is the obvious one in the context of a book devoted to the analysis of federalism that the findings here suggest that any links between decentralization and economic performance are a function of fiscal rather than political structure. This contrasts with the findings of the literature linking decentralization and spending policy outcome, where federalism and constitutional structure are the crucial institutional parameters. Probably, though, we should not be surprised at a contrast, which fits with our earlier speculation that the political and fiscal dimensions of decentralization could have quite different implications for policy. Spending outcomes are directly shaped by government decisions, so the way in which political structures shape the scope and domain of decision-making is immediately relevant to outcomes. In the economic arena, the choices of firms, employers and employees are constrained, but not shaped by political choices. That the institutional structure of the tax system proves to be prominent amongst these constraints is a finding wholly consonant with the speculations of public choice theory.

The second point is that interest in the consequences of political and fiscal decentralization is not merely a topic of academic concern. Governments initiate centralization of functions, devolve their powers and promote tax reform programmes. Governments also are in the game of seeking optimal trade-offs between macro-economic policy objectives. So if changes of the former type could make the latter kinds of policy dilemmas easier to resolve, it would matter not merely in the sense that we would know more, but in the sense that we could, as a community, do more. A dramatic instance of what is potentially at stake is the finding here that fiscal centralization is significantly associated with a weaker record of post-war economic growth and with poorer inflation outcomes. These outcomes can be quantified. If the implications of our models are taken at face value, we can say that, if the United Kingdom had been characterized by the OECD average level of fiscal centralization (i.e. if the level of fiscal centralization had been on average 16 percentage points lower across the post-war era), that country would have experienced a post-war economic growth rate on average 0.27 percentage points higher and an average post-war inflation rate 0.97 points lower than was actually the case. Countries like New Zealand, Ireland and Australia, with still more centralized fiscs, would have stood to make proportionately greater gains.

Clearly, if demonstrated, economic performance gains of this kind would be regarded by most politicians as heaven-sent. My third point, however, is that the findings here are quite inadequate for demonstrating such relationships to the satisfaction of any sane policy-maker. The modelling we have undertaken is designed to be exemplary rather than comprehensive. The big question is whether relationships seemingly characterizing the period as a whole in fact characterize its separate parts. There are good reasons to suppose that the magnitude of the effects with which we are concerned will have been at their greatest during the periods when the cross-national variances of particular performance parameters were at their greatest: economic growth before the First Oil Crisis, inflation from the mid-1970s to the mid-1980s and unemployment from the early 1980s to the mid-1990s. If that is so, the relevance to present-day policy-makers of our various findings will depend on whether the story told by reading the entrails of long-term outcomes is picking up on contemporary effects or on ones long since dead and buried.

So why a study of long-term aggregates, if long-term aggregates offer us little relevant in the way of immediate policy implications? The answer is to stimulate further research. It is axiomatic that much of that research effort should be empirical: that we should systematically disaggregate into policy components and time-periods and establish within what parameters political and fiscal decentralization is relevant to policy outcomes. My final point, however, is that, in this instance, theoretical work is a no lesser priority. In the case of the 'politics matters' paradigm, the mechanism of policy impact was, in crude outline, obvious enough. Voters choose candidate, at least partly on the basis of their policy platforms, so class and party preferences translate into legislated expenditure programmes. The mechanisms by which decentralization impacts on outcomes are far less transparent. Nowhere is this truer than in respect of the linkages between fiscal arrangements and economic performance. Usually in the field of comparative public policy analysis, theory suggests the hypotheses that require empirical testing. If some of the relationships located here pass the test of a more detailed empirical analysis, it will be time to reverse the process and demand of theory answers to the question of how decentralization matters.

Notes

1 This chapter is a somewhat modified and shortened version of a paper with the title of 'Decentralization and the Post-war Political Economy' which appeared in the *European Journal of Political Research* in 1999.

2 Post-war strike coefficient $= -93.382 - 174.475$ (51.129) corporatism $+22.445$ (4.827) 1960–1993 sectoral transformation. Adj $R^2 = 0.594$. 21 cases in regression. Figures in parentheses are standard errors. The strike coefficient is defined as the number of working days lost per 1,000 employees in non-agricultural sectors of the economy and is calculated for the period 1967–1992 from ILO, *Yearbook of Labour Statistics*, various years.

3 Such discrepancies will occur where there is Vertical Fiscal Imbalance (VFI), i.e. where central governments levy a higher proportion of taxes than they spend, passing on revenues to be spent at lower levels. Where VFI is high, as in Australia, it means that the fiscal difficulty of central governments will be higher on the expenditure than the tax side of the budget. It seems quite probable that a measure of the ratio of the relative ease with which central governments may boost public expenditure as compared with initiating tax cuts could explain a great deal about some countries' post-war policy development.

References

Alesina, A. (1989) 'Politics and Business Cycles in Industrial Democracies', *Economic Policy* 8: 55–98.

Barwise, K and Castles, F.G. (1991) 'The New Federalism, Fiscal Centralisation and Public Policy Outcomes', *The Australian Quarterly* 63, 2: 165–77.

Baumol, W. (1967) 'The Macroeconomics of Unbalanced Growth', *American Economic Review* 57, 2: 415–26.

Brennan, G. and Buchanan, J.M. (1980) *The Power to Tax: Analytical Foundations of a Fiscal Constitution*, Cambridge: Cambridge University Press.

Bruno, M. and Sachs J. (1985) *Economics of Worldwide Stagflation*, Cambridge, MA: Harvard University Press.

Busch, A. (1993) 'The Politics of Price Stability: Why German-Speaking Nations are Different', in F.G. Castles (ed.), *Families of Nations: Patterns of Public Policy in Western Democracies*, Aldershot: Dartmouth, 35–92.

Cameron, D. (1978) 'The Expansion of the Public Economy: A Comparative Analysis', *American Political Science Review* 72, 4: 1243–61.

—— (1984) 'Social Democracy, Corporatism, Labour Quiescence and the Representation of Economic Interest in Advanced Capitalist Society', in J.H. Goldthorpe (ed.), *Order and Conflict in Contemporary Capitalism*, Oxford: Oxford University Press, 143–78.

Castles, F.G. (1982) 'The Impact of Parties on Public Expenditure', in F.G. Castles (ed.), *The Impact of Parties*, London: Sage Publications, 21–96.

Castles, F.G. (1998) *Comparative Public Policy: Patterns of Post-war Transformation*, Cheltenham: Edward Elgar.

Castles, F.G. and Dowrick, S. (1990) 'The Impact of Government Spending Levels on Medium-term Economic Growth in the OECD, 1960–85', *Journal of Theoretical Politics* 2, 2: 173–204.

Castles, F.G. and McKinlay, R. (1979) 'Does Politics Matter?: An Analysis of the Public Welfare Commitment in Advanced Democratic States', *European Journal of Political Research* 7: 169–86.

Crepaz, M.M.L. (1992) 'Corporatism in Decline? An Empirical Analysis of the Impact of Corporatism on Macroeconomic Performance and Industrial Disputes in 18 Industrialized Democracies', *Comparative Political Studies* 25, 2: 139–68.

Crouch, C. (1985) 'Conditions for Trade Union Restraint', in L.N. Lindberg and C.S. Maier (eds) *The Politics of Inflation and Economic Stagnation*, Washington: Brookings Institution, 105–39.

Dogan, M and Pelassy, D. (1990) *How To Compare Nations*, 2nd edn, London: Chatham House.

Dowrick, S. and Nguyen, D.T. (1989) 'OECD Comparative Economic Growth in the Post-War Period: Evidence from a Model of Convergence', *American Economic Review* 7, 5: 1010–30.

Gregory, R.G. (1993) 'Aspects of Australian and US Living Standards: The Disappointing Decades 1970–1990', *Economic Record* 69, 1: 61–76.

Grilli, V., Masciandaro, D. and Tabellini, G. (1991) 'Political and Monetary Institutions and Public Financial Policies in the Industrial Countries', *Economic Policy* 13: 341–92.

Huber, E. Ragin, C. and Stephens, J.D. (1993) 'Social Democracy, Christian Democracy, Constitutional Structure and the Welfare State' *American Journal of Sociology* 99, 3: 711–49.

ILO (various years) *Yearbook of Labour Statistics*, Geneva.

OECD (various years) *Historical Statistics*, Paris.

—— (various years) *Revenue Statistics*, Paris.

Pierson, P. (1995) 'Fragmented Welfare States: Federal Institutions and the Development of Social Policy', *Governance* 8, 4: 449–78.

Scharpf, F.W. (1991) *Crisis and Choice in European Social Democracy*. Ithaca: Cornell University Press.

Schmidt, M.G. (1996a) 'When Parties Matter: A Review of the Possibilities and Limits of Partisan Influence on Public Policy', *European Journal of Political Research* 30: 155–83.

— (1996b) *Die parteipolitische Zusammensetzung von Regierungen in demokratischen Staaten (1945–1996)*, Heidelberg: Institut für Politische Wissenschaft.

Stockholm International Peace Research Institute (SIPRI), *Yearbook*, various years.

Summers, R. and Heston, A. (1991) 'The Penn World Table (Mark 5)', *Quarterly Journal of Economics* 106, 2: 327–68.

Wilensky, H.L. (1975) *The Welfare State and Equality*, Berkeley, CA: University of California Press.

9 Federalism and policy performance

A conceptual and empirical inquiry

Hans Keman

Introduction

Federalism as the organizing principle of a democratic state is considered by some authors to be superior to other types of states, because it apparently better safeguards the democratic rights of the citizens at large and of minorities in particular (see Riker 1975; Ostrom 1991; King 1993; Elazar 1995). In addition, so it has been claimed by these authors, federal states are often seen to perform better in terms of social and economic development (see also Lane and Ersson 1997). This begs the question to what extent federalism as a *polity* is indeed different from other democratic states (regarding its constitutional organization of public decision-making) and whether or not its material performance (i.e. enhancing public welfare) is indeed positively different from non-federal democracies (Weaver and Rockman 1993). To put it otherwise: is it true that federal democracies have an advantage over non-federal – often unitary – states in terms of their procedural and material performance? If this claim can be upheld then it would follow that the non-federal format of the national state is not only different from a federal democratic state as a *structure*, but particularly regarding its *process* of decision-making and the related *outcomes*, i.e. policy performance (see Elazar 1997).

From this line of reasoning it would follow that the polity is an important factor for structuring the political process, which – eventually – would result in an optimal democratic performance. This type of argument comes close to those of Shepsle (1995), who claims that polities, or institutional arrangements, do indeed structure the process of government toward an equilibrium (or optimal performance). Riker (1975: 111ff.) pushes this argument even further by stressing the fact that an optimal combination of centralized government and constitutional power division is conducive to 'rational bargaining among its constituents' rather than by majority decision-making or by consensus politics which is necessitated by the constant struggle of minorities in a unitary democratic state.

These arguments, however, neglect in my view the simple fact that non-federal states are not to the same degree unitary, as compared amongst each other, or conversely do have alternative institutional provisions for effective countervailing powers that can be seen as functional equivalents of the highly praised system of 'checks and balances' in federal states.

Some protagonists of federalism also tend to overlook the fact that most democracies are quite variable in their institutional complexion (see Colomer 1996; Lijphart 1999). Hence, there is not a clear-cut distinction between these two types of democratic polity as regards their governmental process (Dahl 1956: 22). Another point of contention is that, more often than not, the process of decision-making is considered by many political scientists as being (almost) identical with the process of *policy*-making (Heywood 1997; King 1993). Conceptually this means that these two distinctive processes are collapsed (see also Colomer 1996: 12). However, it can be argued that the 'right to decide' (i.e. decision-making) and the 'right to act' (i.e. policy-implementation) can be organized differently in any democratic polity, independently from its federal or unitary status (see also Hague et al. 1993; Lane and Ersson 1997).

Finally, and this is perhaps the strongest objection to the claim of federalism being the superior form of the democratic state, there is little convincing evidence that there is a *direct* relationship between the democratic state format, or polity, and the eventual performance in terms of its democratic politics and material outcomes (e.g. Castles 1982; Weaver and Rockman 1993; Keman 1993; Lane and Ersson 1997). In sum, one may indeed argue that the distinction between federal and unitary states is an important institutional *difference* of any democratic state, but not that the one is superior to the other because of its institutional features *per se*. On the contrary!

In this chapter I shall therefore argue that:

1   federal polities may well differ from non-federal ones, but this is rather a matter of degree than a fully fledged dichotomy which, in addition, would have direct implications for the decision-making process of the two types;
2   the differences between federal and unitary states should thus rather be addressed as different *types* of democratic policy-making and not as the one being superior to the other in this respect;
3   the conceptual distinction between a federal and unitary state format often confuses the matter of who has the 'right to decide' as regards policy-making with what state agency has the 'right to act' as regards policy-implementation;[1]
4   the cross-national variation in federal or unitary state *structure* and the *process* of policy-making is not a causal factor with respect to the material performance of a democratic polity.

I shall discuss these four propositions by investigating the cross-national variation in 18 democracies (see Table 9.1 below for the countries under review) with respect to their (constitutional) features regarding the 'right to decide', on the one hand, and who has the 'right to act', on the other. This conceptualization of the distinction between unitary and federal systems is often used in a confusing way which renders them invalid (see also Lane and Ersson 1997). Most authors tend to confound the 'right to act' with the 'right to decide' and vice versa. Instead I rather see this distinction as two sides of the same coin, which empirically hardly ever has the same imprint in each democratic state.

The 'right to decide' in a democracy refers to the extent to which citizens and organized interests are fairly represented and can exert influence on the political decision-making of the state (Bellamy 1996). Given the *indirect* nature of most democracies, the 'right to decide' is delegated by means of an electoral mandate to political actors (like MPs in parliament representing parties and, in turn, parties in government). The question is then on which level of the state this right is exercised: nationally or also subnationally? If the decision-making process takes place in the political 'centre' alone I consider this as a unitary type of decision-making. If the 'right to decide' is also organised at the subnational level (like for example in Australia and Germany) or is functionally delegated to other decision-making bodies (like in the Netherlands after the Second World War or in the UK recently) one can consider this as forms of non-unitary decision-making, or power-sharing (Lane and Ersson 1999: 170–1). In short, the 'right to decide' refers to the organization of democratic decision-making in relation to the level – national or not – and the competencies involved. An important indication of this can be found in the (constitutional) rights and safeguards of citizens, organized interests and (semi-)public bodies.

The 'right to act', conversely, concerns the operational and material *organization* of the (democratic) state with respect to policy-making, i.e. implementing decisions democratically made. The question here is then: which agencies have the legitimate right to public regulation (including the right to levy and allocate taxes)? In essence one can distinguish here between central and non-central governance. I define 'central' as those situations where one agency has a nation-wide authority to organize and implement public policies as opposed to those situations where either this authority is shared with other agencies (either public or private ones) or is delegated to territorial or functional bodies (Toonen 1990; Scharpf 1994). For example, in many federal states the 'right to act' is devolved across their states, but not all (e.g. regarding defence or the infrastructure), whereas in most unitary states most functional activities are centrally organized, but not necessarily all.[2]

In many studies, however, the 'right to act' is included in the measurement of the *distinction* between unitary and federal polities (see, for example, Lane and Ersson 1999: 187–8; Lijphart 1999: 186–91; Colomer 1996: 12). Yet, I contest that the degree of federalism of the *polity* (i.e. the 'right to decide') and decentralization of *governance* (i.e. the 'right to act') are in reality identical and therefore by nature strongly interrelated in a straightforward fashion. As will become clear, the variations in the structuration of the state and the concomitant variation in governance is greater than one often would expect from the literature. In part this is a consequence of how federalism is conceptualized, and more often than not includes the *organization* of the state (i.e. being more or less centralized or not).

On the basis of this discussion I shall develop two empirically founded scales, namely: *federal–unitary*, representing the constitutional indicators for the 'right to decide', and *central–decentral*, indicating the extent to which non-central state agencies have indeed the 'right to act'. I shall confront both scales with indicators representing the size of the public sector and public welfare (see also Schmidt 1996b; Castles 1998; Lane and Ersson 1997). This will enable me to say more on the matter of the material performance of both types of democratic politics and its eventual consequences for society.

In addition, these two cross-national variables allow me to to examine the issue of whether or not federalism matters as regards to democratic decision-making by controlling federal–unitary differences for *consensus democracy* (see also Linder 1994) and variations in central–decentral for *corporatism* (see also Vergunst 1998). Finally, I shall investigate the question to what extent these political processes are influenced by the features of *party government* (Budge and Keman 1990). These three institutional factors are seen as important regarding the question of who *decides* and makes policies and the related performance. The relations between politics and policy-making are examined to scrutinize the potential differences of *procedural* performance. I shall first elaborate on the conceptual issues regarding federalism and decentralization and the related empirical consequences.

Federalism as a distinctive state format

According to a *Dictionary of Politics* (Robertson 1985: 123–4), federalism is 'a form of governance in which power is constitutionally divided between different authorities in such a way that each authority exercises responsibility for a particular set of functions and maintains its own institutions to discharge those functions'. Such a definition would imply in theory that there exists within a (national) polity a number of sovereign bodies that may be interdependent but are constitutionally autonomous (i.e. functionally or territorially). What remains unclear, however, is how this division of powers actually works and what binds the various autonomous agencies within the greater framework of the federal state. It has been argued therefore that in the long run federations tend to disintegrate if and when the common good is not, or cannot be identical with the separate interests of the constituent parts (Wilcox 1989).

These matters are taken up by Schmidt (1996b: 167–8) when he discusses the distinctive features of federalism *vis-à-vis* unitary systems. His point of departure is that a federal polity is characterized by 'sharing power' and 'dividing power' in a *vertical* fashion between the federation and its constituting parts. This state structure serves the purpose of regional autonomy, on the one hand, and the protection of the rights of minorities, on the other. In his definition of what a federal state is, Schmidt adds two important features, namely: the *territorial* dimension and the idea of *power-sharing* (see also Linder 1994; Elazar 1995; Colomer 1996). Yet, like Robertson's definition, it is not clear to what extent a federal polity – apart from its organizational features – is fundamentally different from many unitary polities (where minority rights and power division are also safeguarded through a number of constitutional veto options).

Other definitions – like those of Vincent Ostrom (1991), Maurice Vile (1977), or Schultze (1992) – do not clarify the *specifica differentia* of federalism either. The same observation can be made regarding King (1993: 94–101), who claims that federalism is a decentralized government which is constitutional and thus non-absolutist, not to say democratic (see also Hague et al. 1993: 268–9). Again, such a definition still begs the question why this is fundamentally different from other types of democratic governance which are not considered as federal. Elazar (1995: 474–5) provides perhaps an answer as he states that federalism must be considered as a 'mother form of democracy like parliamentary democracy or direct democracy' since this type of polity is unique for its constitutionalized power-sharing through systems that *combine* self-rule and shared rule. Hence, a federalist polity is specific amongst (constitutional) democracies for its features of multi-level *representation* and territorial (or functional) *autonomy*. In Elazar's view a federalist state structure is not only superior since it combines features of other types of democratic rule, but also by avoiding the drawbacks of parliamentarism (majority rule in the centre of the polity) or of direct democracy (i.e. veto-power at the subnational level). Given these multiple interpretations, the question which is begging for an answer is: why would federalism be superior to the other forms of democracy, and how exactly does this work in practice regarding national political decision-making and policy-making and related performances?

In particular German scholars (Schultze 1992; Scharpf 1994; Schmidt 1996a) have pointed to the impediments of decision-making in a federal state due to (what Schmidt calls) 'veto points' at the lower levels within the polity. The accompanying bargaining structures which emerge in the process of policy-making and the (apparent) tendency towards a more unitary system over time (Wilcox 1989; Abromeit 1992; Heywood 1997: 121) are considered to be different from politics in non-federal types of democracy (Elazar 1997). Hence such a claim implies that indeed federalism matters as regards the 'democraticness' of the polity (i.e. accountability and responsiveness) (Keman 1997): the relation between decision-making and policy performance enhancing the 'public welfare' or the 'common good' would therefore be quite different from unitary states (e.g. Lane and Ersson 1997). From this discussion the following questions arise:

- How different are federal states from unitary polities with regard to decision-making?
- What are the *specifica differentia* that make federalism matter with respect to policy-making?
- To what extent are these differences relevant regarding the eventual policy performance?

These questions are in need of an answer since the claim of many a 'federalist' researcher is that federalism is not only different from but also superior to other types of democracy.

Federalism and unitary systems as democratic polities

At first glance it appears fairly simple to distinguish between federalism and unitary systems in terms of their state structures. In the literature the federal type is conceptualized as follows:

- having a written constitution which spells out the formal relationship between the federal government and its constituting parts as well as having a system of 'checks and balances' (for instance by means of symmetrical bicameralism) (Lijphart 1999);
- having a functional division in terms of policy competencies (e.g. regarding foreign policy, defence and infrastructure at the national level) and formal powers between the federation or national government and its constituting parts in terms of the 'right to decide' and the 'right to act' (i.e. the degree of subnational autonomy);
- having set rules regarding disputes between the federation and the 'states', on the one hand, and between the 'states', on the other, by means of legal review and an independent judiciary (Lane 1996).

Yet, how different is this from many unitary states? Most democratic states under review here have a written constitution, albeit that the relations between the 'national government' and the lower tiers of government are based primarily on the delegation of powers and co-government. This is indeed different, but at the same time it is obvious that in many unitary states there is quite some variation in the extent to which and in what way the 'centre' devolves powers, including fiscal autonomy, to subnational levels of the state (see Castles, in this volume). Hence, the organization may be different but not necessarily the mechanisms of power sharing within the polity. It can also be observed that most democratic states have similar institutions for solving conflicts within the polity. Judicial review and legal regulation of the state organization are features of any modern democracy, as bicameralism and (often compulsory) types of policy review by means of advisory boards and functional competencies (Irwin and Andeweg 1993; Heywood 1997; Woldendorp 1997). Once again, the apparent distinction between federal and unitary democratic states is less self-evident and straightforward than is often suggested in the literature on federalism (Elazar 1991; Ostrom 1991; Burgess and Gagnon 1993).

Lane and Ersson demonstrate this by comparing a number of listings of federal states (Lane and Ersson 1997: 87–94). They conclude that most of these focus on the formal side of the federalism and neglect more often than not the real organization and working of the federal state vis-à-vis unitary ones. The various listings also demonstrate that some classifications are rather strict, excluding some states that could well be considered as federal. For instance, most listings converge on the fact that Australia, Canada, Germany, Switzerland and the US are 'federalist' states. Yet, this would not be true for Austria, Belgium, Italy and Spain (Ducacheck 1970; Riker 1975; Sullivan 1991). Conversely, Elazar (1991) makes life even more difficult by including: states with 'federative arrangements' (which includes any type of home rule, devolution, regionalization), through which Denmark, the Netherlands, New Zealand, Portugal and the UK could also be considered as 'federative' (Lane and Ersson 1997: 91). Apart from the counter-intuitive character of such an inclusion, I would object to such classifications because they are either unnecessarily rigid (e.g. Riker 1975) or unduly extensive (e.g. Elazar 1991). Second, I think that – given the various dimensions of federalism that were discussed – it is more appropriate to develop a *comparative scaling* of federal and unitary systems. The reason for this is twofold:

1   A number of features are shared between federal and non-federal polities; they may differ in degree but are not mutually exclusive.
2   Existing classifications of federalism show not only disagreement between them, but appear also to be incomparable among themselves and often overlapping with unitary democracies.

In view of our discussion and the four contentions made at the beginning of the chapter, it is methodologically required to avoid simple dichotomies or fuzzy operationalizations. Arend Lijphart (1999: 312) has already developed a scale of federal–unitary. This scale is derived from constitutional features like: written constitution, bicameralism, minority representation and decentral governance. Although I concur with the idea that these features are important, Lijphart's operationalization has two drawbacks: first, it stresses the formal side of federalism only; and second, it includes decentral governance as a part of the constitutional federal polity (see also Burgess 1993: 5; Hague et al. 1993: 269).

First of all, in my view, in a scale of federal–unitary only the relevant competencies and related mechanisms concerning the 'right to decide' should be taken into account. This would imply more precise indicators of the way powers are shared (or not) between the constituting parts of the polity, whether these are separated and equal (or not) and the extent to which subnational governance is protected from interference from the national state. Furthermore, fair representation on the national level as well as decision-making at both levels of the state must be taken into account (Colomer 1996; Braun 1996; Anckar 1999).

Second, in most conceptualizations of federalism the *territorial* dimension is justifiably emphasized as an important feature. However, this feature is almost always equated – more or less explicitly – with the dichotomy *centralization/decentralization* of the state organization.

Various definitions of specific types of federalism have been developed to indicate this relationship: dual federalism (Switzerland and the US) implementation federalism (Germany), centralized federalism (Austria) or functional federalism (Belgium).[3] However useful these divisions may be to depict and describe a specific case of federalism, I do not think it proper to include this dimension – centralization/decentralization – in a comparative analysis of federalism and unitary systems. Such a scale would confuse the characteristics of the (constitutional) polity of the state with the structuration of implementing decision-making, i.e. the state organization.

Instead I propose to focus, on the one hand, on the organization of decision-making, i.e. the 'right to decide', as a *continuum* which runs from the formal separation of powers across levels of governance which are characterized by territorial features to power concentration on the national level for the whole territory. On the other hand, I shall develop an additional variable which focuses on characteristics of delegation and co-governance on other levels than that of the national state with respect to the 'right to act'. In sum, I propose to develop two cross-national measures in order to investigate empirically the research questions under review in this chapter:

1 *federal–unitary*: the complexion of the 'right to decide' (polity);
2 *centralization–decentralization*: the organization of the 'right to act' (policy).

The first scale will be used to scrutinize the extent to which federalism differs indeed from other types of democratic polities, as well as how different federal states are among themselves. The second scale is then an additional measure to analyse the question to what extent federalism does matter in terms of material policy-performance as compared to non-federal democracies, controlling for their organization of the state.

Scalability of federalism and decentralization cross-nationally

In the previous section I criticized Lijphart's operationalization of the federal–unitary scale for being too formal and too constitutionally driven.

In addition his scale (and other classifications as well) includes certain elements which I consider to belong to the dimension of centralization–decentralization. For these reasons I have employed a number of indicators developed by others, to construct a scale of federalism in addition to the constitutional classification of a polity being federalist or not. These indicators are: institutional autonomy vs. delegated governance (Lane and Ersson 1999); sovereignty of the constituting parts vs. political dominance of the national 'centre' (Schmidt 1996b); institutional barriers to national dominance (Colomer 1996); and balance between the executive and legislative (Lijphart 1999). All four indicators tell us a part of the story of how independently the national state can operate from lower levels of governance or territorial units, and hence, to what extent subnational units within the nation-state are capable of autonomous political actions. For instance, sovereignty and institutional barriers focus on the power division within democratic states from below, whereas autonomy and balance refer more to what extent the national state, or the 'centre', is capable of governing independently without the interference of other political actors. The various indicators, which are reported in Table 9.1, have been transformed into one (factor) score representing the extent to which the 18 states under review can be characterized as polities in which power-sharing in terms of self-rule, shared rule and national rule is more or less formally institutionalized (final column of Table 9.1).

The results reported in Table 9.1 show first of all that most polities can be characterized as having more devolutionary elements than not. Only Finland, France and Portugal can be considered as polities without features of local autonomy. In terms of institutional barriers and of power sharing (i.e. sovereignty) between the national state and the subnational units, the variation is quite mixed. All constitutionally defined federal states (i.e. Australia, Canada, Germany, Switzerland and the US) have scores above the mean. Yet, this is also the case for Belgium on Sovereignty and for Italy on Barriers. In addition, the institutional barriers are relevant in Austria, Finland, France and Spain. Obviously the institutional mix regarding subnational independence is shaped in a more varied way than is often thought and empirically indicated. This also implies that the cross-national variation is indeed more a matter of degree and is not a dichotomy.

Second, although the listings of federalism we discussed earlier are by and large correct, this seems less the case with countries like Austria, Belgium, Italy and Spain. Obviously these polities also have features in common with the established and recognized federal systems. This only reinforces my claim that the differences between federal and unitary states are less distinctive and more nuanced than is often put forward. Nevertheless it can be observed that there are indeed 'true' federal polities: Australia, Canada, Germany, Switzerland and the US. This confirms most existing listings, however, now reliably confirmed on the basis of indicators and shaped by means of a *continuum*, rather than a simple dichotomy or

Table 9.1 Features of federal and unitary democratic states

Country	Autonomy	Balance	Sover-eignty	Barriers	Federalism (Lijphart)	Federal (Maddex)	Unitary–federal
Australia	6	−1	3	4	−0.99	3	0.93
Austria	4	−0.5	2	3	−0.37	2	0.05
Belgium	5	−1	3	3	0.19	2	0.41
Canada	8	−1	3	5	−1.22	3	1.22
Denmark	4	−0.5	2	2	0.49	1	−0.25
Finland	4	−2.5	0	3	0.46	1	−0.96
France	0	−2.5	0	3	0.36	1	−1.23
Germany	6	1	5	4	−1.79	3	1.56
Ireland	0	0	1	2	0.76	1	−1.02
Italy	3	0	2	4	0.01	2	0.21
Netherlands	2	−0.5	1	2	0.33	1	−0.74
Norway	4	0	2	1	−0.08	1	−0.26
Portugal	1	0	1	2	0.61	1	−0.98
Spain	2	−0.5	2	3	−0.23	1	−0.23
Sweden	4	−1	0	1	−0.06	1	−0.89
Switzerland	7	0	5	6	−1.53	3	1.72
UK	3	−1	1	1	1.40	1	−1.00
USA	7	−1	5	6	−1.62	3	1.44
Mean	3.89	−0.86	2.11	3.06	2.18	1.72	0.004
SD	2.35	1.11	1.64	1.55	0.9035	0.89	1.00
Range	8	5	5	5	3.19	2	2.95

Sources and notes: *Autonomy*: additive index of non-central independence, based on Lane and Ersson 1999: 187 (high values indicate more independence from the central state).

Balance: relations between parliament and government, based on Lijphart 1984: 121ff. (+=parliament>government; −=government>parliament).

Barriers: additive index of constitutional safeguards for subnational governance and modes of representation, based on Colomer 1996: 12 (high values indicate higher barriers against national dominance).

Sovereignty: additive index of power-sharing features in democracies, based on Schmidt 1996b (high values indicate stronger formal powers at the sub-national level).

Federalism: scale of federalism as developed by Lijphart and taken from Schmidt 1996b (−=federal;+=unitary).

Federal: scores of federalism as provided in the respective constitution, based on Maddex 1998 (3=federal; 2=mixed; 1=unitary).

Unitary–federal: scale of federal unitary features by means of explorative factor analysis (R^2=66.4%; Varimax, One-solution) based on the listed variables except for *Federalism* (*Lijphart*) and *Federal* (*Maddex*) (+=more federal; −=more unitary).

(SD=standard deviation.)

trichotomy as is the case in most listings (and is illustrated by the variable 'Federal (Maddex)' in Table 9.1). This is demonstrated in the variable unitary–federal (see also Figure 9.1). In effect the values clearly show that indeed the federal cases, as well as Austria, Belgium and Italy, tend to have federal features. Figure 9.1 also shows that the cross-national variation among non-federal states is less dramatic than is the case with federal systems. Hence the scale of unitary and federal features appears to confirm my argument with respect to its scalability (see also Pennings et al. 1999).

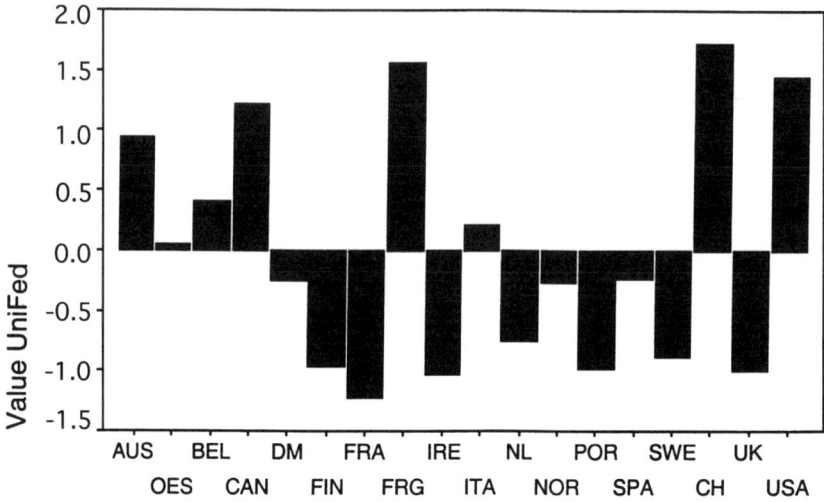

Figure 9.1 Comparative degree of unitary and federal features.

The other objection I have put forward with respect to the division often made in the literature between federal and unitary systems is that the conceptualization tends to be fuzzy. By including features of the state organization as regards centralization/decentralization, the distinction between decision-making and policy-making becomes blurred, if not contaminated. To avoid this, a measure of the degree of *decentralization* of a nation-state has been developed, also by means of factor analysis (see Table 9.2 and Figure 9.2). In this case a number of indicators were used that reflect the extent to which on *other* levels of governance than national government not only revenues and expenditures are not only collected independently, but also (more or less) autonomously allocated. Hence, this indicates to what extent non-central governing agencies like regions, provinces and communities indeed (materially) are able not only to decide on certain matters by themselves, but also to produce policy outputs more or less independently from central government.

The scale of decentralization demonstrates that – contrary to what is often thought – centralization and unitary systems do not go together in most cases.[4] Yet, what is more interesting in Table 9.2 (see last column) is that in a number of countries a mixed relation exists. On the one hand, there are moderately federalized systems – like Belgium and Italy – which are not strongly decentralized. On the other hand, in a number of unitary states a relatively high degree of decentralization exists: Denmark, Norway, Spain and Sweden (see Figure 9.2). Hence it can be concluded that the degree of federalism of the *polity* and decentralization of *governance* are neither identical nor strongly interrelated in a straightforward manner.

Table 9.2 Indicators of centralism and decentralization in democratic states

Country	Public sector	Central revenues	Decentral revenues	Decentral transfers	Fiscal difficulty	Fiscal centrality	Decentral- ization
Australia	34.9	22.2	6.2	6.7	4.1	0.14	1.03
Austria	48.6	21.2	8.9	6.1	4.2	−0.07	0.65
Belgium	53.1	26.6	1.9	7.0	3.3	0.71	−0.56
Canada	46.9	15.4	13.0	4.3	5.8	−0.95	1.74
Denmark	56.6	32.2	14.9	19.5	2.8	1.42	0.51
Finland	45.4	22.6	9.7	12.3	3.8	0.42	−0.20
France	49.9	18.1	4.0	1.9	4.7	−0.42	−0.19
Germany	46.0	13.3	11.4	3.5	6.7	−1.21	1.34
Ireland	41.9	28.9	1.4	8.7	3.1	1.01	−1.05
Italy	49.8	23.9	1.8	14.3	4.4	0.81	−0.37
Netherlands	51.7	27.3	1.3	14.3	3.4	1.20	−0.59
Norway	51.6	24.6	9.8	12.1	3.5	0.58	0.75
Portugal	39.3	20.4	3.5	1.4	4.3	−0.23	−1.04
Spain	36.2	18.3	4.3	9.5	6.2	−0.21	0.29
Sweden	59.1	18.0	15.2	5.9	3.6	−0.41	1.04
Switzerland	32.3	8.7	11.9	3.9	11.3	−2.25	1.21
UK	38.1	27.4	0.9	9.1	3.4	0.91	−0.59
USA	34.6	11.3	9.5	3.6	7.9	−1.46	1.53
Mean	45.3	21.1	7.2	8.0	4.8	−0.001	0.31
SD	8.0	6.4	4.9	4.9	2.1	1.0	0.90
Range	26.8	23.5	14.3	18.1	8.50	3.66	2.79

Sources and notes: *Public sector*=public expenditures of general government in % GDP (source: Lane et al. 1997).

Central tax=total tax revenues of central government in % GDP (source: Lane et al. 1997).

Decentral tax=total tax revenues of non-central government in % GDP (source: Lane et al. 1997).

Fiscal difficulty=taken from Castles (in this volume) indicating the impact of the fiscal pressure of central government on total tax revenues (the lower the value, the higher the fiscal pressure).

Fiscal centrality=degree of fiscal centralization (factor scores of central and non-central government expenditures as a % of GDP (source: Lane et al. 1997).

Decentralization=based on factor analysis of non-central public expenditures and revenues (R^2=63.7%; Varimax, One-solution); += decentralized, and −=centralized.

(SD=standard deviation.)

The cross-national variation is demonstrated in a scatterplot of both variables (see Figure 9.3).

On the basis of this scatterplot four clusters of countries can be distinguished. Those polities that are clearly federal regarding their state format and combine this feature with a high degree of fiscal and policy decentralization appear at the right hand top corner. Their counterparts are to be found in the left-hand lower corner. Both these clusters conform to common-sense ideas, but the remaining systems in the other cells do much less. The conclusion to be drawn is (again) that there is much more cross-

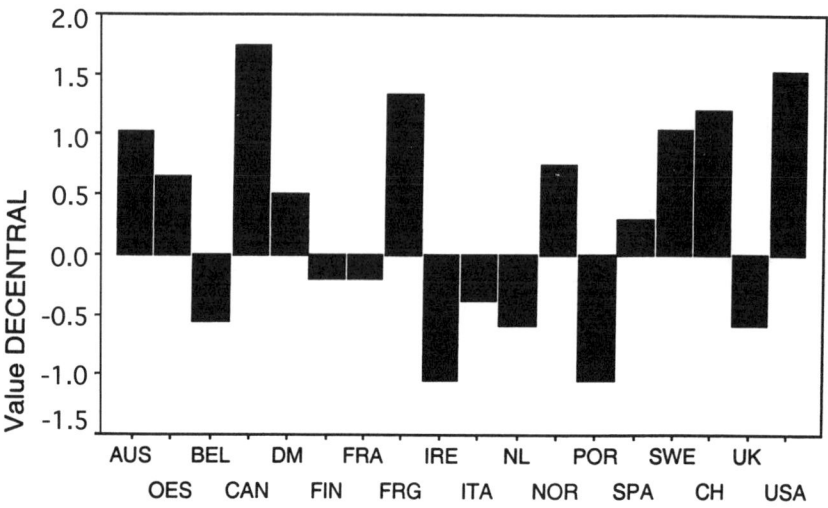

Figure 9.2 Comparative degree of centralizing and decentralizing features.

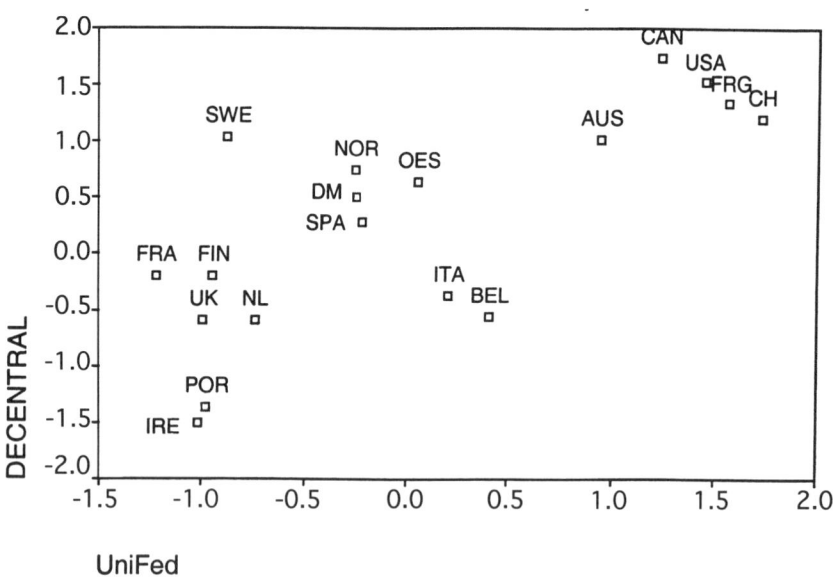

Figure 9.3 Scatterplot of unitary–federal and centralization–decentralization.

national variation in terms of federalized and non-federal states and decentralization than is often put forward. In addition, it is clear that by distinguishing between state *format* (i.e. federalized or not) and *organization* (i.e. decentralized or not) the cross-national distribution of the 18 democracies (in Figure 9.3) sheds new light on the questions that are raised in this chapter. The four clusters detected in this analysis show that there is indeed considerable cross-national variation in how the 'right to decide' (i.e. level and type of decision-making) is related to the 'right to act' (i.e. policy-making and implementation). In fact, it appears analytically worthwhile to suggest the following typology on the basis of the empirical analysis so far:

Type 1: Federal–Decentral (N=6): Australia, Austria, Canada, Germany, Switzerland and the US.
Type 2: Federal–Central (N=2): Belgium and Italy.
Type 3: Unitary–Decentral (N=4): Denmark, Norway, Spain and Sweden.
Type 4: Unitary–Central (N=6): Finland, France, Ireland, the Netherlands, Portugal and the United Kingdom.

In types 1 and 3 the 'right to decide' is clearly differently organized. The 'right to act', however, appears to be distributed across the different levels of government according to the type of decision-making (shared vs. centred). Conversely, in types 2 and 4 the 'right to act' is more or less identical, but the 'right to decide' is variable as regards the dimension of more or less unitary. Bearing these types in mind, it will be interesting to proceed this exploration by turning to the next research question: does federalism make a difference with respect to the procedural and material performance of the democratic systems under review?

Federalism and decentralization: the public sector and policy-making

The distinction between federal–unitary, on the one hand, and central–decentral, on the other, can serve a useful purpose. By considering these as mutually influencing factors determining the policy performance of a democratic system, the nature and direction of policy-making can be researched in a more meaningful way than has been hitherto the case. To be sure, the implications of a differently organiszed polity regarding the related mode of policy-making makes sense. The division of power and the degree of power-sharing in a political system are obviously deliberate choices with regard to the working of a democracy. Hence, it is perfectly sensible to expect that political actors are in different ways constrained in their room to manoeuvre regarding decision-making (Keman 1997). In addition, if the organization of the state regarding policy implementation is also a relevant feature of the policy-making process, one may well expect it to affect the eventual performance (Castles 1998: 108). Yet, before assessing policy performance and related outcomes, the actual implications of the polity features and of the organization of the state will be examined in view of the size of the public economy and the so-called overheads of the state (i.e. government consumption).

Federalism and decentralization and the size of the state

It is often suggested that federal polities are different from non-federal ones regarding the size of the state, i.e. the level of the public economy, and the degree of welfare state organization (see, for example, Schmidt 1996b; Lane and Ersson 1997; Vaubel 1995). This kind of Leviathan-type of argument is understandable if one follows the political-economic ideas regarding 'scales of economy' and transaction costs. The first argument is that smaller units (here subnational agencies) are more efficient than large-scale organizations (North 1990). The second argument is derived from the idea that the degree of co-ordination and monitoring within an organization – if and when goal oriented – is slack-avoiding and thus more effective (Czada et al. 1998). Hence, following these arguments small-sized states with a decentralized organization will be spending less and have less organizational costs (e.g. for employing people and related overheads). It may therefore be expected that federalized countries will have a lower level of public expenditures and revenues as well as less government consumption, whereas the other types (i.e. 3 and 4) will show an opposite development. In Table 9.3 two indicators of the size of the state and the public economy are compared for each of the four types of states.

The claims that state format and organization does make a difference cannot be considered a strong one. However, type 1 – the 'true' federalist systems – have indeed the smallest public sector within the universe of discourse. Not only have these states experienced lower levels of public expenditures, they remain so over time (and firmly below the cross-national average). What is remarkable, though, is the fact that also type 4, the unitary and centralised state, shows the same pattern, especially in 1990. Hence, we must conclude that the cross-national differences in the size of the public economy do not confirm the hypothesis put forward. It is rather the mixed bags, i.e. the countries belonging to types 2 and 3, which are characterized by higher levels and growth rates of the public sector.

With respect to the level of the 'Overheads' of the state organization, we can observe that type 2 (i.e. federal and central) is lagging behind in 1960, but clearly has caught up in 1990. The type 3 states, unitary and decentral, are by far the leaders in this category of public expenditures. Yet, it should be noted that in type 3 the range and standard deviation demonstrate that the within-variation is quite high, whereas this is less within the other types used. All in all, I conclude that the typology does yield cross-national differences as regards the public expenditures and the size of the state. However, these differences do not yet corroborate the hypothesis that federalism does really make a difference in this respect.

Table 9.3 Types of polity and state organization related to the size of the public sector

Type		Fed/ Dec (1) (N=6)	Fed/ Central (2) (N=2)	Un/ Dec (3) (N=4)	Un/ Central (4) (N=6)	All cases (N=18)
Public economy						
In 1975	Mean	34.8	39.8	37.9	38.8	37.6
	Range	15.8	2.9	23.7	23.9	29.9
	SD	6.03	2.05	11.17	8.30	7.55
In 1990	Mean	40.6	51.5	50.9	44.4	45.3
	Range	16.3	3.3	22.9	13.6	26.8
	SD	7.35	2.33	10.27	5.59	8.00
Change 1975–90		5.3	12.3	13.0	5.6	7.7
Government consumption						
In 1975	Mean	17.5	12.4	19.2	17.8	17.9
	Range	8.2	0.5	15.4	7.6	15.4
	SD	3.07	0.35	7.08	2.71	3.84
In 1990	Mean	17.8	17.5	21.8	18.3	18.8
	Range	6.8	0.4	13.4	5.6	13.8
	SD	2.47	0.28	5.98	2.15	3.50
Change 1975–90		0.3	5.1	2.6	0.5	0.9

Source: Lane et al. 1997.
Notes: *Public economy*: total outlays of general government.
Government consumption of general government.
All data in percentages of GDP.
(SD=standard deviation.)

State format and organization and public policy-making

Another claim is that federalist polities not only tend to have a smaller state and public economy, but also differ with respect to policy performance. This is not only a consequence of their rules of decision-making and existing veto-points (see Castles 1998: 82–3), but also result from their state or implementation structure (Vaubel 1995; Linder 1994; Lane and Ersson 1997). The reasons for this appear obvious enough: if the 'states', in particular the federalized polities, are indeed 'smaller' and with lower levels of expenditure, then it follows (seemingly) suit that 'politics does matter', but differently. Contrary to a 'bigger' and non-federalized state, one may well expect a more restrained policy profile in type 1 and 4 and to some extent also in type 2. The first two types are characterized by a decentralized state organization, whereas type 2 is closer to federalism than type 3 is. If this argument is correct, then it can be expected – given the mixed economy that is characteristic of all democracies under review here – that the social and economic performance in these countries will be different from those in type 4 (unitary and centralized).

In order to scrutinize these propositions, the various types of polity and state organization will be examined in view of two policy indicators. The first concerns transfer payments to households, which is not only an indicator of welfare statism but is also quite differently organized in the states under review (see Castles 1998) and is one of the most prominent policy areas in most democracies. The second policy indicator is government employment, which can be seen as an indicator of employment policy as well as of how extensively the state is organized. It may be expected that the welfare statist policies are more extensive in the centralized types of states (types 2 and 4), since the 'right to decide' and the 'right to act' appear to converge here. Hence, both decision-making and policy-making are organized on various levels of governance and thus may well tend to complement each other in a reinforcing manner.

The conclusion that can be drawn from Table 9.4 is that the 'true' federal and decentralized states are indeed (slightly) different from the other three types. Both in terms of level and change they make policies that are below the average for all cases included (n=18). What is striking, though, is that the more unitary but decentralized polities are 'catching' up with the other types (2 and 4) with respect to Transfer Payments and are

Table 9.4 Types of state format and organization related to welfare statism and public sector employment

Type		Fed/ Dec (1) (N=6)	Fed/ Central (2) (N=2)	Un/ Dec (3) (N=4)	Un/ Central (4) (N=6)	All cases (N=18)
Transfer payments						
In 1975	Mean	12.8	17.4	12.8	15.2	14.1
	Range	9.6	2.8	5.8	17.1	17.1
	SD	3.92	1.98	2.53	6.81	4.69
In 1990	Mean	14.2	19.4	17.0	17.3	16.4
	Range	10.2	4.1	2.7	15.5	15.6
	SD	3.93	2.90	1.29	6.32	4.49
Change 1975–90		1.4	2.0	4.2	2.1	2.3
Government employment						
In 1975	Mean	17.3	14.9	19.6	14.3	16.5
	Range	16.0	1.7	15.5	12.6	17.4
	SD	5.48	1.20	6.91	4.00	5.16
In 1990	Mean	17.2	17.7	26.2	17.2	19.3
	Range	11.8	3.7	18.8	13.8	24.3
	SD	4.15	2.26	8.25	5.12	6.32
Change 1975–90		−0.1	2.8	6.6	2.9	2.8

Source: Lane et al. 1997.

Notes: *Transfer payments* in % of GDP; *government employment* in % of total labour force. (SD=standard deviation.)

'leaders' regarding government employment. Belgium and Italy are to some extent different from the other countries. Probably this is a consequence of being a 'mixed' federalized polity and having a long tradition of nation-wide governance. Only recently is this changing. The four unitary and decentralized states (type 3) are different from the others because of the fact that three of the four countries belong to the Scandinavian family (Castles 1993). Here the local communities have always had a strong position regarding public policy formation and employing people by the state. Generally speaking, however, one can surmise that neither in terms of levels of expenditure nor in growth rates, are the federal and decentralized systems among the 'big spenders' on income maintenance programmes. Actually, the differences with the other types of states, as can be seen from Table 9.4, are growing over time. The same conclusion can be drawn with respect to the increase in government employment. Apart from type 3, all other polities experience the same level, but not in terms of growth.

I conclude that the federal and decentralized polities do indeed differ from the other types, but also that the cross-national variation between the remaining types does not yet warrant a firm statement as regards the impact of institutional and organizational factors on decision-making and policy performance. It rather appears that our polity types 2, 3 and 4 manifest certain differences. It seems that the mix of institutional arrangements in these polities is relevant, albeit in a varied way.

Federalism and decentralization and policy performance

Lane and Ersson (1997) and Castles (1998) ask to what extent the state format and its organisation affect the eventual social and economic performance of governmental policy-making. The question under scrutiny here is thus: do 'polity' and 'organization' matter in terms of societal outcomes? This question ought to answer one of the issues at stake in this chapter, namely whether or not federalism is superior to unitary systems with respect to material performance. In order to test the plausibility of such a claim, Table 9.5 shows variables which indicate the affluence of a country (by GDP per capita), and the rate of unemployment and of inflation. The former variable indicates the wealth of the nation, whereas the other two are indicators of the relative degree of 'misery' in a country (Schmidt 1982; Keman 1993). We expect that the various types of state format and organization will yield significant differences between the four types.

Obviously the respective types do perform quite differently as regards socio-economic development. In all respects the federal and decentralized states have experienced high rates of affluence and low rates of unemployment and inflation. Even after omitting Switzerland and the United States – reputedly the wealthiest nations of all – this category still performs above average. The semi-federal states (Belgium and Italy) perform worse

Table 9.5 Types of polity and state organization and socio-economic performance

Type		Fed/ Dec (1) (N=6)	Fed/ Central (2) (N=2)	Un/ Dec (3) (N=4)	Un/ Central (4) (N=6)	All cases (N=18)
Affluence						
In 1975	Mean	10.638	8.595	10.640	7.815	9.471
	Range	6.025	3.570	8.765	8.680	12.390
	SD	2.148	2.524	3.708	3.515	3.107
In 1990	Mean	19.333	17.177	15.994	14.528	16.750
	Range	6.120	555	4.900	9.035	13.015
	SD	2.405	392	2.216	3.433	3.208
Change 1975–90		8.695	8.582	5.354	6.713	7.279
Unemployment						
In 1975	Mean	2.8	3.6	2.5	2.7	2.8
	Range	5.3	0.8	2.0	3.6	5.3
	SD	2.18	0.57	0.91	1.35	1.57
In 1990	Mean	5.4	11.4	8.0	7.3	7.1
	Range	8.6	7.1	13.5	10.3	14.4
	SD	2.49	5.02	5.02	3.73	3.75
Change 1975–90		2.6	7.8	5.5	4.6	4.3
Inflation						
In 1975	Mean	2.9	3.9	5.3	4.9	4.2
	Range	1.0	2.8	2.7	6.0	7.0
	SD	0.46	1.98	1.34	2.27	1.75
In 1990	Mean	7.4	9.8	11.1	13.0	10.5
	Range	6.3	2.1	7.1	12.3	14.9
	SD	2.42	1.49	3.24	4.23	4.02
Change 1975–90		6.5	5.7	5.8	8.1	6.3

Source: Lane et al. 1997.
Notes: Affluence is GPPpC in $; inflation is % change in consumer prices; unemployment is % of total labour force.

and the unitary systems – decentralized or not – show high levels of 'misery'. Various authors offer an explanation for these findings (see Busch 1993; Lijphart 1999). On the one hand, it is suggested that corporatist structures in federalized states are an important asset to keep down inflation and unemployment (Schmidt 1982; Woldendorp 1997). On the other hand, it is put forward that central bank independence tends to go together with federalism and has an ameliorating effect on economic welfare in general, and on inflation in particular. I shall explore these hypotheses in more detail below. Hence, it appears that the state format and organization do matter with respect to socio-economic performance. At the same time one should observe that the degree of homogeneity as regards the policy performance *within all types* is relatively low (indicated by a high SD), whereas it is increased

in 1990. This would imply that other factors than state format and organization may well have caused the cross-national differences. Nevertheless it is
obvious that particularly the 'true' federal states (type 1) and, albeit to a
lesser extent, the decentralized states appear to be more capable of con-
troling the economy than unitary and centralized ones.

All in all, the conclusion is that the various types of federalism and
decentralization do yield different socio-economic performances, and that
federalism and decentralization appear to matter here. Unitary systems do
not perform well, particularly not around 1990. In particular the unitary
and centralized states are below the cross-national averages in all respects.

This section has made clear that we ought to dig further as to find out
whether or not federalism (or not) and decentralization (or not) do indeed
matter, if and when these relations are controlled for specific modes of
political decision-making and socio-economic policy-concertation (Keman
1997; Woldendorp 1997). In the next section I shall therefore employ the
concepts (and related measures) of *consensus democracy* and *corporatism* as
intervening variables that may account for the cross-national variation
between federalism and decentralization and the size of the state and public
economy, on the one hand, and policy and the performance of a country, on
the other. In addition, I shall take into account whether or not the variation
in the ideological complexion of government may have an impact on policy-
making and performance. This will allow us to explore to what extent actors,
i.e. partisan influences, do play a role and whether or not these influences
are mitigated by the institutional design of democratic states.

Modes of democratic decision-making and policy-making

It is by now obvious that the institutional design of state format (the 'right
to decide') and organization (the 'right to act') are *not always nor directly*
relevant for cross-national variations with respect to the public sector and
public policies. In my view, however, this does not imply that differences in
the degree of federalism and decentralization do not matter. What needs to
be investigated is the extent to which the behaviour of the relevant socio-
political actors is more or less shaped by these institutional configurations,
and, conversely, to what extent different types of political actors and
informal modes of decision-making may well account for the cross-national
variation in policy performances (Castles 1998; Keman 1990; 1993; 1997).
This will be the subject of analysis in this section.

Decision-making and policy-making capabilities and federalism and decentralization

I shall make use of the well-known concepts which are considered to represent informal modes of decision-making: corporatism and consensus democracy (Keman 1999). The basic idea underlying both concepts is that in

non-majoritarian or non-win situations socio-political conflicts can only be solved by the emergence of *coalescence* between actors and by *co-operative* behaviour of all actors involved. Hence, it may well be expected that these informal modes of decision-making and policy-making are crucial links between the polity and state organization as regards the public policy and socio-economic performances.

Both variables used in the analysis which represent consensus democracy and corporatism are taken from Lijphart and Crepaz (1991; but see also Keman and Pennings 1995). As these variables are not interrelated with the variables representing the scale of federal–unitary systems nor with the measure of centralization–decentralization,[5] it is therefore possible to apply regression analysis (Pennings et al. 1999). In other words, I suggest to control for the linkage between the polity and state organization with policy capacities and performance by the degree to which there exist consensual and corporatist modes of decision-making in the different states under review here (see also Linder 1994; Schmidt 1982; Woldendorp 1997; Lehmbruch 1998).

In addition to these informal institutions I shall also include in the analysis the partisan governance factor, i.e. differences in complexion of government. The rationale for this inclusion is that by now it is an accepted idea in comparative politics policy analysis that party differences matter and that left-wing parties in particular tend to use the public sector to influence socio-economic performances (Castles et al. 1988; Keman 1993; Schmidt 1996b).

Before presenting the results of the regression analysis I shall first discuss the bi-variate correlations (Table 9.6). The regression analysis is then employed in order to explore the relative impact of the degrees of federalism and decentralization on the various indicators of the size of the state, public policy formation and socio-economic performance (Table 9.7). Finally, the impact of consensus democracy and corporatism, as well as the role of political actors in democratic government, are analysed for their intermediating effects.

From Table 9.6 it emerges that federal states are indeed not in the category of 'big' government, nor are they at the forefront of active policy-making. As regards socio-economic performance, federal states are positively related to 'affluence' (or wealth) and to low levels of inflation (see also Table 9.5). Decentralized states are similarly related to socio-economic performance, but (apart from transfer payments, or income redistribution and social security) not to public policy-making and the size of the public sector. Equally striking is that one of the modes of conflict regulation, i.e. consensus democracy appears not to be relevant, but that the corporatist mode of conflict regulation as well as the complexion of government are significantly related both to the size of the state and public policy-making and to lower levels of unemployment, but less so to the other indicators of socio-economic performance.

Table 9.6 Bivariate relations between institutional variables and indicators of the public sector and policies and socio-economic performance

	Unitary/ federal	Decentral- ization	Consensus democracy	Corporatism	Complexion of government
Size of public sector	−0.47	−0.20	0.27	0.53	0.57
Government consumption	−0.40	0.12	−0.13	0.28	0.65
Government employment	−0.46	0.10	−0.01	0.41	0.84
Transfer payments	−0.47	−0.50	0.28	0.46	0.14
Affluence (GDPpC)	0.72	−0.71	0.09	−0.08	−0.14
Unemployment	−0.19	−0.50	−0.19	−0.52	−0.55
Inflation	−0.58	−0.59	−0.16	−0.46	−0.15

Sources: See Table 9.1 and 9.2 for the values of unitary/federal and centralization/ decentralization; see Lijphart and Crépaz 1991 for consensus democracy and corporatism; see Woldendorp et al. 1993 for complexion of party government.
Note: Pearson Product Market Correlations.

From this survey the preliminary conclusion may be drawn that the way socio-economic interests are represented in government and are organized through corporatist arrangements appears to matter. The questions that are therefore in need of an answer are, first, to what extent federalism and decentralization matter with respect to the state and policy capabilities (Weaver and Rockman 1993), and second, to what extent do party governments and institutionalized systems of intermediation influence these capabilities of policy-making and the related socio-economic performance? To find an answer I have modelled these questions in such a way that we may observe the relative influence of the various institutional variables. The results of this analysis are presented in Table 9.7 and discussed below:

The results of the model are quite remarkable. Apart from the fact that the models representing the size of the state are robust, whereas this is not the case with public expenditures, it appears that the two dimensions employed – federalism and decentralization – cancel each other out. In other words, the 'true' types of state format and organisation (1 and 4) developed earlier in this chapter affect significantly the cross-national distribution, but in opposite directions. This may then well explain the relatively small cross-national variation between the types in relation to features of size of the state and related policy capacity (i.e. level of expenditures). In addition, the equations 1 to 3 demonstrate that across-the-board there is some truth in the contention that federal states do have lower levels of public expenditures and size of the state (see also Schmidt 1996b; Lane and Ersson 1997). However, the most important result is that

Table 9.7 Multiple regression analysis of unitary–federalism and centralization–decentralization

Dependent variable				Independent variables
1. Size of the public sector 1990	=	Federalism	+	Decentralization
44.3%	=	−5.2%	+	3.1%
		(−1.80)		(1.30)
R² (*adjusted*) = 9%				
2. Government consumption 1990	=			
17.8%	=	−3.2%*	+	3.3%
		(−3.11)		(2.98)
R² (*adjusted*) = 33.8%				
3. Government employment 1990	=			
17.1%	=	6.5%*	+	7.0%*
		(3.83)		(4.57)
R² (*adjusted*) = 46.0%				
4. Transfer payments 1990	=			
16.6%	=	−1.1%	+	0.65
		(−0.71)		(−0.36)
R² (*adjusted*) = 13.2%				
5. Affluence	=			
16.254 $	=	1.083 $	+	1.624 $
		(1.32)		(1.80)
R² (*adjusted*) = 49.3%				
6. Inflation 1990	=			
11.1%	=	2.98	+	1.98
		(−0.82)		(−0.1.5)
R² (*adjusted*) = 33.9%				
7. Unemployment 1990	=			
7.7%	=	0.82	+	−2.02
		(1.36)		(1.51)
R² (*adjusted*) = 9.0%				

Notes: t-values are between brackets; the results are non-standardized; *=significant.

– apparently – the more federalist the polity and the more decentralized the state organization (type 1), the less difference this will make in the end as compared to unitary and centralized states (type 4). This conclusion is supported by the coefficients (compare this also with Table 9.3). One may conclude that federalism matters with respect to the size of the public sector, but to what extent it makes a difference depends (also) on the related degree of decentralization (as, for example, in Belgium and Italy; i.e. type 2).

Conversely government employment is typically shaped by the degree of decentralization. In fact, given the knowledge that more states than only federal ones are often decentralized, the result of equation 3 explains why type 3 states (unitary/decentral) have a much higher level of government employment than the other states. The causal relationship between affluence and federalism (or not) and decentralization (equation 5) appears to be strong. Yet, a closer inspection of the separate cases shows that the institutions may matter, but not for all the countries of type 1 (federalist and decentralized). The positive outcome is by and large due to the US, Switzerland and Austria, whereas Ireland and Portugal are negative outliers influencing the results of the opposite type (=4). The performance as regards Inflation and unemployment is rather insignificant indicating that other factors than state format and organization need to be taken into account. The overall conclusion with respect to Table 9.6 is that cross-national differences in federalism and decentralization do certainly matter but also that they appear to be mitigated by other (f)actors as well. To these factors we shall now turn.

The role of consensus democracy, corporatism and complexion of party government

In what way and to what extent can the more informal modes of decision-making and policy-making can be considered as influential? Both the concepts of consensus democracy and corporation are seen as important intermediating institutions which shape political behaviour in such a way that suboptimal outcomes can and will be avoided (Linder 1994; Shepsle 1995; Keman 1999). Hence, it is expected that both modes of conflict regulation are relevant for decision-making and policy-making, if and when veto-points can well induce stalemates. Such a situation may arise in particular in the event that a more left-wing oriented government is in power. As the vast literature on 'does politics matter?' demonstrates, parties in government do matter and the distinction between left and non-left parties is relevant for the direction and level of governmental actions (see, for example, Castles et al. 1988; Schmidt 1996b; Keman 1997). Two models, or equations, have been developed to answer this question:

Equation 1: *Institution, actors and the 'right to decide'*.
Public sector and policy-making and socio-economic performance = consensus democracy (CD)+complexion of government (CoG)+ unitary vs. federal (U/F).

Equation 2: *Institutions, actors and the 'right to act'*.
Public sector and policy-making and socioeconomic performance = corporatism (CoR)+complexion of government (CoG)+ decentralisation (Dec).

Equation 1 represents the interactions between the state format (the 'right to decide') and the institutional arrangements and government with respect to the state and related public expenditures and socioeconomic performance. In other words, how institutions and actors are indeed intermediating, if not shaping, the political decision-making in unitary or federal states. Equation 2 focuses on the intermediating role of the same institutions and actors in relation to the existing state organization (the 'right to act'). In Table 9.8 the results of the multiple regression analysis are reported in which this line of reasoning has been modelled.

Table 9.8 Multiple regression analysis of unitary and federal systems and decentralized states in relation to consensus democracy, corporatism and party government

Public sector activities	*Equation 1*		*Equation 2*	
Level of expenditures	=	34.1	=	35.1
	CD	1.3	CoR	1.4
	CoG	4.8*	CoG	4.6
	U/F	−1.5	Dec	−1.5
	R^2 =	21.6	R^2 =	19.1
Level of government consumption	=	12.7	=	9.0
	CD	−0.7	CoR	−1.6
	CoG	2.7*	CoG	4.2*
	U/F	−0.3	Dec	0.9
	R^2 =	26.7	R^2 =	33.0
Government employment	=	5.3	+	−0.6
	CD	−0.7	CoR	−2.7
	CoG	6.0*	CoG	8.5*
	U/F	−0.3	Dec	0.5
	R^2 =	46.1	R^2 =	54.7
Transfer payments	=	16.5	=	22.0
	CD	0.9	CoR	3.4*
	CoG	−0.09	CoG	−1.3*
	U/F	−1.5	Dec	0.5
	R^2 =	1.6	R^2 =	22.3
Affluence (= GDPpC)	=	15.614	=	20.485
	CD	315.0	CoR	908.0
	CoG	470.0	CoG	−1.857
	U/F	2.331*	Dec	2.773*
	R^2 =	37.3	R^2 =	49.7
Unemployment	=	3.8	=	10.8
	CD	−0.6	CoR	−0.8
	CoG	−2.8*	CoG	−1.4
	U/F	−1.3	Dec	−1.2
	R^2 =	22.8	R^2 =	16.4
Inflation	=	14.4	=	4.2
	CD	−0.5	CoR	−3.3*
	CoG	−1.7	CoG	3.2*
	U/F	−2.8*	Dec	−3.2*
	R^2 =	32.0	R^2 =	58.3

Notes: The coefficients are non-standardized; *=significant; R^2=adjusted; CD=consensus democracy; CoG=complexion of government; CoR=corporatism; U/F=scale of federal/unitary; Dec=scale of decentralization (see Tables 9.1 and 9.2). The variables CD and COR are taken from Schmidt 1996b, CoG from Woldendorp et al. 1993.

Most of the equations are statistically not robust nor do they yield many significant results. However, this is not an overriding concern since we are more interested in the interactions per se and the direction of each component in the model. Hence Table 9.8 should be seen as a descriptive tool for analysis.

As regards the outcomes of equation 1 it can be observed that the role of government is relevant (except for 'transfer payments' and 'affluence'). It really makes a difference whether or not there is a (more or less) left-wing government regardless of whether it is a federal or unitary state. However, it must be added that the difference between federal and unitary remains an important factor: almost all state activities are affected by this distinction in a downward direction if it concerns a federal state. This implies that however 'radical' government may be in federal democracies, the effect of government will be less pronounced than in unitary ones. Consensus democracy as an intermediating mode of decision-making appears hardly relevant. The working of this phenomenon is rather restricted and must be considered as an additional factor that appears only relevant in certain countries, namely the low countries and the 'Germanic' family of nations (Castles 1993; Schmidt 1996a).

In summary, equation 1 tells us that the complexion of government is crucial for the direction of decision-making and if it is left-wing oriented that this effect is dampened in the more federalist types of democracy. Conversely, the intermediating effect of consensus democracy is, comparatively speaking, weak and restricted to a certain group of nations. The overall significance of this model of the 'right to decide' is that the distinction between federal and unitary systems is important. This is particularly true as regards the socio-economic performance of a nation.

The results of equation 2 – where the decentralized organization of the state and the existence of corporatism figure in combination with the complexion of government – yield roughly the same results: the role of government is by and large the driving factor as regards the public sector and policy activities. What is different from the first equation, however, is that in certain areas the statistical results are not only characterized by a higher explained variance (like government employment, transfer payments, affluence and inflation), but also that decentralisation does affect the direction and levels of governmental activity. It makes a difference whether or not a democratic state is more or less decentralized. This is visible in the socio-economic performance of a country: in particular affluence and inflation, and to some extent government employment, show this trend. Yet, one must be wary of making too strong statements in this respect because, for instance, affluence is quite a structural feature of any economy and it is exactly the type 1 polities (i.e. federal and decentralized) which belong to the stronger post-war economies (like Germany, Switzerland and the USA). Inspecting the outliers with respect to inflation and affluence shows that the weaker economies (i.e. Ireland, Portugal and

Spain) are lagging behind. Hence, it would be a too rash conclusion that both government and the institutional features are decisive regarding the policy performance. It seems more proper to suggest that the results of equation 2 demonstrate that in decentralized states corporatism and the complexion of government are of *equal* significance (or are cancelling each other out) as regards policy-making and the related socio-economic performances. In short, the way that the 'right to act' is organized within a democratic state seems to enhance socio-economic development.

Conclusions

In this chapter the claim that federalism per se is superior to other types of democratic states in terms of their performance has been challenged both conceptually and empirically. I have demonstrated that existing concepts of federalism cannot only be contested, but appear often to be elaborated in a fuzzy way. In order to improve on this, I have, first of all, made a distinction between those institutional features that can be considered to structure the process of decision-making or the 'right to decide' (i.e. degrees of 'self-rule' in contribution with 'power-sharing'), on the one hand, and those pro-visions that promote the power and thus the 'right to act' on subnational levels of the state, on the other. This distinction appears not only concep-tually useful, but could also be applied empirically. In fact, it could be demonstrated that federalism and decentralization are two distinct cross-national variables, which enable the researcher to categorize the cases under investigation in a more meaningful way than is often the case in the literature.

In this chapter I have constructed four types of democratic state (see Figure 9.1) in order to examine the claim that federal and decentralized states produce different, if not superior, policies and related performances. The comparative cross-national analysis made clear that, although there are certainly differences between the four types, these differences do not result in similar consequences. The most significant finding remains that the strongly federalized polities and highly decentralized states tend to have a 'smaller government' than others and produce higher levels of affluence and less 'misery'. At the same time it must be added that this pattern is also quite variable among the countries that make up the other three categories. Hence, another conclusion must be that the cross-national differences between federal and unitary polities, and decentralized and centralized state organizations, are more a matter of degree. As cross-national variables, however, it should be noted that these should be amplified by intermediary institutional constellations in empirical analyses of their effects.

The second part of this chapter has been devoted to the investigation of the relationships between the structural features of the 18 democracies under review and the processes of decision-making and policy-making. As expected, there are no strong relationships between structure and process. Yet, it should be noted there are significant relations between the size of government and socioeconomic performance (see Table 9.6). We extended therefore our investigations by means of multiple regression analysis to inspect the extent to which both the processes of decision-making and policy-making are also influenced by intermediating institutions like consensus democracy and corporatism, on the one hand, and by differences in the complexion of government, on the other. The results of the analysis showed that the role of party government in particular is relevant across the 18 democracies under review here. The effects of consensus democracy and corporatism *can* strengthen policy outcomes and socio-economic performance, but only to a limited degree. Overall, we conclude that the state format and organization is a latent but relevant feature of liberal democracy.

So, what have we learnt of the conceptual and empirical inquiry performed in this chapter? First of all, we have found that 'federalism does matter' if and when considered as a cross-national variable with respect to the size and organization of the state. Second, we have observed that 'decentralization' is not by definition absent in non-federal states and this has implications for policy-making capabilities. Third, the socio-economic performance of federal-cum-decentralized states appears to be better than that of other states, but one must bear in mind that – at least partially – this finding is affected by some economies that can be seen as 'catching up' or as laggards (e.g. Spain, Portugal, Ireland).

Notwithstanding these observations, it can be concluded that, *ceteris paribus*, federalism is a distinctive feature of the democratic state and it appears to matter with respect to its policy capacities and policy performances in particular. The results of the cross-national analysis presented in this chapter have demonstrated that:

- The distinction federal–unitary is indeed a matter of degree and they should therefore not be considered as mutually exclusive concepts. Instead one should focus more explicitly on how the 'right to decide' *per se* is organized in the democratic policy.
- The central–decentral organization of the state should always be taken into account, preferably as a separate variable, otherwise the independent impact of the 'state' as an organization is underrated and may lead to compromised conclusions.
- The material performances of the polities under review here are relatively different from each other, but, this does not lead to the conclusion that federalism is *by definition* superior to unitary systems in terms of public policy-making and socio-economic performance.
- The distinction between the 'right to decide' (format) and the 'right to act' (organization) is particularly useful for studying democracies, as regards their procedural performance.

- The cross-national analysis by means of bi-variate and regression analysis has shown that polity features and organization of the state are *conditional* factors with respect to the material performances and influence decision-making and related political behaviour.

As a final statement I contend that the analysis presented is not only food for thought, but will also be contested by those who focus on federalism exclusively and apply this concept and related mechanisms to specific cases, instead of investigating it from a truly comparative perspective. In doing so an important point is missed: namely that although institutions matter, in the final analysis cross-national differences in terms of context and actors matter equally in any type of democratic state.

Notes

1 The right to decide refers to the situation in which actors (parties, government) are in a formal position to impose their will in the process of decision-making, whereas the right to act refers to those situations in which (one or more) actors are independently responsible for executing policy decisions.
2 For example, in the Netherlands 'water management' is organized on the level of the nation-state, but the actual implementation is regionally organized, including the right to tax and of rule-making.
3 See Abromeit 1992; Schultze 1992: 108–9; Burgess and Gagnon 1993; Hague et al. 1993: 268–76; Scharpf 1994; Lane and Ersson 1997: 97; Heywood 1997: 128–30.
4 Pearson's r between decentralization and uni-fed=0.75 implying a R^2 of only 53 per cent.
5 Pearson's r of unitary–federal with consensus democracy=−0.10, and with corporatism=−0.23; Pearson's r of centralization–decentralization with consensus democracy =−0.27 and with corporatism=0.0

References

Abromeit, H. (1992) *Der verkappte Einheitsstaat*. Opladen: Leske & Budrich.
Anckar, D. (1999) 'Try Federalism', *Scandinavian Political Studies* 22, 2: 99–128.
Barwise, K. and Castles, F.G. (1991) 'The "New Federalism". Fiscal Centralisation and Public Policy Outcomes', Discussion Paper no. 27, Australia: Australian National University. Graduate program in public policy.
Bellamy, R. (1996) 'The Political Form of the Constitution: The Separation of Powers, Rights and Representative Democracy', in R. Bellamy and D. Castiglione (eds), *Constitutionalism in Transformation: European and Theoretical Perspectives*, Oxford: Blackwell, 25–44.
Braun, D. (1996) *Der bundesdeutsche Föderalismus an der Wegscheide. Interessenkonstellationen, Akteurskonflikte und institutionelle Lösungen*, Heidelberg: Institut für Politische Wissenschaft, Universität Heidelberg.
Budge, I. and Keman, H. (1990) *Parties and Democracy. Coalition Formation and Government Functioning in Twenty States*, Oxford: Oxford University Press.
Burgess, M. (1993) 'Federalism and Federation: A Reappraisal', in M. Burgess and A.-G. Gagnon (eds) *Comparative Federalism and Federation*, Hertfordshire: Harvester Wheatsheaf.

Burgess, M. and Gagnon, A.-G. (1993) (eds) *Comparative Federalism and Federation*, Hertfordshire: Harvester Wheatsheaf.

Busch, A. (1993) 'The Politics of Price Stability: Why the German-Speaking nations are Different', in F.G. Castles (ed.), *Families of Nations: Patterns of Public Policy in Western Democracies*. Aldershot: Dartmouth, 35–92.

Castles, F.G. (ed.) (1982) *The Impact of Parties: Politics and Policies in Democratic Capitalist States*. London: Sage Publications.

—— (ed.) (1993) *Families of Nations: Patterns of Public Policy in Western Democracies*. Aldershot: Dartmouth.

—— (1998) *Comparative Public Policy*, Cheltenham: Edward Elgar.

Castles, F.G., Lehner, F. and Schmidt, M.G. (eds) (1988) *Managing Mixed Economies*. Berlin: De Gruyter.

Colomer, J. (ed.) (1996) *Political Institutions in Europe*, London: Routledge.

Czada, R.M., Héritier A. and Keman, H. (eds) (1998) *Institutions and Political Choice: On the Limits of Rationality*, Amsterdam: VU University Press.

Dahl, R.A. (1956) *A Preface to Democratic Theory*, Chicago: University of Chicago Press.

Ducachek, I.D. (1970) *Comparative Federalism: The Territorial Dimension of Politics*. New York: Holt, Rinehart and Winston.

Elazar, D.J. (ed.) (1991) *Federal Systems of the World*, Harlow: Longman.

—— (1995) 'Federalism', in: S.M. Lipset (ed.), *The Encyclopedia of Democracy*, London: Routledge, 2: 472–82.

—— (1997) 'Contrasting Unitary and Federal Systems', *International Political Science Review* 18, 3: 237–51.

Hague, R., Harrop, M. and Breslins, S. (1993) *Comparative Government and Politics*, 3rd edn, Basingstoke: Macmillan.

Heywood, A. (1997) *Politics: An Introduction*. Basingstone: Macmillan.

Irwin, G.A. and Andeweg, R.B. (1993) *Dutch Government and Politics*, Basingstoke: Macmillan.

Keman, H. (1990) 'Social Democracy and Welfare Statism', *Netherlands Journal of Social Sciences* 26, 1: 17–34.

—— (1993) 'The Politics of Managing the Mixed Economy', in H. Keman (ed.), *Comparative Politics, New Directions in Theory and Method*, Amsterdam: VU University Press.

—— (1996) 'Political Institutions in the "Low Countries": Confrontation and Coalescence in Segmented Societies', in J. Colomer (ed.), *Political Institutions in Europe*, London: Routledge.

—— (1997) *The Politics of Problem-Solving in Postwar Democracies*, Basingstoke: Macmillan.

—— (1999) 'Political Stability in Divided Societies: A Rational-Institutional Explanation', *Australian Journal of Political Science* 34, 2: 249–68.

Keman, H. and Pennings, P. (1995) 'Managing Political and Societal Conflict in Democracies: Does Consensus and Corporatism matter?', *British Journal of Political Science* 25, 2: 271–81.

King, P .(1993) 'Federation and Representation', in M. Burgess and A.-G. Gagnon (eds), *Comparative Federalism and Federation*, Hertfordshire: Harvester Wheatsheaf.

Lane, J.E. (1996) *Constitutions and Political Theory*, Manchester: Manchester University Press.

Lane, J.E., McKay, D. and Newton, K. (1997) *Political Data Handbook: OECD Countries*, 2nd edn, Oxford: Oxford University Press.

Lane, J.E. and Ersson, S.O. (1997) 'Is Federalism Superior?', in B. Steunenberg and F. van Vught (eds), *Political Institutions and Public Policy: Perspectives on European Decision Making*, Dordrecht: Kluwer Academic Publishers.

—— (1999) *Politics and Society in Western Europe*, 4th edn, London: Sage.

Lehmbruch, G. (1998) 'The Organisation of Society. Administrative Strategies and Policy Networks', in R.M. Czada, A. Héritier and H. Keman (eds), *Institutions and Political Choice: On the Limits of Rationality*, Amsterdam: VU University Press.

Lijphart, A. (1984) *Democracies: Patterns of Majoritarian and Consensus Government in 21 Countries*, New Haven and London: Yale University Press.

—— (1999) *Patterns of Democracy: Government Forms and Performance in Thirty-Six Countries*, New Haven and London: Yale University Press.

Lijphart, A. and Crepaz, M.M.L (1991) 'Notes and Comments. Corporatism and Consensus Democracy in Eighteen Countries: Conceptual and Empirical Linkages', *British Journal of Political Science* 21: 235–56.

Linder, W. (1994) *Swiss Democracy*, London: Routledge.

Maddex, R.L. (1998) *Constitutions of the World*, London: Routledge.

North, D.C. (1990) *Institutions, Institutional Change and Economic Performance*, Cambridge: Cambridge University Press.

Ostrom, V. (1991) *The Meaning of American Federalism: Constituting a Self-governing Society*, San Francisco: ICS Press.

Pennings, P., Keman, H. and Kleinnijenhuis, J. (1999) *Doing Research in Political Science: An Introduction to Comparative Methods and Statistics*, London: Sage Publications.

Riker, W.H. (1975) 'Federalism', in F.I. Greenstein and N.W. Polsby (eds) *Governmental Institutions and Processes*, Reading. MA: Addison-Wesley.

Robertson, D. (1985) *Dictionary of Politics*, Harmondsworth: Penguin Books.

Scharpf, F.W. (1994) *Optionen des Föderalismus in Deutschland und Europa*, Frankfurt am Main: Campus.

Scharpf, F.W., Reissert, B. and Schnabel, F. (1976) *Politikverflechtung. Theorie und Empirie des kooperativen Föderalismus in der Bundesrepublik*, 2 vols, Kronberg: Scriptor Verlag.

Schmidt, M.G. (1982) 'Does Corporatism Matter? Economic Crisis, Politics and Rates of Unemployment', in G. Lehmbruch and Ph.C. Schmitter, *Patterns of Corporatist Policy-Making*, Beverly Hills and London: Sage Publishers.

—— (1996a) 'Germany: The Grand Coalition State', in J. Colomer (ed.) *Political Institutions in Europe*, London: Routledge.

—— (1996b) 'When Parties Matter: A Review of the Possibilities and Limits of Partisan Influence on Public Policy', *European Journal of Political Science* 30, 2: 155–83.

Schultze, R. (1992) 'Föderalismus', in D. Nohlen, *Lexikon der Politik. Band 3. Die westlichen Länder*, München: Verlag C.H. Beck.

Shepsle, K.A. (1995) 'Studying Institutions: Sum Lessons from the Rational Choice Approach', in J. Farr, J. Dryzek and S. Leonard (eds), *Political Science in History*, Cambridge: Cambridge University Press.

Sullivan, M.J. (1991) *Measuring Global Values: The Ranking of 162 Countries*, New York: Greenwood Press.

Toonen, T.A.J. (1990) 'The Unitary State as a System of Co-Governance', *Public Administration* 68, 3: 281–97.

Vaubel R, (1995) 'Constitutional Safeguards Against Centralisation in Federal States: an international cross-section analysis', unpublished paper, universität Mannheim.

Vergunst, N. (1998) 'Consensus Democracy. Corporatism and Federalism. Do Institutions Matter'? Paper for workshop 'Does Federalism matter?', ECPR Joint Sessions, Warwick.

Vile, M. (1977) 'Federal Theory and the "New Federalism"', in D. Jaensch (ed.) *The Politics of New Federalism*, Adelaide: Australian Political Science Association.

Weaver, R.K. and Rockmann, B.A. (1993) *Do Institutions Matter?* Washington: The Brookings Institution.

Wilcox, K. (1989) 'Australian Federalism', in R. Smith and L. Watson (eds), *Politics in Australia*. Sydney: Allen and Unwin, 140–53.

Woldendorp, J.J.W. (1997) 'Neo-corporatism and Macroeconomic Performance in 8 Small West-European countries (1970–1990)', *Acta Politica* 32, 1: 49–79.

Woldendorp, J.J.W., Keman, H. and Budge, I. (1993) *Handbook of Democratic Government : Party Government in 20 Democracies (1945–1990)*, Dordrecht: Kluwer Academic Publishers.

10 The impact of federalism and neo-corporatism on economic performance

An analysis of eighteen OECD countries

Thomas D. Lancaster and Alexander M. Hicks

'Does federalism matter?' Neo-institutionalists believe that structural arrangements have an independent effect on policy-making and outcomes (March and Olsen 1989; Steinmo et al. 1992). They argue that organizational structures, by affecting incentives, influence the social and political behaviour of groups and individuals. The decentralized institutional frameworks of federalism create different incentives and offer different rewards from those provided by unitary systems, with their emphasis on central state decision-making priority. This chapter asks whether federal or unitary state structures also affect macro-economic policy performance in the world's major industrialized countries.[1]

A large literature already argues that federalism does matter in policy affairs, including intergovernmental co-ordination (Scharpf et al. 1976), public administration (O'Toole 1990; Wright 1994), political parties and representation (Brzinski et al. 1999a; 1999b), interest group organization and mediation (Coleman 1987), social policy (Pierson 1995; Pierson and Leibfried 1995), regional development (Hoffman 1981), European integration (Scharpf 1988; Jeffrey and Sturm 1993), and other areas of public policy. We aim to add federalism – as a specific organizational and institutional variable – to the comparative literature explaining economic performance (see, for example, Grier and Tullock 1989; Zysman 1983; Weingast 1995). Neo-institutionalist economists have already made the case that institutional arrangements encourage individuals and organizations to engage in productive economic activity, producing successful economies (North 1990). They tend to assume that *laissez-faire* approaches to governance and decentralization are economically the most beneficial. Another group of economists argue for the economic superiority of more centralized states, emphasizing the benefits of state collective goods (Zysman 1983; Stiglitz 1986; Summers et al. 1993). We agree with the neo-institutionalists that market incentives are important. In our view, however, they are generally channelled by, and framed in, specific extra-market institutions, of which federalism is an example.

Why should federalism matter?

Two competing arguments guide an inquiry into if, how, and when vari-ation in state structures affects macro-economic performance. According to the first, a unitary state, *ipso facto*, more effectively co-ordinates such issues of macro-economic policy-making as fiscal policy. The logic here is simple. Greater centralized control of policy-making permits more efficient deter-mination of macro-economic targets, less diffusion in the utilization of policy instruments, and a higher degree of economic policy co-ordination. In addition, relatively centralized government facilitates the aggregation of popular and working-class interests by concentrating issues in a single locus of political action. Socialists made this argument (Shonfield 1965), but so did neo-corporatists (Schmitter 1980) and monetarists arguing for inde-pendent central banks (Zysman 1983).

The second contending argument is that federalism enhances economic performance because it institutionalizes a greater degree of political and policy competition and *laissez-faire* economics than unitary systems. All forms of federalism stress decentralization of policy-making along territorial lines (King 1982; Riker 1987).[2] If properly constructed, federal structures can preserve and even enhance market forces. This market orientation, in turn, increases economic development (Streeck 1992; Weingast 1995). As Elazar (1987: 87) states: 'Some proponents of federalism argue that it is important primarily as a means to institution-alize pluralism'. Pluralistic competition, according to this line of argument, facilitates achievement of Pareto-optimal outcomes in many areas, including macro-economic performance.[3]

Both arguments provide essential components to the debate about the advantages of unitary and federal structures, to the determination of the degree to which market forces should guide a country's economy, and to the general literature on macro-economic performance. A certain amount of logical tension exists, however, when these two arguments stand side-by-side. Economically, do we best look to state structures that are more likely to generate fruitful collective goods, to eliminate negative externalities, and to realize positive ones? Or, should we consider state structures that discourage such economic outcomes? Here we test empirically the hypo-thesis that, *ceteris paribus*, federalism is more conducive than unitary struc-tures to strong macro-economic performance and we test this causal linkage against the alternative hypothesis that unitary, not federal, structures are economically most beneficial. Moreover, because of the importance of neo-corporatist institutions as economically consequential ones, our analysis of federalism's economic effects are also elaborated, after a simple first run, into one focusing on federalism in the context of neo-corporatist institu-tional arrangements. The chapter then reports a testing of the impact of federalism on macro-economic performance in 18 of the world's most economically developed countries.

Data

The data for this analysis consists of pooled time-series for 18 members of the Organization for Economic Cooperation and Development (OECD). The countries included were Australia, Austria, Belgium, Canada, Denmark, Finland, France, Germany, Ireland, Italy, the Netherlands, New Zealand, Norway, Sweden, Switzerland, the United Kingdom, and the United States (plus Japan in ancillary analysis). The data for each country were collapsed into five periods, each capturing a phase of the business cycle: 1960–7, 1968–73, 1974–9, 1980–9, and 1990–4. With five time periods and 18 countries, this data set thus contains 90 cases.

The dependent variables

Economic performance can be measured in a variety of ways. For the purposes of this analysis, we considered seven different macro-economic indicators. These measures included five typical indicators of macro-economic performance that frequently appear in economic analyses: growth, investment, a country's trade balance, employment, and inflation. These five measures were operationalized in the following manner:

growth: real per capita GDP growth (OECD 1995, 1996);

investment: gross fixed capital formation as a percentage of GDP (OECD 1995, 1996);

trade balance: exports minus imports as a percentage of GDP (OECD 1995, 1996);

unemployment: as a percentage of the total labour force (OECD 1995, 1996); and,

inflation: as a percentage change in the consumer price index (OECD 1995, 1996).

We also included two other measures that take into consideration social dimensions of economic performance: income transfers and social wage. Income transfers as a distributive and re-distributive variable were measured as government transfers as a percentage of GDP (OECD 1995, 1996). This is spelled out in greater detail in Hicks and Kenworthy (1998). Social wage was measured as the amount of money that a worker earning the median wage at last employment will earn, when severed from the labour market, merely by virtue of his or her citizenship (plus, where relevant, with demonstration of serious resolve to re-enter the labour force). Social wage is expressed as a proportion of the pre-unemployment income of a worker with median income. This social wage measure is compiled from data on unemployment compensation, general public assistance, and other programmes that perform income maintenance functions for the unemployed, as selected nation by nation (OECD forthcoming).[4]

For convenient exposition, we regard unemployment, transfer spending and the social wage as relatively distributive outcomes. Here the progressively redistributive impacts of transfer spending and the social wage are well known (but see Kenworthy 1999), as is the inegalitarian facet of unemployment (see Hibbs 1987: ch. 1). We regard investment, GDP growth, trade balances and (somewhat more equivocally) inflation as indicators of aggregate macro-economic gain. (Equivocation is offered for the case of inflation because of the progressive redistributive consequences often claimed for it (as in Hibbs 1987: ch. 1), at least where in the short run, fixed incomes are not too prominent and where inflation is not too high.)

The independent variables

Federalism is the primary causal factor under investigation. For our purposes, the federal–unitary distinction was coded as a simple 0–1 dummy variable. As federal systems, Australia, Austria, Canada, Germany, Switzerland and the United States were assigned a value of 1. All other countries, as unitary systems, were assigned a value of 0.[5]

Four control variables were also included in our analysis. Two core controls, a 'catch-up' term and a 'pre-OPEC' dummy variable, were quite extensively included. The 'catch-up' control variable is real GDP per capita (in constant dollars) or per person employed at the onset of each time period (Summers and Heston 1988). This 'catch-up' variable was included in the equations to control for growth processes. More specifically, it accounts for the lag in adoption by less advanced economies of technologies developed in richer nations (Baumol et al. 1994; Dowrick and Nguyen 1989; Barro and Sala-i-Martin 1992). The 'Post-OPEC' control variable (equal to 1 for 1974 on and 0 for the preceding panels) is used to purge at least partially the influence of the OPEC oil shock and its correlates. This variable essentially considers economies in the years prior to the oil crisis as fundamentally different from those in the post-1974 period. Both terms, 'pre-OPEC' and 'catch-up,' are important given the fundamentally economic nature of the seven dependent variables. Measures of neo-corporatism and meso-micro political economic co-operation are used in elaborations of the simple analyses of outcomes, federalism and 'post-OPEC' (plus more occasionally 'catch-up'). Analyses adjust for heteroskedastic distortions of standard errors using the Panel-Adjusted Standard Error option suggested by Beck and Katz (1995) and now available from White (1997); and they adjust for longitudinally dependent errors using a simple AR(1) model for autocorrelation that circumvents the problems associated with proliferating implicit parameters that flow from the use of adjustments for contemporaneous, cross-unit error covariances.

Models are kept simple in the belief that the temporally stolid variable for federalism, the once-and-for-all OPEC oil shock, and the intrinsically rather long-term tendencies placed on growth processes by 'lagged' productive capacity (or 'catch-up') are all highly exogenous forces. As such they are utilized without controls for such presumptively more endogenous, short-run factors as the variables of macro-economic and macro-policy models. In short, the effects sought for federalism variables are 'total causal' or 'reduced form' effects that encompass federalism's impact via any and all conduits. Although an absence of detailed controls does not allow for precise, unbiased estimates of conventionally stressed 'direct' or 'structural' regression impacts, it should provide reasonable approximations of more fundamental total effects. Although it would be preferable to employ structural estimates to specify the array of indirect pathways or causal mechanisms whereby effects of federalism are channelled or carried out, specification of such structural equations would be a formidable task even for a study with less numerous and varied dependent variables.

Principal models are confined to the affluent, long-term, post-war capitalist democracies of post-World War II Europe and her settler nations, which is to say that Japan is excluded from such models. The appearance of Japan as a frequent 'outlier' or 'influential' case that tended to render otherwise robust models unstable influenced the Japanese exclusion.

Basic findings

We first regressed the seven different indicators of economic performance on the federalism dummy measure and at least one of the two previously mentioned core control variables.

For the case of distributive outcomes, federalist systems are uniformly relevant. As seen in Table 10.1, federalism tends to dampen unemployment and thus has a modestly redistributive effect (standardized slope estimate or beta equal to -0.088). But it also has an anti-redistributive, or regressively redistributive effect on social policy. Specifically, the federalism dummy variable has highly significant effects on both transfer effort and the social wage.

Federalism is almost as consistently relevant where aggregate economic gain is more at issue. Although federalism has a negligible relation to trade balances in these simple models, it has a statistically significant, positive relation to investment rates and rates of growth in (per capita) GDP and significant, negative effects on inflation.

Overall, preliminary findings indicate that federalism tends to improve macro-economic outcomes relatively tied to the operation of private markets (investment and income growth and even unemployment and inflation), but it tends to inhibit redistributive social policies. This pattern is consistent with the views that (1) federalism tends to inhibit government and social economic activism, that (2) government social policy activism is progressively redistributive, but that (3) *laissez-faire* governmental macro-economic policy tends to be macro-economically beneficial so far as aggregate gain (and distributively benign low unemployment) is concerned. In

Table 10.1 Federalism and economic performance: ordinary least squares

Variable	Unemployment		Social transfers		Social wage		Inflation		Investment		GDP growth		Trade balance	
	Co-efficient	St. B.	Co-efficient	St. B.	Co-efficient	St. B.	Co-efficient	St. B.	Co-efficient	St. B.	Co-efficient	St. B.	Co-efficient	St. B.
Federalism	−0.707 (0.726)	−0.092	−2.06** (1.01)	−0.182	−0.194* (1.00)	−0.216	−0.652 (0.686)	−0.093	1.26 (0.900)	0.150	0.226 (0.299)	0.059	−0.850 (0.571)	−0.155
Pre-OPEC	−3.80*** (0.926)	−0.520	−5.56*** (0.965)	−0.516	−0.253 (0.095)	−0.299	4.47** (0.875)	−0.663	−0.013 (1.15)	0.002	0.907** (0.382)	0.249	0.692 (0.729)	0.133
Catch-up	0.012 (0.027)	0.056	—	—	—	—	−0.001*** (0.000)	0.567	−0.0009** (0.0003)	−.368	0.0006*** (0.0001)	−0.546	−0.0008*** (0.0002)	0.518
Constant	5.65*** (2.13)		16.20*** (0.688)		1.432*** (0.75)		13.82*** (0.000)		26.84*** (2.14)		5.194*** (0.71)		−3.975 (1.36)	
N	90		90		72		90		90		90		90	
R-square	0.322		0.303		0.136		0.280		0.133		0.536		0.176	
Adjusted R-square	0.298		0.287		0.111		0.255		−.102		0.519		0.148	

Notes: *** $p<0.01$ or better; ** $p<0.05$; * $p<0.1$.

this regard, it bears noting that in ancillary regressions of unionization rates on federalism, with and without controls for neo-corporatist institutions, federalism shows a statistically significant tendency to hold down rates of unionization — a key indicator of employee-class interest aggregation for policy ends. But do these effects of federalism persist when viewed in the context of controls for a second major political economic institution: tripartite neo-corporatism?

Elaborated political models

Such a bare institutional approach to understanding federalism's impact on economic performance is not likely to be very accurate or robust. Some 'flesh' must be added to such a 'skeleton' institutional approach to understand more fully federalism's influence on macro-economic outcomes. One way to do this is to include greater institutional complexity in the analysis. Neo-corporatism is perhaps the most frequently discussed political economic institution in recent social science.

Schmitter (1974), Katzenstein (1985), and many others have suggested that neo-corporatism is an alternative method to pluralistic modes of economic policy-making. Neo-corporatism is an interesting and succinct way to incorporate politics into the analysis because, in some ways, it is the opposite of federalism. Federalism is essentially about territorial decentralization of governance. Amongst other things, it disperses power, thus producing multiple points of entry into the policy area. Federalism tends to promote pluralistic forms of interest representation. In contrast, neo-corporatism emphasizes policy-making centralization at the national level (Schmitter 1974; Katzenstein 1985). In corporatist contexts, negotiations over issues of political economy are limited to a few powerful interest groups. In addition, these same groups often hold a degree of monopolistic power in the system. Such contrasting policy-making styles, we believe, provide an efficient test of the assumptions underlying the notion that federalism should help explain macro-economic performance.

We thus included a 'neo-corporatist' variable in the previously discussed seven models, testing the impact of federalism on economic performance. We measured 'neo-corporatism' using a multi-item scale that draws on the previous scales of Lijphart and Crepaz (1991) and Hicks and Swank (1992), plus additional measures of national business organization, wage bargaining co-ordination, interest group cohesion, investment bank prominence and micro-level management–labour cooperation drawn from Hicks and Kenworthy (1998). We believe utilizing the Hicks–Kenworthy index nicely covers the domain of tri-partite neo-corporatism as a policy-making institution, the statist stress of Wilensky (1976) and Hicks and Swank (1992), as well as the more societal emphasis of Lijphart and Crepaz (1991), the prominence of business confederation detailed in Crouch (1993) and of labor in a plethora of studies (e.g. Cameron 1984), and of both informal (as in Soskice 1991) and formal (e.g. Cameron 1984) labour coordination. This index captures the confederal foundations for, and the key co-operative practices of, business–union–state national labour-market negotiation, concertation and state supplementation. The Hicks–Kenworthy neo-corporatist scores, constructed for 1960–89, are the following (with rank in parentheses): Australia 0.22 (13), Austria 0.96 (3), Belgium 0.73 (8), Canada 0.10 (17), Denmark 0.78 (6), Finland 0.86 (4), France 0.42 (11), Germany 0.81 (5), Ireland 0.12 (16), Italy 0.42 (11), the Netherlands 0.76 (9), New Zealand 0.20 (14), Norway 0.98 (2), Sweden 0.99 (1), Switzerland 0.55 (10), the United Kingdom 0.15 (15), the United States 0.08 (18), and the less utilized Japan 0.76 (7) (see Hicks and Kenworthy 1998).

Previous work has suggested that neo-corporatism is an important explanation of macro-economic performance. Our analytical focus on federalism logically led us to hypothesize not only that federalism and neo-corporatism so overlap that they might confound each other's examination, but that they might mediate each other's operations. For example, federalism might restrain any neo-corporatist impact on social policy while neo-corporatism might confound the *laissez-faire* logic of federalism's pro-growth effect (or alternatively reinforce it with complementary public goods). We therefore included an interactive term. We call this 'FedCorp' and operationalize it as the product of the previously discussed federalism dummy variable and the neo-corporatism measure.

In addition, we introduced the Hicks–Kenworthy measure of such meso-micro (or 'firm-level') co-operative practices and institutions as purchaser–supplier co-operation (as in Keiretzu skill-sharing), competitor co-operation (as in German corporate collusion in upgrading human capital), and cross-specialty, even multi-divisional, production teams (as in Scandinavian automobile plants). We added this measure to a variant of the equation for economic growth because neo-corporatist effects in the growth equation of Hicks and Kenworthy (1998) had faded in the presence of such 'firm-level' co-operation.

Table 10.2 reports the estimates of these expanded 'political' models. As in Table 10.1, all seven indicators of economic performance were regressed on the federalism dummy measure and the two control variables. This time, however, the neo-corporatism measure and the federalism-neo-corporatism interactive term were also included.

The models' estimates suggest federalism's complexity as an explanatory variable. Regarding distributive outcomes, neo-corporatism emerges as redistributive across the board. Previous estimates of federalism's effects on unemployment and the social wage – but not on social transfer effort – appear to have been artefacts of the failure to control for neo-corporatism. In particular, as seen in Table 10.2, neo-corporatism appears both to reduce unemployment and to do so unsupplemented by any negative effects of federalism upon unemployment. This suggests that the previous appearance of anti-unemployment effects of federalism's *laissez-faire* consequence

Table 10.2 Expanded OLS models of federalism and economic performance

Variable	Unemployment		Social transfers		Social wage		Inflation		Investment		GDP growth		Trade balance	
	Co-efficient	St. B.	Co-efficient	St. B.	Co-efficient	St. B.	Co-efficient	St. B.	Co-efficient	St. B.	Co-efficient	St. B.	Co-efficient	St. B.
Federalism	-1.08 (0.07)	-0.140	-3.29** (1.60)	-0.291	0.009 (0.129)	0.010	1.32 (1.37)	1.89	5.14*** (1.87)	0.648	0.893* (0.475)	0.364	-0.210 (1.14)	-0.046
Neo-corporatism	-4.12*** (1.11)	-0.381	4.31 (1.66)	0.270	0.943*** (0.135)	0.732	0.197 (1.26)	0.020	7.24*** (1.69)	0.634	1.34*** (0.437)	0.382	1.25 (1.05)	0.193
FedCorp	-0.477 (1.81)	-0.037	4.62* (2.70)	0.244	-0.163 (0.212)	-0.113	-4.27 (2.15)	-0.363	-5.46** (2.83)	-0.428	-1.16 (0.727)	-0.295	0.648 (1.74)	0.090
Pre-OPEC	-3.81*** (0.581)	-0.521	-5.98*** (0.866)	-0.555	-0.304*** (0.067)	-0.360	-5.00*** (0.924)	-0.743	-1.28 (1.25)	0.267	0.811*** (0.300)	0.346	1.34* (0.713)	0.311
Catch-up	—	—	—	—	—	—	-0.001*** (0.000)	-0.693	-0.0012*** (0.0004)	-0.518	-0.0004*** (0.0001)	-0.457	0.0009** (0.0003)	0.617
Constant	8.84*** (0.758)		13.85*** (1.13)		0.907*** (0.093)		15.21*** (1.65)		25.42*** (2.12)		3.53*** (0.62)		6.51*** (1.48)	
N	90		90		72		89		68		68		68	
R-square	0.469		0.457		0.582		0.345		0.316		0.568		0.268	
Adjusted R-square	0.444		0.431		0.557		0.305		0.261		0.533		0.209	

Notes: *** p<0.01 or better; ** p<0.05; * p<0.1.

may have been an artefact of effective active manpower and labour-market policies in such relatively corporatist nations as the federal countries of Austria and (until 1989, West) Germany. Furthermore, conflicting positive and negative effects of neo-corporatism and federalism, respectively, upon social transfer spending as a share of GDP are complicated by a negative interaction between federalism and neo-corporatism. Specifically, anti-redistributive effects of federal state structure are offset, indeed reversed, in neo-corporatist nations (e.g. federal Austria and Germany). However, the actual per-recipient social benefit levels captured by the social wage or social transfer income-replacement rate swamps any federal consequences. Neo-corporatism's impact on the social wage are substantively large (beta= 0.732) as well as significant at far better than the 0.01 level. As seen in Table 10.2, aggregate gain models consistently reveal that federalism has a significant impact on economic performance once neo-corporatism is included along with it. As before, federalism buoys investment rates, income growth and price stability. But now it also appears to contract trade balances slightly and to interact variously with the persistently benign effects of neo-corporatism on aggregate economic gain. Federalist and neo-corporatist modes of investment enhancement appear to conflict by dampening each other's contribution to growth. Perhaps this is because the former are *laissez-faire*, for example entailing tax cuts, and because the latter is statist, for example involving substantial revenue-based public investment. Federalist and neo-corporatist modes of growth enhancement also appear (findings fall short of significance) to conflict with and dampen each other, perhaps for reasons involving conflicting impacts on investment. This conflict, at least, is what results once a control for the measure of 'firm-level' co-operation is entered into the analyses.

With neo-corporatism incorporated into the analyses, federalism emerges as a drag on trade balances but neo-corporatism emerges as a boost to trade balances and the interaction between the two appears to act as an additional source of positive trade balances. Substantively, this finding reveals a recognizable pattern. The very open and long internationally well-disciplined neo-corporatist nations have good trade balances; the set of federal countries that includes such dramatic carriers of trade deficits as Australia, Canada and the United States fares less well; and the set of federal-corporatist states including Austria and Germany does well. Trade findings are less theoretically clear, however, if we stick to the variables directly involved. Neo-corporatist states with their relatively centralized economic policy communities, institutions and practices are perhaps better able to co-ordinate trade policies while the *laissez-faire* component of federalism gives no boost to trade balances in an era of intensifying international competition. Perhaps the greater *laissez-faire* orientations of federalism discipline rather than hamstring the superior capacities of activist economic policy-making capacities in neo-corporatist countries. Without effectively interacting, both appear to help dampen inflation. This is not surprising if we consider that *laissez-faire* governance reduces the likelihood of state-induced inflationary market distortions while neo-corporatist activism – explicitly anti-inflationary in motivation as it has often been called – is unlikely to have spun off inflationary externalities. Overall, then, neo-corporatism appears to have had benign effects on all of the factors considered here, suggesting that, overall, it has been a constructive macro-economic structure during the 1960–94 period. Federalism, though far less viewed with an eye to its economic consequences, appears to have been influential across the same set of outcome variables, although pernicious with respect to the social wage – at least if one regards such a general safety net as benign. Combinations of federal and neo-corporatist institutions appear relevant or irrelevant, benign or pernicious, depending on the particular outcome at issue. Our analysis suggests that federal-corporatism interactively fosters transfer spending as a share of GDP but is irrelevant regarding unemployment, income replacement and inflation rates; it undercuts institutional buoying of investment and (very marginally) aggregate income growth but helps to advance positive trade balances. Federalism, in short, appears to matter for economic outcomes, most visibly when viewed in combination with tri-partite neo-corporatist institutions. Stated differently, federalism matters when viewed with an eye to possible beneficial combinations of state *laissez-faire* and activist governance rather than from one mutually exclusive, fundamentalist free-market or mixed-market point of view.

Conclusion

Does federalism matter in the area of economic performance? We considered seven different macro-economic indicators in 18 different countries of the OECD from 1960 until 1994. We found that federalism does appear to have an influence on some fundamental areas of macro-economic performance such as income transfers and social wage. More interesting, however, federalism's main effects on economic performance appear to be integrative with other institutional arrangements and styles of policy-making. Federalism's impact on GDP growth, investment and social transfers as a percentage of GDP are statistically significant when neo-corporatism is simultaneously considered. Variation in unitary–federal arrangements thus helps provide an explanation of social transfers, investment, and GDP growth. In addition, federalism functions interactively with neo-corporatism in the areas of income transfers. And, as an interactive term with neo-corporatism, federalism also serves as an explanatory variable for inflation, despite the fact that neither of the two variables alone is statistically significant.

In sum, we believe that understanding a state's institutional configuration is crucial to understanding its macro-economic performance. Extra-market institutions such as federalism and neo-corporatism, with their embedded policy styles, are important factors in explaining economic performance despite the fact that they tend to offset each other when they coexist. Federalism's decentralization and neo-corporatism's emphasis on centralized policy-making are not as contradictory as they might first appear. In fact, our evidence suggests that strong economic performance may simultaneously require both centralizing and decentralizing tendencies in policy-making arrangements. Moreover, federalism and neo-corporatism are probably only two examples of such tendencies that work in combination. More work clearly needs to be done to untangle fully why these two work together, and what other arrangements might be acting in a similar manner to enhance economic performance in advanced industrial countries.

Notes

1 The authors would like to thank the participants of the workshop 'Does Federalism Matter?' at the 26th Joint Workshops of the European Consortium for Political Research, University of Warwick, United Kingdom, held 23–28 March 1998, where an earlier draft of this contribution was presented. Special gratitude is extended to Francis G. Castles, Hans Keman and Ute Wachendorfer-Schmidt for their especially insightful comments and criticisms. We also wish to thank Patrick Allitt for reading a later draft of this chapter.
2 We are not interested in this chapter in entering into the debate on definitional considerations of federalism. As important as they are, the reader should turn elsewhere for such definitional or conceptual debate. See, for example, Riker (1964, 1975), Burgess and Gagnon (1993), King (1982), or Beam et al. (1983).
3 The same logic applies, of course, to the creation of a federal Europe in the European Union. See, for example, Garrett and Weingast (1993).
4 The data from this OECD (forthcoming) volume were obtained from Professor Duane Swank of the Department of Political Science, Marquette University, who obtained them from the Geneva office of OECD.
5 Belgium formally became a federal state in 1993. It thus might be considered a federal system in the last panel only. We coded it as a unitary state in this analysis for two reasons. First, it was federal in only part of the final period. Second, a certain lag would be expected in economic effects of federalism.

References

Barro, R.J. and Sala-i-Martin, X. (1992) 'Convergence', *Journal of Political Economy* 100: 223–51.
Baumol, W.J., Nelson, R.R. and Wolff, E.N. (eds) (1994) *Convergence of Productivity*, New York: Oxford University Press.
Beam, D.R., Conlan, T.J. and Walker, D.B. (1983) 'Federalism: The Challenge of Conflicting Theories and Contemporary Practice' in A.W. Finifter (ed.) *Political Science: The State of the Discipline*, Washington, DC: American Political Science Association.
Beck, N. and Katz, J.N. (1995) 'What to Do (And Not to Do) with Time-Series Cross-Section Data' *American Political Science Review* 89: 634–47.
Brzinski, J., Lancaster, T.D. and Tuschhoff, C. (eds) (1999a) *Compounded Representation in West European Federations*, London: Frank Cass.

—— (eds) (1999b) *Federalism and Compounded Representation*, special issue of *Publius: The Journal of Federalism* (Winter, 1999).

Burgess, M. and Gagnon, A.-G. (eds) (1993) *Comparative Federalism and Federation*, London: Harvester Wheatsheaf.

Cameron, D. (1984) 'Social Democracy, Corporatism, Labour Quiescence and the Representation of Economic Interest in Advanced Capitalist Society', in J.H. Goldthorpe (ed.), *Order and Conflict in Contemporary Capitalism*, Oxford: Claredon Press.

Coleman, W.D. (1987) 'Federalism and Interest Group Organization', in H. Bakvis and W.M. Chandler (eds), *Federalism and the Role of the State*, Toronto: University of Toronto Press.

Crouch, C. (1993) *Industrial Relations and European State Traditions*, Oxford: Clarendon Press.

Dowrick, S. and Nguyen, D.-T. (1989) 'OECD Comparative Economic Growth 1950–85; Catch-Up and Convergence', *American Economic Review* 79: 1010–30.

Elazar, D.J. (1987) *Exploring Federalism*, Tuscaloosa: University of Alabama Press.

Garrett, G. and Weingast, B.R. (1993) 'Ideas, Interests, and Institutions: Constructing the European Community's Internal Market', in J. Goldstein and R.O. Keohane (eds), *Ideas and Foreign Policy: Beliefs, Institutions, and Political Change*, Ithaca: Cornell University Press.

Grier, K. and Tullock, G. (1989) 'An Empirical Analysis of Cross-National Economic Growth, 1951–1980', *Journal of Monetary Economics* 24: 259–76.

Hibbs, D. (1987) *The Political Economy of Industrial Democracies*, Cambridge: Harvard University Press.

Hicks, A. and Kenworthy, L. (1998) 'Cooperation and Political Economic Performance in Affluent Democratic Capitalism', *American Journal of Sociology*, 13, 6: 631–72.

Hicks, A. and Swank, D. (1992) 'Politics, Institutions, and Welfare Spending in Industrialized Democracies, 1960–1982', *American Political Science Review* 86: 658–74.

Hoffman, G.W. (ed.) (1981) *Federalism and Regional Development: Case Studies on Experiences in the United States and the Federal Republic of Germany*, Austin: University of Texas Press.

Jeffery, C. and Sturm, R. (eds) (1993) *Federalism, Unification and European Integration*, London: Frank Cass.

Katzenstein, P. (1985) *Small Nations in World Markets: Industrial Policy in Europe*, Ithaca: Cornell University Press.

Kenworthy, L. (1999) 'Do Social-Welfare Policies Reduce Poverty? A Cross-national Assessment', *Social Forces* 77: 1119–39.

King, P. (1982) *Federalism and Federation*, Baltimore: Johns Hopkins University Press.

Lijphart, A. and Crepaz, M.M.L. (1991) 'Corporatism and Consensus Democracy in Eighteen Countries: Conceptual and Empirical Linkages', *British Journal of Political Science* 21: 235–46.

March, J.G. and Olsen, J.P. (1989) *Rediscovering Institutions: The Organizational Basis of Politics*, New York: Macmillan.

North, D.C. (1990) *Institutions, Institutional Change, and Economic Performance*, New York: Cambridge University Press.

OECD (Organization for Economic Co-operation and Development) (1995) *Historical Statistics, 1960–1993* (diskette version), Paris: OECD.

—— (1996) *Historical Statistics, 1960–1994*, Paris: OECD.

—— (forthcoming) *OECD Database on Unemployment Benefit Entitlement and Replacement Rates*, Geneva: OECD.

O'Toole, Jr., L.J. (1990) 'Theoretical Developments in Public Administration: Implications for the Study of Federalism', *Governance* 3: 394–415.

Pierson, P. (1995) 'Fragmented Welfare States: Federal Institutions and the Development of Social Policy', *Governance* 8: 449–78.

Pierson, P. and Leibfried, S. (1995) 'Multitiered Institutions and the Making of Social Policy', in S. Leibfried and P. Pierson (eds), *European Social Policy: Between Fragmentation and Integration*, Washington, DC: Brookings Institution.

Riker, W.H. (1964) *Federalism: Origin, Operation, Significance*, Boston: Little, Brown and Company.

—— (1975) 'Federalism', in F.I. Greenstein and N.W. Polsby (eds), *Handbook of Political Science: Governmental Institutions and Processes*, Vol. 5, Reading, MA: Addison-Wesley.

—— (1987) *The Development of American Federalism*, Boston: Kluwer.

Scharpf, F. (1988) 'The Joint Decision Trap: Lessons from German Federalism and European Integration', *Public Administration* 66: 239–78.

Scharpf, F., Reissert, B. and Schnabel, F. (1976) *Politikverflechtung: Theorie und Empirie des kooperativen Föderalismus in der Bundesrepublik*, Kronberg: Scriptor.

Schmitter, P.C. (1974) 'Still the Century of Corporatism', in, F.B. Pike and T. Stritch (eds) *The New Corporatism*, Notre Dame: University of Notre Dame Press.

—— (1980) 'Interest Intermediation and Regime Governability in Western Europe', in S. Berger (ed.), *Organizing Interests in Western Europe*, New York: Cambridge University Press.

Shonfield, A. (1965) *Modern Capitalism*, London: Oxford University Press.

Soskice, D. (1991) 'The Institutional Infrastructure for International Competiveness: A Comparative Analysis of the UK and Germany' in A.B. Atkinson and R. Brunetta (eds) *Economics for the New Europe*, New York: New York University Press.

Steinmo, S., Thelen, K. and Longstreth, F. (1992) *Structuring Politics: Historical Institutionalism in Comparative Analysis*, Cambridge: Cambridge University Press.

Stiglitz, J. (1986) *The Economics of the Public Sector*, New York: Norton.

Streeck, Wolfgang (1992) *Social Institutions and Economic Performance: Studies of Industrial Relations in Advanced Capitalist Economies*, London: Sage Publications.

Summers, R., and Heston, A. (1988) 'A New Set of International Comparisons of Real Product and Price Level Estimates for 130 Countries', *Review of Income and Wealth* 34: 1–25.

Summers, L., Gruber, J. and Vergara, R. (1993) 'Recent Lessons of Development', *World Bank Research Observer* 8: 241–54.

Weingast, B.R. (1995) 'The Economic Role of Political Institutions: Market-Preserving Federalism and Economic Development', *Journal of Law, Economics, and Organization* 11: 1–31.

White, K.J. (1997) *SHAZAM's User's Reference Manual, Version 8.0*, New York: McGraw Hill.

Wilensky, H.L. (1976) *The 'New Corporatism,' Centralization, and the Welfare State*, Beverly Hills, CA: Sage.

Wright, V. (1994) 'Reshaping the State: The Implications for Public Administration', *West European Politics* 17: 102–37.

Zysman, J. (1983) *Governments, Markets, and Growth*, Ithaca, NY: Cornell University Press.

Conclusion

Ute Wachendorfer-Schmidt

The contributions of this book support the argument that federalism does matter because it generates particular constraints and opportunities for political action. Federalism constrains central and subnational government activity through power sharing, and it may constrain the options of subnational governments through competition. Federalism also creates opportunities for citizens and politicians to pursue their goals, as it provides multiple access points for policy-making within the states and in the federation. No unitary state, regardless of its degree of decentralization, will present such a mix of opportunities and constraints.

The finding that federalism matters is congruent with the results obtained from measuring democracies. Arend Lijphart (1999), for example, discovered that when one examines all of the major institutions of democratic government – executives, parliaments, courts, political parties, electoral systems, patterns of centralization and decentralization, constitutions, interest groups, and central banks – their characteristics form two clusters in modern democracies, and one of these clusters is formed around the distinction between federal and unitary governments. If federalism is a pillar in one out of two institutional configurations of democracy, and if the two democratic configurations differ in their performance, federalism should make a difference.

As to how federalism matters, the cross-national statistical analyses in this volume confirm the view that it tends to be associated with a smaller government (including smaller volumes of income redistribution), and improved macro-economic outcomes, such as higher rates of economic growth and reduced inflationary pressures (see the contributions of Hans Keman, Francis G. Castles, Thomas Lancaster and Alexander Hicks). The explanation of this pattern lies in the barriers federalism imposes on government action. The market economy benefits from a decentralized state structure because it operates at a higher degree of liberty. Inflation control is strengthened because a decentralized fiscal structure impedes policies that may generate inflationary pressures, such as combating unemployment through Keynesian policies on the part of the central government (Scharpf 1987). In most federal systems, control of inflationary pressure is supported by an independent central bank. The development of big government and a generous welfare state is prevented because federal systems have a larger number of veto points and veto players, i.e. individual or collective actors whose agreement is necessary for a change of a status quo (Tsebelis 1995). Beside the parties in the central government,[1] in federal systems there are other players endowed with veto power, such as a significant second chamber, strong supreme or constitutional courts with the power of judicial review, and constitutions that are rigid because they are difficult to amend.[2] When veto players are numerous, the central government cannot get significant pieces of legislation through parliament, such as redistributive social policies.

The veto players theory explains to a large extent why Germany deviates significantly from the federal pattern of political outcomes. In this country, federalism has not been an obstacle to the emergence of a large welfare state. This is largely due to the ideological affinity of the two big parties with respect to social policies. Both Christian Democrats and Social Democrats are advocates of the welfare state, their ideological distance in this policy field being relatively small. As the veto players' theory holds that ideological distance together with an increase in the number of veto players reduces the ability of both government and parliament to produce significant laws, it can be deduced that in Germany, one of two constraints on central government's initiatives in social policy is not too strong. Interlocking politics has not impeded a high level of welfare state intervention either, because the way it has been financed entailed no costs for the *Länder* (the country's social security system is mainly financed by social insurance contributions rather than taxes). In social policy, more often than not, major decisions have been steered through the legislature by a formal or informal grand coalition of the major established parties and a formal or hidden grand coalition of federal government and state governments – what Manfred Schmidt has called the 'grand coalition state' (1996: 95). The German case underpins the contention that policy processes need to be conceptualized as a result of the 'interaction of individual and corporate actors endowed with certain capabilities and specific cognitive and normative orientations, within a given institutional setting and within a given external situation' (Scharpf 1997: 37).

Measuring federal and unitary systems is a complex problem. This volume has demonstrated that it is useful to apply both dichotomous and non-dichotomous measures, such as the distinction between centralized and decentralized federations, as well as centralized and decentralized unitary states. A quantitative index of federalism can be built using the primary federal characteristics – a constitutionally guaranteed division of power between the central government and the regional governments, as well as decentralization – to classify states as either federal or unitary, or place them in an intermediate category, by assigning a score to each category (Lijphart 1999: 188). Hans Keman (in this volume) constructs a comparative scaling of federal and unitary systems. In addition to the constitutional classification of a polity, Keman uses four indicators for the degree to which a state provides for a territorial division of power, transforming them into one (factor) score. Likewise, he uses a number of indicators to construct a measure of centralization – decentralization. His results correspond to most existing listings of polities related to the territorial division of power. The more sophisticated the indicators for measuring federalism are, the more scholars diverge about them, and the more the results differ. For example, Dietmar Braun (2000) finds not only centralized and decentralized unitary states but three clusters of unitary states. The cluster of the Scandinavian states corresponds roughly to the unitary and decentralized category (see Keman in this volume and Lijphart 1999: 189), whereas the unitary and centralized states form two groups, a 'classic' type represented by New Zealand and Greece, for example, and an Anglo-Saxon type that gives local authorities more discretion in some functional areas, delegating decision-making and implementation. For some purposes, it will be useful to follow Braun's suggestion and compare federal states with each group of unitary states separately. An interesting line of investigation would be to see whether the same cultural and historical factors that fragmented a society and shaped the territorial organization of a state make the territorial actors inclined to defend their autonomy (or hierarchical power) or to co-operate in overlapping functions. For comparative statistical analyses focusing on the effects of federalism for political performance, however, a larger number of cases is necessary, and as most of the measurings largely coincide in their classific-ations, a simple dichotomous distinction will suffice (see Lancaster and Hicks in this volume).

Another limitation of cross-national analyses on the role of federalism for policy-making and political performance results from the similar cases design which has dominated most of the research so far. The cross-national studies in this volume and many others concentrate on economically advanced and politically stable Western democracies. There are good reasons for a similar cases design, yet it leaves countries like India, the world's largest federation and largest democracy, out of consideration. Not included are also the many other federations that emerged after the end of the Second World War, like Venezuela (federalized in 1961). Many of them are not even democracies, such as Malaysia (a federation since 1963), Nigeria (1960), Pakistan (1985–99), and the United Arab Emirates (1971), or must be qualified as quasi-democracies, like Argentina, Brazil and Mexico, whose federalization dates back to the nineteenth century (Argentina: 1862, Brazil: 1891) or to the beginning of the century (Mexico: 1910). In the twentieth century, the number of federal states has increased from six (1900) to nineteen (2000). Most of them are economically less developed, and many are politically unstable. South Africa was the last country to federalize in the twentieth century (1997).

The viability of federalism in economically weak and politically unstable countries has only recently attracted fresh scholarly interest, after the demise of communism in middle and eastern Europe. Normatively, it is assumed that federalism is a better solution to post-Communist Europe's multi-ethnic states than self-determination and independence, because federalism alone can protect both the minority in the larger state and that in the constituent states which nationalists aspire to govern (Linz 1999: 384). However, the experience of the three post-Communist states that were organized as federations, Yugoslavia, the Soviet Union and Czechoslovakia, which became 22 independent states in the process of democratic transition, has focused attention on the ambivalent character of federalism. Being an institution, or more precisely a system of rules that structure the courses of action that a set of actors may choose (Scharpf 1997: 38), federalism does not determine the outcome. It is not only a means for integrating multiethnic, multi-cultural, multireligious and multilingual societies, but also an opportunity for ethno-nationalists to press their case.

In Russia, as Klaus von Beyme argues, a true federal system has not (yet) been established. The institutions chosen by the transformational elites in order to grapple with social and ethnic diversity were not appropriately tailored to suit their purpose. For example, the electoral system combined elements of proportional and majoritarian electoral laws, with the majoritarian element predominating on the local level. The electoral law strengthened the autonomy of many local leaders and favoured disintegration rather than integration. A result of this constitutional engineering was that Russia's institutional mix placed the country somewhere between federations with proportional or majoritarian electoral law, and decentralized unitary states with proportional or majoritarian electoral law. The inconsistencies of federalism in the Russian case are not a deliberate adaptation to local conditions, as has been suggested to explain institutional variations departing from classic American-style federalism and now termed 'holding-together-federalism' (Stepan 1999). The inconsistencies of Russian federalism are rather explained by three causes – the ideological and territorial heritage of the Soviet Union, the power struggles in the centre, and the disastrous economic situation in Russia which strengthens the financial egotism of all constituent units. In contrast to Russia, India has a federal system that works. What makes the difference, considering that India was quite as poor and even more fragmented ethnically, linguistically and culturally than Russia is, and that it had to cope its with colonial heritage? One of the reasons seems to be that India's elite, when drafting the constitution, could build on a tradition of Mogul and British rulers that blended strong central control with local initiative. Except for Indira Gandhi's brief interlude of authoritarian rule, the federal system kept its balance by co-operation between the centre and the states, and by the practice of (regional) accommodation and co-optation used by the

Indian National Congress, which had already organized itself on the basis of the federal principle back in the 1920s. The federal balance was maintained during alternating rules of the Congress party and the Janata coalitions, and has endured up to this day under the coalition government led by the Hindu nationalist Bharatiya Janata Party. National surveys of the Indian electorate presented by Mitra corroborate the view that federalism is not only supported by the elites but also by a growing percentage of people who have trust in the government at both the central and the regional levels. India has also been relatively successful in dealing with ethno-nationalist challenge, using strategies of accommodation and repression. The experience of Russia and India underlines that cultural and historical factors, as well as the norms and perceptions of the transformational elites, are of great significance for the success or failure of federalism.

In the economically advanced and politically stable democracies, the strengths and weaknesses of different models of federalism are of particular interest. The contributions in this volume support the view that collaborative federalism, arm's length federalism and mixed types generate specific *patterns* of policy outcomes. It is also shown that federal systems have ways of self-correction that reduce their respective drawbacks, and that the efforts of self-repair in turn are likely to generate, along with the desired increase in the capacity to solve particular problems, new defects. The study on Germany reveals how collaborative federalism reduces its main problem, a tendency for suboptimal policies or even blockage, using devices to oil the interlocking systems, thereby creating problems of viability for the political system in the long run, narrowing the room for manoeuvre available to future governments, and shifting burdens onto future generations (see Wachendorfer-Schmidt in this volume). Arm's length federalism is also capable of generating suboptimal political solutions or gridlock when joint action is desirable, as competitive and collaborative elements of policy-making coexist uneasily. Martin Painter's study on Australia demonstrates that under certain conditions the territorial actors in arm's length federations establish joint decision systems and succeed in resolving problems of collective action without generating the deficiencies normally found in collaborative federalism. Painter attributes this positive outcome to the embeddedness of joint decision systems in an arm's length polity, which makes collaborative forms of decision-making less rigid and fixed in formulae or in the constitution. Yet the second major disadvantage of collaborative federalism – empowering the executives at the cost of parliaments – cannot be mitigated by arm's length federalism. More elasticity in problem-solving and less negative side effects are reported of Switzerland, a federal system that combines features of the American model and of the German model of federalism. Klaus Armingeon (in this volume) argues that Swiss federalism is a success story if evaluated against the criteria of constraints on central government, sustainability, integration, preservation of distinctiveness and people's satisfaction with the way democracy works. The explanation for the superiority of Swiss federalism as compared with the federations of the USA and Germany offered by Armingeon is threefold. Swiss federalism (as the Australian system) avoids the tight coupling (Benz 1998: 563–5) of Germany's federalism, and party competition does not counteract federal co-operation, as it does in Germany (Lehmbruch 1998). On the other hand, Swiss federalism performs better than the American model because it mitigates inter-jurisdictional competition by co-operative solidarity. The study on Canada focuses on the consequences of uncoordinated power and policies. Stephen Tomblin's theme is the attitude of a highly decentralized and competitive federal system towards economic change. The Canadian case warns against expectations (especially on the part of advocates of federal reform in Germany) that dual federalism would promote allocative efficiency, regional integration and institutional reform. Tomblin argues that precisely the high degree of autonomy of the provinces can be used and is used by the poorer provinces to resist regional integration, reminding us that federalism is not merely about economic efficiency but about political sovereignty and cultural values, among other goals.

In sum, this book has stated that federalism makes a difference for policy-making and political performance as compared with unitary states, that different types of federalism produce different patterns of policy outcomes, and that the strengths and weaknesses of each type of federalism can be overcome under certain conditions, if not completely and not without negative side-effects.

Notes

1 'In a parliamentary system, veto players are the parties in government as well as other actors endowed with veto power' (Tsebelis 1999: 593).
2 Federal systems tend to be associated with strong bicameral parliaments, strong supreme courts with the power of judicial review, constitutional rigidity, and central bank independence (Lijphart 1999: 246).

References

Benz, A. (1998) 'Politikverflechtung ohne Politikverflechtungsfalle. Koordination und Strukturdynamik im europäischen Mehrebenensystem', *Politische Vierteljahresschrift* 39, 3: 558–89.

Braun, D. (2000) 'The Territorial Division of Power in Comparative Public Policy Research: An Assessment', in D. Braun (ed.) *Public Policy and Federalism*, Aldershot: Ashgate.

Lehmbruch, G. (1998) *Parteienwettbewerb im Bundesstaat*, 2nd edn, Wiesbaden: Westdeutscher Verlag.

Lijphart, A. (1999) *Patterns of Democracy*, New Haven and London: Yale University Press.

Linz, J.J. (1999) 'Democracy, Multinationalism and Federalism', in A. Busch and W. Merkel (eds), *Demokratie in Ost und West. Für Klaus von Beyme*, Frankfurt: Suhrkamp, 382–401.

Scharpf, F.W. (1987) *Sozialdemokratische Krisenpolitik in Europa. Das 'Modell Deutschland' im Vergleich*, Frankfurt and New York: Campus.

—— (1997) *Games Real Actors Play: Actor-Centered Institutionalism in Policy Research*, Boulder, CO: Westview Press.

Schmidt, M.G. (1996) 'Germany. The Grand Coalition State', in J.M. Colomer (ed.) *Political Institutions in Europe*, London and New York: Routledge, 62–98.

Stepan, A. (1999) 'Federalism and Democracy: Beyond the U.S. Model', *Journal of Democracy* 10, 4: 19–34.

Tsebelis, George (1995) 'Decision-Making in Political Systems: Veto Players in Presidentialism, Parliamentarism, Multicameralism and Multipartyism', *British Journal of Political Science* 25, 3: 289–325.

—— (1999) 'Veto Players and Law Production in Parliamentary Democracies: An Empirical Analysis', *American Political Science Review* 93, 3: 591–608.

Index